NO SENSE OF EVIL

Espionage, The Case of Herbert Norman

JAMES BARROS

DENEAU PUBLISHERS & COMPANY LTD.
760 BATHURST STREET
TORONTO, ONTARIO
M5S 2R6

© 1986
Printed in Canada

This book has been published with the assistance of the
Canada Council and Ontario Arts Council under their block grant
programmes.

Canadian Cataloguing in Publication Data

Barros, James, 1930–
No sense of evil: espionage, the case of Herbert
Norman

Includes index.
ISBN 0-88879-142-9

1. Norman, E. Herbert, 1909-1957. 2. Diplomats -
Canada - Biography. 3. Canada - Foreign relations -
1945- . I. Title.

FC611.N67B37 1986   327.2'092'4   C86-094143-4
F1034.3.N67B37 1986

In Memory of Colleagues

George Heiman, 1926-1985

Stephen E. Koss, 1940-1984

Gentlemen, Teachers, Scholars

Contents

Preface

It is now possible to examine in some depth the tragic career of the Canadian diplomat Egerton Herbert Norman, and the tortuous road he followed throughout his life. He was a well-meaning person of gentle persuasion. Like many of his contemporaries, he was caught up in a web of history and, although much has been said about him, what follows could not have been written until recently.

Governments in general, and the Canadian government in particular, have been less than forthright in disclosing substantive details of the arcane and murky world of subversion, espionage, and counter-intelligence. By avoiding discussion they have held their electorate ignorant about important aspects of modern international relations. The arguments they have advanced against public debate were justified by "reasons of state." The wall of silence they maintained was meant to defend national security, but it was also used to hide the peccadilloes and gaffes of politicians and mandarins.

Cracks in the wall began to appear with the passage of the Freedom of Information Act in the United States, and they were widened when the analogous Access to Information Act became law in Canada. In addition, through the years, there has been an enormous increase in knowledge of the history, structure, objectives, personalities, and tradecraft of the Russian intelligence services. This greater understanding is based on the works of academics, interested laymen, perceptive journalists and, especially, on the memoirs, recollections, and sworn testimonies of those who defected from the Russian, and the intelligence services of satellite states in Eastern Europe. It is also based on archival materials and the evidence accumulated and published by numerous government bodies. The dusty tomes of royal commissions, American congressional committees, and other agencies can prove invaluable, if systematically examined. Testimonies and information culled from these volumes, if blended with such archival material and subsequently juxtaposed with legislative debates and official statements, can uncover a detailed mosaic of revealing information. These developments now allow us to examine past events and activities of individuals, as well as of organizations, in a manner and with a thoroughness never before accomplished.

This ultimately leads us to a wider issue, so succinctly defined in the memoirs of former United States Secretary of State Henry L. Stimson:

"Accurate information is
the raw material of policy."[1]

It was the experience he gained when serving in the cabinets of three American presidents that allowed him to make so wise an observation. Yet, his comments leave us with the impression that the acquisition of information and its subsequent utilization is a flawless process devoid of bureaucratic wrangling. In addition, it suggests that acquired information is readily accepted by the political leadership who receives it, and who is supposedly free from personal and other prejudices.

We know now that acquiring, analyzing, and successfully integrating data obtained by the intelligence services of one's country can, even in the best of situations, lead to tragic errors.[2]

These errors and problems are explored in the pages that follow. They occurred and had developed in Canada, a country whose bureaucracy is, by international standards, considered to be one of the best in the world. It operates within a system of government that, at least on the surface, appears both diligent and fastidious. This fact alone should caution even the most optimistic from believing that the safety of the State can, to a marked degree, be secured by an effective and wide-ranging information-gathering capacity. The pitfalls connected with these assumptions are illustrated in the case of Egerton Herbert Norman.

His story can be compared to seeing a giant web draped over a tall building or free-standing structure. The plucking of one of its strands leads to the tightening of other strands on the reverse side of the web; simultaneously, a vast network of ties and relationships becomes apparent for the very first time.

Acknowledgments

A long journey of discovery is often made easier by the encouragement and assistance of others. Accordingly, special thanks are due to Maureen Hoogenraad of the Public Archives of Canada in Ottawa for her help in examining the papers of the Canadian prime ministers, and to Milton Gustafson, Ronald E. Swerczek, and J. Dane Hartgrove at the National Archives in Washington, D.C., for their assistance in inspecting the papers of the Department of State. Likewise, I owe special thanks to Michael Straight and Victor Kiernan for corresponding with me about E. Herbert Norman.

In the world of the ivy tower, no academic accomplishes very much or can do so quickly without the aid of expert library personnel. Fortunately, the Robarts Library of the University of Toronto is blessed with a reference staff whose grace under pressure is exceeded only by its ability to trace the arcane: Carla Hagstrom Bissada, Jane Clark, Patricia Fysh, Marjorie Horsley, Susan Johnston, Jana Kalish, Jane Lynch, Mary McTavish, Patricia Norman, Sofia Skorić, and Mary-jo Stevenson. Similar expertise has been displayed by Peter Hajnal, director of the Robarts Library government publications section, and by Kent Weaver.

Most importantly, I am grateful to my son Andrew for discovering the name of Alexander George Heakes, the culinary talents of Emma Woikin, the Canadian activities of Dmitri Stepanovich Chuvakhin, and other facts that led to the title of the book.

Although parts of this study were read by colleagues and many others, two people deserve special mention because they went beyond the call of duty by reading the entire manuscript not once but several times. Special thanks are due to Richard Gregor of the Department of Political Science, and Robert Bothwell of the Department of History, University of Toronto. Their comments and criticism, along with the invaluable advice given by my wife Anne, have gone far toward making this a better book. I alone, however, am responsible for the pages that follow.

J.B.
Erindale College
Department of Political Science
University of Toronto

Chapter 1

Discovering Marx

On the morning of April 4, 1957, Egerton Herbert Norman, the Canadian Ambassador to Egypt, entered the modern eight-storey Cairo apartment building where his friend the Swedish minister resided. He took the elevator to the top floor and walked up to the roof. Observed by passers-by from the street below, he paced up and down and then sat down on the roof's parapet, placing his head between his hands. Then he rose, and in a manner described as "ritualistic," removed his wrist watch and glasses and placed them in his coat pocket. Next, he carefully folded his coat and laid it on the parapet. He then took a backward step and jumped. . . . He was dead when he landed on the pavement below.[1]

Self-destruction is a horrific act, and when it involves a person of talent and intelligence it is a blow to the social fabric of any civilized society. Such was the suicide of Egerton Herbert Norman. His tragic death in Cairo at the age of 47 removed from the western scene an accomplished Japanologist,[2] and from the Canadian Department of External Affairs one of its most gifted career officers. The suicide opened a wound which time has done little to heal—witness a recent book of essays on his life and scholarship.[3] The question remains as to whether his suicide was triggered by the activities of the United States Senate Subcommittee on Internal Security which had investigated him, or whether it was due to less discernible causes.

As the years go by, more and more information appears in public print, is discovered in archival depositories as well as in documents culled from the files of American and Canadian government departments and agencies. The government documents have become available under the freedom of information acts of these countries. This information creates reasonable suspicions about Norman's real political loyalties. Partisans can easily be found for either side of the question but the canons of scholarship dictate that any scrutiny of Norman and the events that led to his tragic death should be empirical, measured, and plausible.

Norman was not an ordinary Canadian. He was born in Karuizawa, Japan, on September 1, 1909, the youngest child of Daniel and Catherine Norman, Ontario-born Methodist missionaries who loyally served their congregation in the small city of Nagano. They retired in Japan and did not return to Canada until 1940, after the outbreak of the Second World War. Herbert's uneventful childhood in which he was initially tutored by his mother and then taught at the Methodist academy at Kobe, was marred by poor health. This led to admission to a Japanese sanatorium, and in 1926–1927 to confinement in a hospital outside Calgary, Alberta. Cured of tuberculosis in the autumn of 1928, he entered Albert College in Belleville, Ontario, a secondary school where Howard, his older brother taught. Like his father, Howard took up the cloth and, we are told, "developed moderate leftwing views and had a strong influence" on his younger sibling.[4]

In the autumn of 1929, Herbert entered Victoria College, University of Toronto. Due to his long residence in Japan, he had acquired considerable knowledge of the country and its language. His extensive reading while convalescing from tuberculosis, coupled with his intelligence, made him an atypical first-year student who specialized in the classics.[5] It therefore should come as no surprise that he was an excellent undergraduate as mirrored in the prizes and scholarships awarded to him at Victoria College.[6]

In 1926, even before entering Albert College, Norman's fascination with Marxism had already commenced. His initial reaction to Marx, whom he inaptly called the "old Teuton," was negative. Ostensibly, still committed to Christianity, he rejected both Red Square's communism, and Wall Street's capitalism, hoping to find some other moderate and less perilous methods[7] to tackle the world's ills. The following year, 1927, he began to revise his position. While rejecting Marx's anti-Christianity—an understandable reaction from the son of a missionary—he wrote to his brother Howard in July that he nevertheless found Marx's critique of capital's ruthlessness attractive. In support of this stance, he cited an epigram which he attributed to the King of Sweden: If someone under the age of thirty avoids being a socialist he lacks heart; if he is a socialist after thirty, he lacks wisdom.[8]

Norman's introduction to the world's harsh realities began at Victoria College in the years which coincided with the world depression. The economic and social chaos it generated and the human misery it caused were quickly brought home to him when he assisted a minister of the United Church (the Canadian union of Methodists, Congregationalists, and Presbyterians) to deliver food parcels to Toronto's unemployed. For someone who, up to this point, had been sheltered from life's buffeting winds, this was a wrenching experience. There had to be a basic flaw with a society, he told friends, which was forcing some of its members to live and barely survive under such appalling conditions.[9]

During these years, Norman lived in the college's dormitories, across the hall from Israel Halperin. The two students were interested in music, and although Halperin was a year ahead, they became friends.[10] Halperin, whose family had immigrated to Canada from Czarist Russia, was a brilliant student of mathematics and physics.[11] Perhaps owing to the temper of the times, he was on the far Left in student politics, serving on the executive committee of a radical Marxist sheet called *The Soap-Box*.[12] These students "adopted the usual Communist method of discrediting all those who do not share their revealed truth," noted their University College contemporary H. Gordon Skilling who, subsequently, became one of the West's leading experts on the politics and governments of Soviet Russia and Eastern Europe, especially, Czechoslovakia. All those who disagreed with them, he observed, were "ipso facto convicted of cowardice and crime." Skilling's strong advice from the "standpoint of rational self-interest," was for them "to confine their opprobrious harangues to their private meetings." Strong words indeed, considering the undergraduate civility that prevailed at the University of Toronto in the early 1930s.[13]

Herbert's years at Victoria College certainly led to his intellectual maturing, matched by his increasing radicalization. Events in Canada, more so than in Europe—Hitler was not yet in power, and Mussolini was quiescent—contributed to his leftward drift.

Specifically, he was vexed by the government's 1931 crackdown on the leaders of the Canadian Communist Party and by the imprisonment of other radicals. To him, the cruelest part of their incarceration was the denial of reading matter, a prohibition he found diabolic and which, he believed, placed Canada even lower than Bulgaria in terms of human repression. There could be no further complaints about Soviet Russia, he wrote to his parents in Japan, for whatever Moscow did to the bourgeoisie, Ottawa had politely reciprocated. Father Daniel Norman who had never succumbed to the idea of the inevitability of a class struggle and had been very unimpressed by the new utopia when he crossed Soviet Russia by train in 1930, was perturbed, pointing out the system's tyranny. Herbert did not deny it but, like others before and since, argued that the revolution was still maturing and that the enormous upheaval it had effected needed time to simmer down. Soviet Russia, he insisted, had nothing to be ashamed of, nor did it need to apologize to a soulless capitalism with its pursuits of endless wars.[14]

He found the Conservative government of Prime Minister R. B. Bennett particularly objectionable, calling it " 'reactionary' " for using a democratic façade in order to disguise its attempts to protect a decaying capitalism.[15] At one point, however, he appeared to waver. Although he thought the Marxist path was an excellent way to approach historical phenomena, he did confess that it could easily be distorted. He also considered Stalin narrow, lacking an international approach and, like many critics, he feared that the deepening bureaucratization of Russian society could undermine the revolution's goals. If he was attracted to anyone, it was to the fallen and exiled heretic Leon Trotsky whose belief in "permanent revolution" dovetailed with his own immediate *Weltanschauung*.

Father Daniel Norman objected. Trotsky was a fanatic, he wrote. Herbert retorted that if that were true then any man who held to his ideals, however wrong they appeared to someone else, must be a fanatic. Accordingly, every church saint was a fanatic, just as every man who was true to his conscience. Skeptics and cynics who followed the Epicurean path and accomplished nothing were the only humans devoid of fanaticism.[16]

In the spring of 1933, Herbert Norman still drifted between the evils and drawbacks of a revolution, and the possibility "of gaining a more hopeful and equitable society."[17] By mid-May, however, he nailed his flag to the mast and embraced revolutionary Marxism. By quoting Marx and Reinhold Niebuhr, he justified the overthrow of capitalism, a system he held to be absolutely stupid and a burden on civilization and whose historical role had long since ended. What was necessary could not be achieved, he wrote to his brother Howard, "without revolution," in view of the capitalists' desire to remain in power to preserve their privileged position.[18] One writer sympathetic to Norman tells us that even at this point he was not a total convert to the communist cause.[19] There is no evidence to support it, but it is not an unreasonable assertion. Certainly, it can be safely said that the waters were running swiftly, carrying Herbert Norman steadily to the extreme Left. Indicative of this drift was his support, in 1932, of the affirmative side in the debate of the University of Toronto's Historical Club that "in the opinion of this Club 'We are all Socialists now'."[20]

However, his inner religiosity, the one anchor that might have held him firm had broken. Though "badly shaken" in 1927 as he had struggled to recover from tuberculosis,[21] it had lasted until that time. His commitment to Marxism, as well as the social and economic impact brought about by the world depression, undoubtedly explains what occurred. Like so many others, Norman had found a new and exciting secular faith which could explain the past, the present, and the future. In 1937 he succinctly expressed this conversion to his brother, when he disagreed with him that preaching the teachings of Christ was life's highest endeavor. On the contrary, he wrote, communism was the "real standardbearer for humanity, for liberty and man's right to develop freely."[22]

Norman's disillusionment with established Christianity and his loss of faith were registered in two allegorical stories he wrote for the Victoria College literary magazine. Imaginative, well crafted, and cleverly written, their message was the futility of religion as even the most pious Christian could be fooled to do the devil's work, while an established Christianity would inevitably be corrupted from within, "stubbornly defending . . . property and wealth."[23]

For these and other reasons, he now was ideologically ripe for recruitment into the Communist Party. In 1933 he entered Trinity College, Cambridge, after receiving a scholarship to study history.

Chapter 2

Cambridge *Rezidentura*

Norman was impressed by Trinity's ambience, and the apparent worldliness of his tutors and fellow classmates—a far cry from the provincialism of Victoria College in the Toronto of the early 1930s. Within weeks of arriving in Cambridge, he joined the university's Socialist Society[1] which, by the time he departed in 1935, had become a communist-penetrated organization.[2] Admitting that he had read *The Coming Struggle for Power*, a "clear, sophisticated and closely reasoned Marxist" tract by John Strachey, was probably entrée enough,[3] as Strachey had moved from Sir Oswald Mosley's extreme Right to the Communist Party.[4] Who talent spotted Norman in Cambridge is not known, though dimly, through the years, an unidentified fellow Canadian has been recognized as his possible "inductor."[5] At the same time, it is worth noting that some of Norman's contemporaries included Anthony Blunt, Guy Burgess, Donald Maclean, and Kim Philby.[6] He was certainly a friend of David Haden Guest, the Trinity man who had organized one of the first communist cells in the college. He belonged to the most ardent of the breed and ultimately gave his life during the Spanish Civil War, fighting in the International Brigade on the Loyalist side.[7]

At the minimum, Norman would have been viewed by any Communist Party talent spotter on the Cambridge campus as a "C" contact, that is to say, someone who had been encountered and was considered good raw material for possible recruitment. He also could have been perceived as a "B" contact, someone under indoctrination, which was certainly true in his case. He was, after all, interested in socialism, was an outspoken critic of the government in power and a supporter of "peace" drives. Most likely, he was viewed as an "A" contact, someone who was ripe for immediate recruitment into the Communist Party.[8]

No talent spotter could have failed to see all these desirable qualities and talents: commitment to the new secular faith; intelligence and sensitivity; knowledge of Japanese and an appreciation of Asian cultures and history, especially Japan's. Though we do not know who Norman's talent spotter was, we do know who recruited him into the Communist Party. John Cornford, whose classicist father had translated Plato's *Republic*, had joined the Young Communist League at an early age, and by the time he arrived at Cambridge he was already a dedicated communist. It was under his " 'tutelage' ", as Norman subsequently admitted to his parents, that he joined the Communist Party. Charismatic, talented and committed to propagating the faith, Cornford can safely be described as a driven ideological fanatic.[9] Anyone who could speak with glee about the machine gunning by the Hungarian communist Bela Kun of 5,000 prisoners during a hasty retreat in the Russian civil war,[10] easily falls under that rubric. In fact, his commitment led him, like Guest, to volunteer for the International Brigade which fought on the Loyalist side in the Spanish Civil War. He had just turned twenty-one when he was killed in December 1936 in a battle on the Cordoba front.[11] Norman was deeply affected by his death.[12]

It is however also possible that James Klugmann was involved in Norman's recruitment. A Trinity contemporary, he has been described as "sinister" and a "committed Stalinist"[13] who would rise high in the Communist Party hierarchy,[14] and chronicle its history.[15] Certainly he had recruited others,[16] working closely with Cornford to enlist Norman's Trinity contemporaries, the American Michael Straight[17] and the Englishman Victor Kiernan.[18] Years later, after Norman had committed suicide in Cairo, Straight identified him to the FBI as a member of the party cell.[19]

In view of Norman's proclivities before arriving in Cambridge, neither Cornford nor those who might have assisted him could have encountered many difficulties. Indeed, one can cogently argue, that some of the values which run through the fabric of Canadian society, had gone far to bring about his recruitment. Foremost, one could suggest, was his Canadian Methodism which, unlike the religiosity that had developed south of the 49th parallel, emphasizing individualism and free initiative, expressed itself in a personal idealism that was dissociated from political considerations. For want of a better term it has been branded the "social gospel,"[20] a creed that had evolved from Canada's agrarian roots, prior to the germination of an industrial base. Metamorphosed, this religiosity could generate "radical opposition to capitalist industrialism," whenever world conditions, such as depressions or wars, demanded it.[21] This creed can rightly be described as "compassionate," concerning itself with "social tasks" that were reflected in a transnational "utopianism and a sense of brotherhood." It explains the paramount role that Methodists played in Canada's socialist parties, and is the reason why Herbert Norman had an "instinctive international outlook," and what has been labeled "libertarian instincts." It, likewise, engendered a social outlook that involved defending the weaker side to form the moral foundation of his anti-establishment politics.[22] This mind-set goes far to explain his initial movement toward the extreme Left, sparked as it was by world depression and, subsequently, accelerated at Cambridge by the expansionist foreign policies and integral nationalisms of a Fascist Italy and a Nazi Germany. Norman was not the only Canadian to soldier through life with this peculiar and mellow creed.[23]

There is another aspect that deserves mention, and it is best adumbrated by the French expression, *déraciné*. This does not mean that Norman was without roots but his upbringing in Japan, so to speak, had cut him off from his Canadian antecedents. It had produced an individual who, though legally a Canadian national, was by his absorbed values something less than that, especially in that tenuous connection between himself and, for want of a better word, the abstraction we call the "State." Keeping in mind his Methodist transnationalism and the international outlook that flowed from it, it can be suggested that in Norman's makeup loyalty to the State was a less tangible ingredient than in that of other Canadians. It never developed as strongly, let us say, as it did in the youths of his own day who grew up in Canada and savored, on an everyday basis, the loyalty symbols that bound them to the Crown: the rendering of *God Save the King* and the Union Jack flapping on the flagpole.

Norman was raised in rural Japan in a period devoid of the benefits of satellite communication and rapid international transportation.

Canada was far away, metaphysically, as well as geographically. Although evidence for this is fleeting and subjective, it can be glimpsed nevertheless. Over a telephone he could be taken for a Japanese because of his command of the language. Portraits of eminent Canadians may have graced the dining room walls of his home and he may have been regaled with stories of Canada's settlement and frontier life, yet in the corpus of his prolific writings there are few references to Canadian events and personages.[24] Moreover, while studying at Harvard, it appears, he voluntarily attempted to acquire American nationality.[25]

Norman was, to use the Greek expression *digenos*, not someone of two races,[26] but someone of two worlds and cultures. Never really of one nor of the other, he had been "conditioned" from childhood, as someone who knew him in his youth has written, "to feel part of his adopted society." This condition was buttressed by the Canadian and, probably by Norman's own "weak sense of identity" which manifested itself when abroad "as openness to other cultures and manners." It was stronger in Norman's time than it is today, and can be traced to the peculiar aspects of Canada's Anglophone society which found it difficult to develop a clear sense of identity because of its proximity to a much larger and vibrant English-speaking neighbor, and the continuous influx of immigrants from the British Isles.[27]

It, therefore, is fair to say that these two streams converged: the internationalism of Norman's Methodism and the ambiguity of his Canadianness. Each may have played an important role in assisting Cornford and perhaps others to recruit him into the Communist Party. It also has been alleged that he was a homosexual. Although this could have been manipulated to help draw him into the party, there is no empirical proof of this, and the subsequent allegations made to the staff of the Senate Subcommittee on Internal Security are, therefore, unconvincing.[28] The canons of scholarship dictate its rejection until proof can be furnished. Indeed, RCMP information acquired in 1963 would appear to point to his heterosexual orientation.[29]

Upon his return to Canada he did not conceal to one of his former Victoria College classmates that his experience with the Cambridge Left had greatly excited him.[30] The Marxist-Leninism he had embraced there had been an "intellectual" resurrection, he wrote in 1935.[31] Many years later, however, Victor Kiernan, his Trinity classmate and fellow party member came perhaps closer to the truth when he pithily observed that "Norman was 'in it for life.' "[32]

Until recently the conventional wisdom was that Norman's party activities at Cambridge were benign and probably entailed nothing more than "attending meetings and study sessions."[33] Nothing could be further from the truth. He proposed and his cohorts agreed that the party should attempt to acquire control of the Majlis, a long-established Indian society on campus. He hoped this would give the party a tangible objective of leading the Majlis to concentrate on serious political subjects.[34] His primary role, therefore, was the recruitment of Indian students into the party. Thanks to his long residence in Japan and his appreciation of Asian culture and history, he was the perfect man for the job. Accordingly, it would not be unfair to say that his task for the party was sinister in the extreme.

His nationality was an additional attribute when recruiting these Indian students. In attempting to convert them to the new faith he could cleverly claim to understand the injustices that were perpetrated under imperialism, a system with which his own country had been saddled. It was an effective and persuasive argument and as one Indian student admitted to Kiernan, all white men made him suspicious, but Norman had "won his confidence with the clinching argument that he was not an Englishman, but a Canadian."[35]

Norman's task, therefore, explains why he was constantly seen in the company of Asian, and especially Indian students.[36] It had little to do with intellectual ruminations or social conviviality, and much with executing the plan that he had proposed. Thanks to his efforts, control of the Majlis was easily achieved, and the organization was soon turned into the political organ that Norman and the Communist Party wanted it to be. The Indian students, it appears, were under official surveillance, and the task of recruiting and organizing them into the party therefore required great discretion.[37] For security reasons, it was also necessary that they not be issued party cards.[38] Norman himself also had to conceal his commitment to the Communist Party and, in general, eschew the activities of Cambridge's left wing.[39] These instructions easily fit the pattern of those who were recruited at Cambridge to toil for Russian intelligence. As the knowledgeable Christopher Andrew tells us, they "began by becoming members of secret communist cells rather than open members of the Communist party."[40] Norman ably executed these instructions, with the exception of a public foray on November 11, 1933, when he joined an anti-war march and wreath-laying ceremony that had been organized by Guy Burgess at the Cambridge War Memorial.[41] The clandestine life Norman led may partially explain why his name never surfaced in any thorough examination of communist activities at Cambridge during the interwar years.[42] Only once was there a breach in his placid security. While ill, he was visited by his conservative tutor, the historian George Kitson Clark who was taken aback by the amount of left-wing literature he noticed in his student's lodgings. Subsequently, when Norman requested a letter of reference from Kitson Clark, it proved less than laudatory. Only when he remonstrated did his tutor issue a more helpful missive.[43] To quote the Duke of Wellington, the incident was "the nearest run thing," yet Norman escaped unscathed.

Leading a double life of deception and duplicity must have proved easy for him. By this point he had already absorbed, as part of his personal code, the Epicurean dictum of the discreet life which demanded the avoidance of public political activity. Such activity inevitably would lead to the loss of tranquility and the trauma of public involvement. It was a code that neatly dovetailed with what Herbert described to his parents as a "too taciturn and reticent" nature which, in turn, manifested itself in having a less than loquacious disposition. Developed during his confinement for tuberculosis,[44] and coupled with his particular Epicurean code, it had produced a personality amalgam that also had served him well at Victoria College. It would continue to do so during his years in government service, and perhaps in other endeavors as well. This is not to say, however, that when conditions demanded, Norman was not capable of projecting publicly a different personality façade.[45] But, by and large, one can suggest that deep down he was an evasive and withdrawn person and there is much evidence to support both these suggestions.

Chapter 3

Toronto, Harvard, and Columbia

Arriving in Toronto in the summer of 1935, Kitson Clark's reference letter in hand, Norman found himself in an impecunious state and trying to find a job in the middle of the Depression. Fortuitously, he encountered Alexander George Heakes, a contemporary of his from their days at Toronto and Cambridge universities. Heakes was then tutor to Alistair Buchan, the youngest son of Canada's Governor General Lord Tweedsmuir. While at the University of Toronto, he had not been aware of Norman's political affiliations, however, at Cambridge he had observed him in the company of "a group of students interested in Communist affairs and theories."

In the course of their Toronto conversations, Norman admitted to being a communist, a member of the Canadian Communist Party, and employed by it. He also told Heakes that he wanted to get married but lacked the necessary funds. Heakes, who had obtained his job through Terence MacDermot, the Headmaster of Upper Canada College, approached him and recommended Norman for the vacant position of instructor in classics at the college, warning MacDermot of Norman's political orientation. He was appointed but cautioned by MacDermot not to interject politics into his teaching.

During that period, Heakes had a "photographic recollection" of seeing Norman in a booth at the Canadian National Exhibition in Toronto, distributing pamphlets for the Canadian League Against

War and Fascism—a communist-front organization—and giving "pep talks to the onlookers."[1]

Norman was subsequently dismissed from Upper Canada College. He later claimed it was because of his unpopular political views, and his opposition to Hitler's expansionist foreign policy. He also alleged that some of the other masters appeared to sympathize with that policy, and that, in fact, "he had been deprived of his livelihood by political prejudice."

There is no evidence to support these statements, as during that period the political leanings of the teaching masters would have been slightly to the left of center rather than to the right; certainly, none was known as a Nazi or fascist apologist. The recollections of those who were associated with Upper Canada College at the time are that Norman's departure was solely due to his inability to maintain discipline—a necessary skill in a secondary school classroom. Moreover, Headmaster MacDermot, by all accounts, was known as an even-handed person who was not likely to penalize someone for his political orientation.[2]

It was during that same year and following Norman's return from Cambridge, that he became acquainted with Philip J. Jaffe,[3] a man who had made his fortune in greeting cards. This information was given to American naval intelligence by Jaffe after Norman had committed suicide.[4] Jaffe admitted that "although not a Party member, [he] was certainly a very close fellow traveller of the American Communist Party," to which many incorrectly assumed he belonged.[5] He had been introduced to Norman by Chi Ch'ao-ting,[6] his cousin by marriage who was a well educated, skilled, and longtime clandestine Communist Party operative. He was loyal to the cause and served it well until his death in Peking in 1963 when he was given a hero's funeral.[7]

Jaffe and Norman became good friends and, according to Jaffe, Norman was Chi Ch'ao-ting's "intimate" until he entered External Affairs in 1939.[8]

The next time Jaffe and Norman met was in 1936.[9] It is unclear whether he or Chi Ch'ao-ting had urged Norman to organize a Canadian counterpart to the American Friends of the Chinese People.[10] Jaffe was attending a meeting in February 1936[11] organized by his longtime friend Alexander A. MacLeod[12] who was chairman of the Canadian League Against War and Fascism. On that occasion,

Norman was elected a member of a provisional committee to establish the Canadian Friends of the Chinese People.[13]

MacLeod has been described as a "very able Communist," the moving spirit of the Canadian League, one of many organizations launched by the Moscow-directed Comintern, "to mobilize intellectuals prepared to combine opposition to war and fascism with support" of Soviet Russia's foreign policy. A similar group had been established in the United States as early as 1933.[14] The American counterpart of the Canadian Friends of the Chinese People, also organized in 1933, was later identified as a communist-front organization with which Chi Ch'ao-ting was associated.[15]

At these February 1936 meetings, MacLeod introduced Norman as " 'Comrade Norman' " to Patrick Walsh who, at that time, was an unpaid informant for the RCMP. Walsh has since observed that Norman's appointment to the organization would not have been made, unless he had been a Communist Party member or a fellow traveller who, for good reason, lacked a party card.[16] His encounter with Norman and Norman's "obvious Communist zeal," together with a description of the setting in which they had met, was soon reported to John Leopold who was handling RCMP surveillance of communist activities in Canada.[17] As MacLeod admitted in 1942, he was attending secret Communist Party meetings at Norman's lodgings during that period.[18] However, it was only in the late 1960s, well after Norman's death, that the RCMP acquired information alleging that Norman had had a secret party affiliation.[19]

His political coadunation with the Communist Party obviates all speculation as to his subsequent attitudes and comments on the burning issues of the day. Obeying the beat of the party drum, he obsequiously accepted Moscow's changing political desires, at a time when well-meaning people, including a significant number of communists, were appalled by Stalin's liquidation of the old Bolsheviks. The great Moscow Spy Trials took place between January 1935 and March 1938. They were the beginning of what was to become the Great Purge (January 1937 to December 1938) in which countless thousands perished. Yet, Norman could, with equanimity, accept this monstrous and obscene negation of Kant's categorical imperative. He regarded the defendants' confessions in open court as the "literal truth," and unimpeachable proof of a wide-ranging Trotskyite and fascist plot. He rejected the contention that the trials were a sham, viewing them as "a vindication of Soviet Justice." He ignored the evidence, freely available at the time, that the defendants had been coerced by torture, drugs, and other means. As one writer friendly to him has observed, the whole episode appeared "linked to his lack of any strong sense of evil."[20]

Concurrently, the Spanish Civil War with all its fratricidal fury erupted in July 1936. Norman was racked by the knowledge that many of his Cambridge contemporaries had volunteered to fight in the International Brigade, while he was safely ensconced in North America. Cornford's death in Spain touched him deeply, as did the demise near Madrid of a New Zealand friend.

By this point, he had been awarded a Rockefeller fellowship to study Japanese history at Harvard University. Though his monthly stipend was a modest 170 dollars, including a family allowance of fifty dollars, (he had married in August 1935), he sent part of it to the Loyalists each month while his wife collected food and clothing for them. Yet, he did not feel he was doing enough, and seriously began to toy with the idea of volunteering to fight in Spain, like the others. He finally concluded, however, that certain personal inadequacies would make him more of a liability than an asset to the Loyalist side. Like many he was impressed by Moscow's material assistance to the hard-pressed Loyalists, as though Stalin had been moved by mere altruism. Of course, this was not the case, as the Loyalist government and Spain's non-Stalinist-dominated left-wing movements rudely learned. The Anglo-French failure to resist fascism's expansion in Europe demonstrated to Norman that their policies were impotent and futile. Now more than ever, he maintained, it appeared exigent to support Stalin's Russia, especially when Hitler's assistance to Franco's rebel forces made it evident that the Nazi tyrant was using the civil war to further his own interests.[21]

While at Harvard, Norman did not allow his ideological commitments to wither away. Halperin, for one, was on campus as instructor in mathematics, and their Victoria College association was soon rekindled.[22] Also present was fellow Canadian Robert Bryce, a future secretary to the Canadian cabinet. While a student at St. John's College, Cambridge, Norman had made an unsuccessful attempt to recruit him into the Communist Party.[23] Bryce now introduced Norman to Shigeto Tsuru, a Japanese doctoral student in economics and Norman, it appears, introduced him to Halperin. Years later, Tsuru denied ever to have been a communist, yet in late March of 1937 it was he who established a study group which would examine capitalism within a Marxist framework, and discuss freely among its members the question of capitalism in America. One of the papers entitled "American Imperialism"[24] had been written by Norman and discussed by the group. In later years, the FBI made Herculean efforts to discover the whereabout of the paper but was unable to do so.[25]

By 1938, Norman was also busy in New York as member of another study group at Columbia University where he was taking courses in advanced Japanese, Chinese history, and Chinese reading.[26] The group, allegedly run by Moses A. Finkelstein (now Sir Moses Finley, Emeritus Professor of Classics, Cambridge University), invited the noted German academic Karl A. Wittfogel to lead their discussions. Wittfogel expounded on imperialism—a subject of clear interest to Norman—with special regard to the ideas of Marx, Lenin, and the Marxist theoreticians Rudolf Hilferding and Rosa Luxemburg.

Thirteen years later, in August 1951, Wittfogel testifying before the Senate Subcommittee on Internal Security, would, without hesitation, identify Finkelstein as a communist, observing that the alleged study group had been composed of "friends, of people who belonged to [Finkelstein's] political creed." His comment was easy enough to make since Finkelstein himself had admitted to him that he was a communist. On the other hand, Wittfogel's longtime membership in the German Communist Party (1920–1932) had well qualified him to evaluate the interests of the group.[27]

Subsequently, another witness verified under oath Wittfogel's testimony that Finkelstein was a communist during the period in question, stating that the alleged study group sessions which he too had attended at Finkelstein's home, were communist-oriented.[28] Though Finkelstein denied in testimony that such a group had met at his home, he did admit that friends would congregate there on Sunday evenings.[29] These meetings, according to a another witness friendly to Finkelstein and hostile to the subcommittee, were identified as "Sunday evening music circles" during which things were discussed such as Wagner's operas and whether they were bad or good. They listened to Gilbert and Sullivan and discussed art appreciation and similar topics.[30] The consensus, at the very least therefore, might be that congregations did occur on Sundays at Finkelstein's home.

There is one additional point to be made. Finkelstein categorically denied, both in executive session and publicly before the subcommittee, that he had ever met Norman, or had ever heard of him until he had seen his name mentioned in Wittfogel's testimony.[31] Likewise it would have been impossible for Wittfogel to meet Norman in his home when he was not present since no congregations took place during his absence.[32]

As to Wittfogel, he correctly identified Norman to the subcommittee as someone studying Japanese at Columbia University. Most importantly, he identified him as a member of the alleged study group, assuring the senators that Norman would have known that it was communist in nature. Was it "obvious" that he was a communist, Wittfogel was asked. Yes, he replied.[33] Subsequently, he was to supply to the subcommittee Norman's address in Cambridge, Massachusetts which had been entered in his address book.[34] Obviously, he and Wittfogel had met somewhere; suffice it to note that the Canadian authorities never denied that fact.

Several days after Wittfogel had testified, Norman did admit to the former University of Toronto academic George Glazebrook, then Director of External Affairs' Defense Liaison II, that he had talked with Wittfogel. He had done so, he explained, because of the latter's eminence as a Sinologue and someone who when they met had "*recently*" been released from a Nazi concentration camp. Norman claimed that he treated him with "considerable deference," but that Wittfogel had done the talking and he the listening. His recollection was that their conversations had been academic, conceding that contemporary Far Eastern questions might have cropped up. Nevertheless, on the basis of these talks Norman could not imagine how Wittfogel could have characterized them in the manner he did. He might have opined that he, Norman, might have held certain views on specific subjects, but his assertion that he had attended a communist study group, either in Provincetown, Cape Cod, Massachusetts, or in New York was a lie. In particular, he categorically denied knowing Moses Finkelstein, a name he insisted that meant absolutely nothing to him.[35]

Unlike Wittfogel, Norman was silent about where they had held their conversations. Since Wittfogel had been allowed to leave Nazi Germany in early January 1934 when Norman was at Cambridge University, they probably met between May and July 1934 while Wittfogel was at Cambridge University residing with the don Roy Pascal, "in a house that he shared with Maurice Dobb."[36] Pascal has been described as a "keen extremist" and Dobb "as a Marxist intriguer and academic economist of subtlety and virtuosity" who propagated "Marxist theory and Soviet practice."[37] Norman's communist commitment would have brought him into contact with both these men and thus with Wittfogel.

But how can one square that these probable Cambridge University conversations took place between May and July 1934 considering Wittfogel's subsequent knowledge of Norman's Japanese studies at Columbia University in 1938, or of his address in Cambridge, Massachusetts? The explanation, as Norman admitted subsequently, was that they had met again in New York, this time when both were associated with the Institute of Pacific Relations (an organization we will presently examine), at a time when Norman was studying at Columbia University.[38] Whereas Norman initially only appeared to remember the Cambridge University conversations, Wittfogel could only recall those in New York.

However, Wittfogel's testimony was marred by two errors, as his biographer correctly points out. In his exchange with the subcommittee's counsel, he gave the impression that Finkelstein's alleged study group had met in Provincetown, Cape Cod, Massachusetts, during the summer of 1938. Two weeks after testifying, he tried to correct his mistake in a letter to its staff. In it he pointed out that the study group had gathered in the winter of 1937–1938 at Finkelstein's home near Columbia University. This would have only been possible if Norman had come to New York from Cambridge to attend some of these meetings. It also might explain why Wittfogel had his Cambridge, Massachusetts address. If he had meant that the gatherings continued through December 1938, they could have included Norman who had arrived at Columbia in September of that year. In addition, Wittfogel's comment that it was obvious that Norman was a communist, only obfuscated matters. Based on public evidence available in 1951, and on Wittfogel's alleged encounter with Norman at the so-called study group, it was not "obvious" in 1938 that he was a communist.[39] Based on evidence now available, Wittfogel's erroneous statement about Norman's alleged political orientation in 1938, though largely intuitive, was nevertheless correct. Moreover, one cannot help but point out that Wittfogel knew Chi Ch'ao-ting as well as Jaffe, and may have learned something from them about Norman.[40] Wittfogel had confused the whole situation by perhaps telescoping their probable conversations at Cambridge into those admitted by Norman to have taken place at Columbia University. It is also possible that they conversed with each other at the Institute of Pacific Relations. Wittfogel perhaps had blended all these talks with Finkelstein's alleged study group conversations.

The concrete information, lacking at the time but now available, left Wittfogel's 1951 testimony open to attack. It was regarded as inaccurate and irresponsible by well-meaning people who felt increasingly uneasy about the tactics and machinations of Senator McCarthy and his ilk. They had pigeonholed him with the Senate Subcommittee on Internal Security although the senator was not a member. Wittfogel's subsequent and vain attempt to set the record straight could not undo the damage that had been done.[41]

Therefore, Canada's then External Affairs Minister Lester B. Pearson was able to characterize Wittfogel's testimony as an "unimpressive and unsubstantiated allegation" by a former member of the Communist Party.[42] After a thorough investigation he could conclude that Norman was a "devoted and loyal [civil] servant."[43] Six years later the Montreal *Gazette* would cogently editorialize that Pearson's statement, as well as one by an External Affairs "spokesman," had given a "somewhat misleading impression" that not only had Norman never been to Provincetown, Cape Cod, Massachusetts, "but that allegations about his belonging to student Communist groups were absurd."[44]

In London, the Director of the Foreign Office's Far East Department was informed by a member of the Canadian High Commission that Pearson and the Canadian Department of External Affairs "were very indignant" over Wittfogel's mention of Norman's name. It had caused External Affairs "some embarrassment,"[45] and it was now forced to issue an official statement that Norman had been subjected to the normal security clearance by the appropriate Canadian authorities, according to established rules which applied to all officials of External Affairs. Subsequently, the statement admitted, reports had reached the Department which reflected adversely on Norman's loyalty to Canada, alleging that he had, in the past, been associated with the Communist Party. After being "very carefully and fully investigated" by the appropriate security authorities (read here RCMP), "Norman was given a clean bill of health," and, accordingly, remained a "trusted and valuable official" of External Affairs.[46] The statement was deceptive. To the uninitiated reader the inference was that the RCMP had given Norman a "clean bill of health". This was not so. The RCMP's role had merely been to supply whatever information it had about Norman. It was the employing department, in this case External Affairs, that had to make the decision whether or not to keep him on. External Affairs decided to maintain him in its ranks.

If thoroughness is a *sine qua non* in the security clearance of any official who has access to secret and confidential information, this did not prove true in Norman's case, and was partially reflected in the fact that the Canadian authorities never made any attempt to interview Wittfogel.[47] To have done so would have had its risks. Under intelligent questioning by the RCMP, the confusion in his mind about where he had first encountered Norman might have led him to realize that they had probably met as early as May-July 1934 at Cambridge University, as well as at Columbia, and at the Institute of Pacific Relations. Therefore, the RCMP's suspicions about Norman, developed by the autumn of 1950, would have been rekindled. That was the last thing in the world that Pearson or the mandarins at External Affairs would have wanted to see. Indeed, Pearson was wary of any editorializing which might keep the question in public view. No doubt he hoped that interest in Norman would soon disappear.[48] In addition, any questioning of Wittfogel might have revealed other damaging information about Norman, such as Wittfogel's subsequent assertion to the Senate Subcommittee's counsel that the people in Finkelstein's alleged study group "were mature Communists."[49]

In fact, it was so much easier for Ottawa to denigrate the eminent Sinologue who had suffered at the hands of the Nazis, than to invite him to Canada to be questioned by the RCMP. Nor was the government daunted, in the least, by its own brand of McCarthyism in reverse, namely, to vilify Wittfogel on the ground that he was a former communist and hence outside the pale. Waving a maple leaf flag in this situation certainly had its advantages.

It therefore would not be unfair to say that Norman was being treated in a very generous fashion. Even before his studies at Columbia University he became an early contributor to the left-wing journal *Amerasia* and in 1939 started to contribute to the left-wing *Far Eastern Survey*.[50] He was also associated with the Institute of Pacific Relations which, subsequently, published his seminal work, *Japan's Emergence as a Modern State. Political and Economic Problems of the Meiji Period* (1940). Someone sympathetic to him has noted that both the Institute and *Amerasia* were later attacked as being "heavily infiltrated by Communists," and that these attacks were not without foundation.[51] Indeed, in 1950, looking back, one of Norman's colleagues in External Affairs who had been secretary to the Institute's Canadian Council had no doubt that in the early 1940s its American counterpart had been infiltrated by individuals whose convictions varied little from those of the communists. Whether or not they were party members was unclear but they certainly did not challenge the party's stance.[52] Norman echoed these comments in August 1951 at a reception to celebrate Indonesia's independence. He told a member of the Senate Subcommittee staff that though Wittfogel's testimony had been a "matter of guilt by association" he had realized while he had been a member of the Institute that "there were doubtful elements in the IPR and too close association was not desirable."[53]

The Institute was investigated by the Senate Subcommittee on Internal Security. It concluded that its "effective leadership" used the Institute's "prestige to promote the interests of the Soviet Union in the United States"; it was a "vehicle used by the Communists to orientate American far eastern policies toward Communist objectives." This conclusion dovetailed with the sworn testimony of senior Russian intelligence officers who had defected to the West.[54]

Together with the subcommittee's report, the observations by J.H.A. Watson, first secretary of the British Embassy in Washington, were perhaps more to the point. The most interesting aspects of the subcommittee's hearings, he wrote to the Foreign Office's American Department, were those which threw "light on the workings of the Soviet system in general, and in particular on the way in which the Russians were able to infiltrate" into the Institute "men engaged in the operations of disseminating ideas and even espionage." In particular, Watson noted, the report helped explain "*front organizations* founded by the communists to further their international purposes . . . which the communists succeed in *penetrating*." He thought this distinction was especially "important for the understanding of communist operations in the outside world, and [was] still far from clearly appreciated by the lay public."[55]

As to *Amerasia*, it was conveniently located in the same building as the Institute of Pacific Relations. Like its co-tenant, it was a front organization penetrated by the Communist Party. Initially, its editorial point of view and its political orientation were largely anti-Japanese. This dovetailed neatly with Soviet Russia's anxieties about Japan's actions in Manchuria and China, and the integral nationalism and expansionist tactics of its ruling military clique. Then in 1941, following the collapse of the united front between the Chinese Communist Party and General Chiang Kai-shek's Nationalist government led by the Kuomintang Party against the Japanese invaders, *Amerasia* directed its criticism against Chiang Kai-shek's inefficient, corrupt, and authoritarian cabal. Its editorial board was a mixed group but its effective leadership which clearly included Chi Ch'ao-ting, was communist oriented. Jaffe was *Amerasia*'s publisher, managing editor, and editor-in-chief. Far more committed to the Communist Party than he was Frederick Vanderbilt Field, scion of a wealthy family and sugar daddy to many a communist or communist-dominated organization. Although he held the title of Chairman of the Board of Editors, Field played no real role in editing *Amerasia*. All correspondence was handled by Jaffe in Field's name; Field shared equally with Jaffe the cost of *Amerasia*'s yearly operating deficit which was far from modest in those days. Field's claim that he had never carried a party card is probably correct but meaningless, since he was never out of step with the party's political zigs and zags.[56]

Lastly, there was The Johns Hopkins academic Owen Lattimore who was also part of the inner circle at the Institute of Pacific Relations. His interests were Inner Asia—Mongolia, Manchuria, and the Turkic areas of Soviet Russia and China. In 1952, he was charged by the Senate Subcommittee on Internal Security with having been "a conscious articulate instrument of the Soviet conspiracy" in the 1930s, someone who had perjured himself on at least five occasions. Sworn testimony, direct and indirect, by senior Russian intelligence officers who had defected to the West, connecting him to their former employers, lent substance to the subcommittee's charge.[57] Though indicted, some of these charges were subsequently dismissed on the ground that they were too vague and indefinite, and infringed on Lattimore's constitutional rights. In 1955 the Justice Department dropped all the charges against him because of lack of evidence. Lattimore had been sifted through the legal mesh.

Despite this, the remarks about Lattimore by First Secretary Watson to the Foreign Office's American Department are not without interest. Though they were concerned with Lattimore's activities at the Institute of Pacific Relations, they would, no doubt, equally apply to his work at *Amerasia*, as well as to his editorship of *Pacific Affairs*, a journal to which Norman contributed articles after Lattimore resigned in 1941. "Reputable scholars," Watson observed, who associated with Lattimore at the Institute of Pacific Relations, such as the

West's pre-eminent Japanologist Sir George Sansom, were "aware that Lattimore was at any rate guilty of endeavouring by covert methods, to impose a clear political line on what was proclaimed to be a body engaged in objective, academic research—a serious enough offence to a scholar, but hardly indictable." Indeed, Lattimore's works on Manchuria and Mongolia were "regarded as dangerous and misleading in their pro-Soviet plausibility by experts on communism in the State Department and in the Foreign Office." As to what the subcommittee actually uncovered about Lattimore, "some of the evidence [was] certainly more impressive than the vague and often absurd charges produced against State Department officials."[58]

In early June 1945, Jaffe and others were arrested by the FBI and charged with violating the Espionage Act following a search of *Amerasia*'s offices, albeit without a proper search warrant. That led to the discovery of hundreds of official documents, some highly classified. Probably only a handful were sensitive, and no evidence was ever produced that they had been conveyed to a foreign power. Jaffe subsequently denied that he had been involved in espionage, however, he and another co-defendant were later tried, convicted and heavily fined. The Grand Jury failed to indict three of those arrested because of insufficient evidence.[59]

By this point, Norman was serving in External Affairs in Ottawa and was in no way involved. Nevertheless, his earlier association with *Amerasia* is important for it brought about a close relationship between the Normans and the Jaffes that lasted until Norman went to External Affairs. During that period, the two couples often saw each other and, at times, the Normans enjoyed the hospitality of the Jaffes' home. Jaffe's repeated observation, therefore, that until Norman joined External Affairs in July 1939, he knew him as a member of the Canadian Communist Party[60] has to be noted and cannot be doubted in view of other available information.

During the time when Norman allegedly attended Finkelstein's gatherings, was associated with the Institute of Pacific Relations, and contributed to *Amerasia* and *Far Eastern Survey*, he was also, according to Jaffe, "close" to V. Frank Coe, as reported by American naval intelligence to the FBI.[61] Since Coe taught in the Department of Political Economy at the University of Toronto from 1934 onward, Norman probably had met him upon his return from Cambridge.[62] Coe—who also knew Chi Ch'ao-ting[63]—would, in later years, be implicated as a member of an alleged communist spy ring within the

Treasury Department; he was summarily removed as Secretary of the International Monetary Fund. Along with his chief, Assistant Secretary of the Treasury Harry Dexter White—later identified as a Russian agent by Whittaker Chambers, Elizabeth Bentley, and Gouzenko through the documents he removed from the Russian Embassy in Ottawa—Coe had, during the war, contributed toward undercutting the economic stability of the Chinese Nationalist government of General Chiang Kai-shek. His prosecution proved impossible, however, once he had established residence in Communist China.[64] As to Chi Ch'ao-ting, he was recruited to serve in the Ministry of Finance by the Chinese Nationalist government under General Chiang Kai-shek on the ground that he would be "useful because he knew" Harry Dexter White.[65]

In March 1939 Norman's Rockefeller fellowship was renewed,[66] however, in early July he decided to accept the appointment as language officer for the Canadian Legation in Tokyo. This posting had been no snap decision by the Department of External Affairs, but rather was based on Norman's assiduous persistence, both by mail and by personal visits to Ottawa, to acquire a position with External Affairs. His initial probe had been made in August 1935, soon after his return from Trinity College, Cambridge University, and probably before being appointed teaching master at Upper Canada College. In the years that followed he continued to express interest in joining External Affairs.[67] As we have seen, he was, during that time, a member of the Canadian Communist Party and allegedly held secret party meetings in his lodgings. The story, therefore, that in 1939 after becoming aware of External Affairs' interest in experts on the Far East, Norman applied and was accepted, is erroneous in the extreme.[68] No, the evidence overwhelmingly points to the fact that he had set his sights long ago and that Jaffe's advice to reject a position with External Affairs[69] naturally went unheeded.

Once ensconced in the Department, Norman openly admitted that he had been a member of a communist cell while at Cambridge.[70] Wisely, his activities with his Indian classmates do not appear to have been mentioned, nor his attendance at the Tsuru and Finkelstein study groups. With the signing of the Ribbentrop-Molotov Pact in August 1939 and the outbreak of the war in September, the Canadian government banned the Communist Party and arrested its leaders. Norman was frightened that he might be arrested along with his Victoria College contemporary Charles P. H. Holmes who, like Norman, had attended the Methodist Academy at Kobe and was employed by the Civil Service Commission.[71] Holmes, who had been an official witness at Norman's wedding, was allegedly "a secret member of an underground branch of the [Communist] Party in Ottawa and was very active in the Communist movement."[72] After the war, he raised the suspicions of American military intelligence in Tokyo.[73] Norman maintained that they might be arrested "not because they were leaders or even members of the party, but because of their past associations."[74]

The question might be raised how thorough a security clearance Norman was subjected to before entering External Affairs. The assertion that he "underwent his first security check" at that time is factually incorrect.[75] In essence, he did not undergo any clearance procedure as that term is understood today. As the ubiquitous "old boys" network appears to have been the order of the day, most individuals were accepted by External Affairs because they were known to an officer in the department, or their teacher, also well known in the department, had written a letter on the candidate's behalf. Clerical and secretarial personnel were not cleared at any level. It was only after Gouzenko's defection and the revelations that followed—and based on the recommendations of the Royal Commission which investigated Gouzenko's disclosures—that a vetting system was instituted under the auspices of the RCMP.[76] This lax procedure was not unique to Canada. An analogous "old boys" network functioned in Great Britain which helps to explain how Guy Burgess and Donald Maclean were accepted into the Foreign Office, Kim Philby into MI6, and Anthony Blunt into MI5.[77] Of course, one could cogently argue that during the late 1930s, the worry was not whether Stalin's disciples were entering government service, but rather those of Hitler or Mussolini who were correctly perceived to be the immediate and objective enemies. Yet, by no stretch of the imagination, were the scandalously lax security procedures adequate to filter out potential Nazi or fascist agents. Consequently, Ottawa's 1951 statement following Wittfogel's testimony, that Norman had been subjected to normal security clearance was deceptive in the extreme.

There is one additional point. When Norman was appointed, the Under-Secretary for External Affairs was Oscar D. Skelton, sometimes referred to as the "father of the civil service." In his youth he had been interested in socialist theory having authored a well-received volume entitled *Socialism: A Critical Analysis* (Boston: Houghton

Mifflin, 1911). His work attracted the attention of an obscure Russian refugee who, in a letter to Skelton from Switzerland, stated that it was "the best work on socialism by a bourgeois scholar" he had ever read. That refugee was none other than Vladimir Ilich Lenin.[78]

If we can accept as reasonably accurate the reminiscences of Tim Buck, the Canadian Communist Party's longtime leader, it would appear that Skelton's weakness for the dialectic had not withered with the years.[79] Indicative of this, for example, were the kind of questions posed to candidates taking the 1936 civil service examination for third secretary in External Affairs. In the historical section of the paper, they were asked, among other things, to trace socialism's development in any one European state and the role it had played in that state's economic and political life. In the political science section they were requested to discuss individual liberty under socialism.[80] This is not to imply that Skelton was disloyal to his country but that his youthful intellectual curiosity would probably have moved him to overlook what he may have considered the not dissimilar wanderings of a Herbert Norman, or indeed, of other Norman-like individuals who applied for positions with External Affairs. Yet his attitude would not have been unique. There is abundant evidence that it was not uncommon among officials in London as well as in other places. However, Skelton's early wanderings through the ideological thicket did not go unnoticed by the RCMP who, many years after his death in 1941, made him the subject of an investigation. They concluded that "his appointments at External Affairs showed no evidence of packing the department with suspected communists."[81]

Chapter 4

Tokyo: Prewar–Postwar

Norman's first External Affairs posting abroad came in May 1940, as language officer at the Canadian Legation in Tokyo. He was subsequently promoted to third secretary, and following the outbreak of hostilities in the Pacific, and the Canadian declaration of war against Japan, he was interned, as were his American, British, and other allied counterparts.

It was not until arrangements had been made through the neutral states of Portugal and Sweden that these nationals of the belligerent powers could be exchanged. Disembarking at Lourenço Marques in the then Portuguese colony of Mozambique in East Africa, Norman encountered Shigeto Tsuru at the quayside. It was night and, according to Norman, Tsuru informed him in hurried conversation that he had left books, papers and some historical works in his apartment in Cambridge, Massachusetts. He wanted Norman to have them "as a gift," and he was sure the apartment's janitor would give him the material.[1] It was a fateful arrangement.

Arriving in New York in late August 1942 on the Swedish liner *Gripsholm*, Norman was briefly interviewed by the FBI. Understandably, Washington and, indeed, all the allied capitals, were interested in amassing as much information as they could about the Japanese and their allies. The interview, therefore, was a *pro forma* debriefing of a diplomatic officer from an allied and friendly power and not, as one author tells us, an intrusion into his life.[2] Queried whether he had "information to offer regarding [the *Gripsholm's*] other passengers"—no doubt, a fear that American or foreign nationals friendly to the Japanese might have been planted on the ship—Norman answered in the negative.[3] Since the FBI did not inquire about other matters, Norman did not have to answer beyond what had been asked of him. He would only have been obligated to divulge specific other information to the RCMP or to some other Canadian authority. The fact of the matter is that, upon his return to Ottawa, there is not a scintilla of evidence to show that he ever mentioned to any Canadian government official his chance encounter with Tsuru and what they had discussed.

General Sherman has told us, "War is cruel and you cannot refine it." There can be no friendship in war. Accordingly, Norman was duty bound to report to the proper Canadian authorities his contact with Tsuru, who was, after all, a subject of the Emperor of Japan, a country at war with Canada. His conduct raises serious doubts about his sense of proportion and his sense of responsibility. When faced in Lisbon with an almost analogous situation, Pearson had held his tongue and had avoided speaking to a Harvard-educated German official he had known during the Geneva disarmament discussions in the 1930s. "I realized," Pearson tells us, "as he may have too, who we were and where and when."[4] Keeping in mind Pearson's behavior, "mendacious" may be the uncharitable adjective one might use to describe Norman's actions.

Repairing to Cambridge, Massachusetts in early November 1942, Norman attempted to acquire Tsuru's possessions. His version of the event, given about a year after his trek, was that he called on the janitor of the apartment building and identified himself. When asked if he had anything to show that might entitle him to receive Tsuru's belongings, Norman responded in the negative, suggesting that if the janitor wished further assurances, he had merely to consult the Cambridge police and the authorities at Harvard University. They agreed that Norman should return once the janitor had verified his credentials. When he came back to the apartment he was met by the janitor and two FBI officers. Norman asserted that these officers were "hostile," "abusive," and impolite to boot. He gave his identity, explaining that he was Tsuru's friend, and a Canadian civil servant. They abused him because he was an alien, Norman recounted, asking what right he had as an alien to acquire the belongings of a Japanese. Supposedly, Norman had to explain that Canada, like the United

States, was at war with Japan, and that he was not intent on causing the United States any harm.[5]

Norman's version of the Cambridge episode that he supposedly gave to Tsuru immediately after the war was recounted by Tsuru to the Senate Subcommittee on Internal Security. It is devoid of much of the substantive detail Norman had given in 1943—the confrontation with the FBI and their alleged less than gentle handling of him. Tsuru, perhaps due to a lapse of memory, failed to mention to the subcommittee that it had been at his request, during a quick conversation at Lourenço Marques, that Norman had journeyed to Cambridge to retrieve his possessions.[6] With the passage of time, it is inevitable that distortions develop when events are reconstructed, however, only the most naive would accept Norman's account of what had occurred; the FBI's depiction is far different.

On November 9, according to the FBI, Norman contacted them to secure Tsuru's possessions. Exhibiting his Canadian diplomatic passport which identified him as a third secretary of External Affairs, he mentioned that he had recently served as the language officer at the legation in Tokyo. To secure possession of the property and to establish his authority to do so, Norman produced Tsuru's personal calling card, addressed to someone else. The card, introducing Norman, was dated June 1942 and signed by Tsuru. He explained that it had been given to him by the addressee who was working at the War Production Board. It had been mailed to the addressee by Tsuru in August 1942, with instructions that it be given to Norman once he arrived in Washington. No mention was made of the meeting at Lourenço Marques, when the calling card probably was given to him by Tsuru.

Initially, Norman had claimed that he was on an "official mission for the Canadian government," to obtain the books for use by Ottawa in a "special investigation." Mentioning his diplomatic immunity, he had observed that "he was on a highly confidential mission" whose details he could not disclose. His original instructions, he explained, had been to contact the Canadian Legation in Washington. On his return to Ottawa he had stopped at Cambridge to take control of Tsuru's possessions, giving the name of an External Affairs official who could verify his mission to Washington and that he was a member of the department. If need be, Norman had boldly asserted, he could "go as high as the Prime Minister of Canada" in order to acquire possession of these books.

Norman's name-dropping, his waving of credentials, and claims of diplomatic status, in a society far less deferential than the Canadian one, and especially his story, must have made no impression on his FBI interlocutors and, indeed, may have raised some doubts in their minds. He must have sensed that, for he soon beat a quick retreat indicating that he did have a "personal interest" in Tsuru's possessions. He backed down on earlier assertions that he was on a "special mission" to secure the material for Ottawa.[7]

If the FBI version of this encounter is even remotely accurate, Norman's whole performance was breathtaking. Initially, he had been less than candid, yet credence to either version would have to be based on the intangible. Surely, it is difficult to believe that FBI officers serving in Boston during the war could have been as politically obtuse or ill-mannered as Norman had claimed, especially vis-à-vis a diplomatic officer of an allied and friendly power. The slightest objection to their alleged misconduct would have been ruinous to their careers in the Bureau. There is no evidence that he ever registered such an objection, but then again the whole encounter would not have been something he would have wanted bandied about. Should it have come to the attention of his superiors at External Affairs, he would have had to explain his silence after meeting Tsuru in Lourenço Marques. Therefore, any conversation about the matter was to be wisely avoided.

Undoubtedly, Cambridge had been on Norman's itinerary during that trip, however, its purpose had been to consult with people at Harvard University on official matters. For inexplicable reasons the encounter with the FBI was not reported to its Washington office until four years later, when Norman was attached to General Douglas MacArthur's Headquarters in Tokyo. Nor, it appears, was an account of what transpired in Cambridge ever communicated to the Canadian authorities. Norman had escaped unscathed; in the debit column, however, the reports on this chance encounter in Boston and on his debriefing interview in New York on disembarking the *Gripsholm*, were the first two papers in a growing FBI file on Herbert Norman.

His track record on this matter does not inspire faith in his candor and his alleged remarks to the FBI interrogators about his diplomatic status and credentials, smack of Norman's confidence that his polish and panache would carry the day. Surely, he was assuming great risk in such an enterprise, and it is exceedingly difficult to believe that he did this merely to acquire Tsuru's books, no matter how great a bibliophile he might have been on all things Japanese.[8]

Neither can one accept the almost absurd interpretation that he would have assumed so great a risk to acquire these possessions consisting of Marxist books and papers, which, if reported to the wartime Japanese authorities, would have undoubtedly placed Tsuru's life at stake. How or why this would have been done by the American authorities is not explained.[9] No, the answer to his bizarre conduct must lie in the nature of the papers which, unknown to Norman, had been examined and confiscated by the FBI the day before he arrived at the apartment.

What was in these papers? According to the FBI, they included writings in five languages (English, French, German, Japanese, and Russian). They were largely composed of "Communist literature and propaganda," including a memorandum of over twenty pages "regarding the procedure of the Communist Party in approaching the intelligentsia of the United States, and comparing the approach with that of the Communist Party Workers School for the lower classes." There was also Tsuru's address book which, understandably, contained Norman's name; likewise there was personal correspondence relating to Tsuru's study group at Harvard, including the mention of Norman and his paper on American imperialism. Was Tsuru a communist, the FBI officers had asked Norman during their discussion. No, he had replied.[10] As the Senate Subcommittee's counsel assured Tsuru in 1957, perhaps ironically, some of these papers which had come to the committee's attention had provided "valuable information" about all sorts of matters.[11]

Between his arrival in Ottawa and his departure for Cambridge Norman was made head of a special intelligence section within External Affairs. Its personnel was very limited, Norman heading its Japanese operations, into which he later seconded his brother Howard, because of his knowledge of Japanese. Even before his repatriation on the *Gripsholm*, however, the question had been raised on the American side whether Norman could be assigned to Washington by the Canadian authorities, to help establish liaison regarding Japanese studies between Canadian and British intelligence agencies, and the Office of Strategic Services directed by Colonel William Donovan. The proposal had been tendered by Charles F. Remer, Director of the Far Eastern Division of Donovan's group and a well-known economic historian from the University of Michigan who specialized in Far East questions. The Institute of Pacific Relations had helped support Remer's scholarly work and, since he had often been invited to its meetings and social functions and was acquainted with Owen Lattimore, one can speculate where the idea to assign Norman to this important role had originated. Remer had flown to Rio de Janeiro, had boarded the *Gripsholm* and, on the trip to New York, had discussed with Norman and the Canadian diplomat E. D. McGreer "the securing and handling of information on the Far East from the Canadian point of view." From this exchange it had become clear to Remer that "closer relations between the Canadians and ourselves in Far Eastern research" were desirable. Accordingly, he had proposed that the idea be informally conveyed, perhaps by Colonel Donovan personally, to a Canadian official who would be in a position to pass it on to the right person or persons in Ottawa.

On November 4, 1942, a few days before going to Cambridge, Norman received a letter of introduction to Colonel Donovan from Lester Pearson, now Minister-Counsellor of the Canadian Legation in Washington. Donovan's acceptance of Norman's appointment soon followed,[12] and in turn, was also sanctioned by the British. Thus he was allowed "to check his political analyses against" those of his American and British counterparts. Indeed, his Japanese reports not only had attracted Donovan's attention, but had also influenced Canadian wartime intelligence services which had been guided in their assessments by Norman's critiques. This had been of special importance when Japan had held the initiative in the Pacific fighting. Norman, therefore, "was able to direct Canadian thinking on post-war Japan" which he would subsequently be "charged with translating into policy."[13]

No sooner had he been repatriated to Canada than Philip J. Jaffe and his wife hurried from New York to greet him and Mrs. Norman who had been evacuated from Japan before the outbreak of hostilities in the Pacific. It soon became very apparent to Philip that Herbert was not pleased with the visit. When during their conversation Jaffe casually used the abbreviation CP—often used when alluding to the Communist Party—Norman admonished him to lower his voice as though they might be overheard. Jaffe then quickly retorted that the only thing he meant by CP was the Canadian Pacific Railway Company.

It would appear that Norman had started distancing himself from the Jaffes from the moment he entered External Affairs. Even when Mrs. Jaffe had visited Tokyo before the outbreak of hostilities in the

Pacific, Norman had appeared embarrassed by her presence. Considering the barely reciprocated hospitality the Jaffes had often offered to the Normans in New York, this unexpectedly cool reception greatly surprised Mrs. Jaffe.[14] In the years that followed Norman visited Jaffe in New York only once, in 1943,[15] thereafter avoiding him altogether, despite his frequent official visits to New York. Even when Jaffe was involved in the *Amerasia* case, there was no letter of sympathy from Norman, nor did he write to him when Senator McCarthy attacked him in 1950.[16] This might help to explain Jaffe's "grudge against" Norman and his feeling of being "slighted by being dropped."[17] According to American naval intelligence, Jaffe believed that the reasons for this snub might have been traced to the testimony of Elizabeth Bentley—a defector from the American communist apparatus—for whom she had been a courier. According to Bentley, those on the Left had been warned to give Jaffe a wide berth as he was overly loquacious with his communist comments.[18]

But the Jaffes were not the only ones. MacLeod, who had attended secret Communist Party meetings in Norman's lodgings, was also cold-shouldered by Norman who would cross to the other side of the street whenever he saw him.[19]

Initially, Jaffe had come to the conclusion that Norman was an agent of the communist apparatus. His argument might have been that, according to established procedure anyone recruited as an agent must sever all links with the party, and with anyone who can be clearly identified as sympathetic to it, or an actual party member.[20] Certainly, Norman's behavior toward Jaffe and MacLeod could perplex even the most skeptical. In turn, they might cogently argue that Norman, loyal to the Crown, wanted to avoid his old communist associates as they would only cause him embarrassment. However, the fact of the matter is that in 1947 he visited Kiernan at Cambridge University when Kiernan was still a member of the Communist Party. But Kiernan did not have the high profile of a Jaffe or a MacLeod and, during a return to his alma mater, who would have noticed his visit anyway? Kiernan concluded from their talk that Norman's "heart was still in the right place," but that he no longer had organized contacts with the party. Then came Norman's pregnant request that Kiernan "not mention him to others," and especially not to fellow Canadian Henry Ferns who, Norman held, had been forced to resign from External Affairs "because he was too indiscreet." Ferns had run afoul of its astute Under-Secretary Norman

Robertson, especially on the advice he had given to Prime Minister Mackenzie King on what Canada's policy should be toward India. Using this policy difference to force Ferns out of the Department appears to have been nothing more than a smoke screen to disguise Robertson's real motive: he did not want Ferns within External Affairs. [21]

The Norman-Ferns connection goes back to the time when Norman had surrendered to Kiernan the task of being the liaison between the Indian students and the Communist Party on the Cambridge campus. Later, Kiernan had passed on the job to Ferns, despite the fact that he had never actually taken out a party card. [22]

With time, Jaffe changed his mind about Norman being an agent of the communist apparatus. He based his new view on Pearson's misleading comments, following Norman's suicide, that neither he, Pearson, nor the Canadian authorities, including the RCMP, had ever known of any "contacts or actions" by Norman during his career in External Affairs "which could in any way be questioned from a security point of view." [23] Because of these comments and, especially, because of Pearson's use of the word "contacts," Jaffe concluded that it was Pearson who, by 1942, had admonished Norman to avoid the Jaffes and the MacLeods of the world—people he had known prior to entering External Affairs. According to Jaffe, it was a ploy by Pearson not only to protect Norman but also the Canadian government. [24]

It is incumbent upon anyone investigating these murky waters to examine Jaffe's rethinking. His contention is not without merit. Pearson did return to Canada from London for a long-delayed home leave in late June 1939. He vacationed in Manitoba and hurriedly returned to London as it became increasingly obvious that Europe would soon plunge into war. [25] Since Norman entered External Affairs on July 5, 1939 and stayed until October 7, at which point he got unpaid leave to go to Harvard to finish his doctoral dissertation (he returned to External Affairs on December 17, 1939), there would have been a short overlap before Pearson's return to London. External Affairs, during those years, was a limited body and the chances of a very junior officer such as Norman, seeing and talking with a senior officer such as Pearson were clearly probable. By the time Norman returned to Ottawa in the late summer of 1942, Pearson was Minister-Counsellor at the Canadian Legation in Washington. Why he might have discussed Norman's associations before entering External Affairs is unclear, although he may have been alerted by his admissions that he had been a member of a communist cell at Cambridge. There were several connecting links between these two men—both had gone to Victoria College and, indeed, Herbert's brother Howard had gone there with Pearson; both were Methodists, both their fathers had been Methodist ministers,[26] both worked for the Canadian government, in fact, in the same subdivision, namely the Department of External Affairs. It is possible that these links could have moved Pearson to advise Norman about what the former might have considered wayward behavior. The probability, however, is miniscule, in view of the short period of time Pearson spent in Canada during that long-delayed home leave.

The war years in Ottawa soon brought Norman into contact with Ferns who had first been introduced to him, from a distance, when Norman had recommended the Japanese academic Kei Shibata, a Marxist but non-communist economist, to Kiernan at Cambridge; he, in turn, had introduced him to Ferns. Since both Norman and Ferns had participated in the Cambridge ideological experience, the relationship between them was warm. They also shared "an optimistic view of the potentialities of the masses for good" which, Ferns tells us, was not inspired by Marxism. Understandably, they reminisced about their Cambridge days, and their friendship, based on "ideological and philosophic agreement," led to free and wide-ranging discussions on many matters. Unlike Ferns, whose loquaciousness did not allow him to appreciate that his "enthusiasm for the liberating experience of discovering Marxism generated hostility and disapproval in others," Norman had already undergone "several encounters that made him cautious and close-lipped about his underlying ideas in the presence of the generality of society." His encounters, however, had not been without trauma. They had affected him to the point of fearing what he "called 'proletarianization,' " that is to say, the denial of being able to intellectually ruminate which "would oblige him to become a casual labourer." Ferns' pithy description is that he and Norman "who were colleagues at work and Marxist historians in private, formed a little island of freedom in an intellectually hostile environment." His openness, described by Norman as indiscreetness, caused Norman to warn Ferns that "active political prejudice against Marxists was a lot stronger" than he supposed, regardless of the wartime enthusiasm manifested for Soviet Russia's struggle against Nazi Germany.

For example, articles in the American Communist Party weekly journal *New Masses,* deriding the anti-communist activities of the so-called Dies Committee of the American House of Representatives, moved Norman to observe that American communists should reside in Japan to really appreciate what anti-communism could be like. He felt that Americans were living in a "comparatively" open society which "had not yet developed a comprehensive system of political police." The FBI wanted a role in this anti-communist endeavor but, in general, it was the bailiwick of politicians seeking to obscure their plunder of the public treasury. Since some of these well-known anti-communist politicians were later convicted of such offenses, Ferns tells us Norman was right. Yet, his whole analysis appears sophomoric, lacking in the kind of depth and subtlety expected of someone whose livelihood was the close dissection of far more complicated political phenomena than the shortcomings and meanderings of the Dies Committee and its successors.

If there was one flaw in Norman's armor, according to Ferns, it was his desire to be within the charmed circle of insiders, proximate to the "centres of power and authority." He had an "insatiable interest in people who had power: how they behaved, what motivated them, how skillful they were, and so on." An offer of a full professorship at Yale University had caused him to waver, but in the end he decided against resigning from External Affairs: "there was no doubt that the attractions of being 'in the know' were too great," Ferns tells us.

Within External Affairs, Norman apparently did not generate any policy differences. No one referred to him as a "red," unlike Ferns who says that during that period he was a red, a "disaffected red." He further assures us that he was not a communist and that he is "sure"—not positive—that neither was Norman. Being a communist, he notes, requires activity within the party organization which neither he nor Norman undertook. In the 1940s and 1950s it meant obedience to Moscow's discipline. This is correct, but does not apply if you are an agent of the communist apparatus. Quite the contrary, distancing yourself from the party is standard procedure. It also means distancing yourself from anyone who is even remotely associated with it. Perhaps this might explain Norman's comments to Kiernan in 1947 not to mention him to others, specifically not to Ferns, and Ferns' relative lack of contact with Norman, especially upon his return to Japan after the war.

What was Norman during these Ottawa years? Well, again according to Ferns, a Marxist as he was. The problem was, however, that Norman did not appear "to have made the effort to separate communism as a political activity from Marxism as a body of ideas and historical insights." Had he done so he would not, in later years, have been so open to attack by the Senate Subcommittee on Internal Security.[27]

The Japanese surrender in mid-August 1945 soon led to Norman's return to the Pacific area, first to the Philippines and then to Japan, to arrange for the repatriation of Canadians who had been held prisoners by the Japanese. Owen Lattimore believed that he was the best man for the job.[28] In early October 1945, while in Tokyo, Norman was seconded—with Ottawa's consent—into the United States Army's Counterintelligence Corps attached to the headquarters of General MacArthur[29] whose ponderous, official title was Supreme Commander for the Allied Powers for the Occupation and Control of Japan. Norman's assigned task was that of Chief of the Research and Analysis Section of the Chief Counterintelligence Office at General Headquarters in Japan. This entailed supervision of about thirty Americans in "interrogating and classifying thousands of Japanese politicians, military leaders, businessmen and intellectuals—both those who had supported the military regime during the war and those who had been imprisoned for opposing it."[30]

In an official communication to American counterintelligence in Tokyo, External Affairs bestowed its blessing on the new assignment by incorporating Owen Lattimore's laudatory comments about Norman's scholarly work, comparing him, perhaps with some hyperbole, to the West's pre-eminent Japanologist Sir George Sansom. In a marginal comment to the official note, an unidentified hand had scribbled that Norman's modesty had prevented him from bringing Lattimore's evaluation of his work to anyone's attention, pointing out that Lattimore, an outstanding academic on China, was teaching at The Johns Hopkins University in Baltimore, Maryland.[31] In view of a subsequent report about Lattimore by the British Embassy in Washington, this was an interesting aside, not to mention his initial support of Norman's transfer to the Pacific area to help repatriate imprisoned Canadians.

Though General Elliot Thorpe, Norman's superior, would on Norman's departure from Tokyo in late January 1946, praise his work in a letter to Prime Minister Mackenzie King,[32] it is a fact that it was in Tokyo where the first American suspicion about Norman began to develop. The initial objection to employing him, it would appear, was raised by General Charles Willoughby, General MacArthur's chief of intelligence.[33] He was opposed to accepting him into General Thorpe's counterintelligence section on the ground that though a diplomat of an allied and friendly power, he would, nevertheless, be privy to highly secret security information.[34] Willoughby's objections were not without merit, but one suspects they were perhaps also motivated by the hostility that existed between him and General Thorpe, based on Willoughby's desire to bring under his control all counterintelligence activity in Japan.[35]

Willoughby's opposition to Norman, initially based on security considerations, soon changed to suspicions. How they developed chronologically is difficult to fathom, but what they were can be related. According to Willoughby, Norman had first attracted his attention when the Hungarian diplomatic mission in Tokyo closed. The Hungarians were destitute and probably needed money to buy their passage home. As Hungary had been a member of the Axis coalition, the files of the Hungarian mission would have been important to General Willoughby; and the monetary plight of the Hungarians would have been a golden opportunity to acquire custody of these papers. But when he inquired about them, he was informed that they were already in Norman's possession.[36] Considering his assigned role for American counterintelligence in Japan, his interest in, and acquisition of, these files are distinctly odd. Certainly, they do not appear to have been of any interest to the Canadian authorities, and what subsequently happened to them is also unclear.

The next incident that attracted General Willoughby's attention involved Norman's role and that of the State Department's John K. Emmerson, in approaching the political prisoners at Fuchu prison in Tokyo.[37] They included the long-incarcerated communist inmates Tokuda Kyuichi and Shiga Yoshio who were to become leaders of Japan's postwar Communist Party. The idea that it might be useful to talk to these political prisoners came from *Newsweek* correspondent Harold Isaacs who, in the past, appeared to have been a communist.[38] Having already interviewed several of the prison's communist inmates, he suggested to Emmerson that someone from MacArthur's Headquarters "might profitably talk with these future political activists." When Emmerson broached the idea to Norman who he had first met in Tokyo in 1941 when they were serving in their respective diplomatic missions, Norman "was enthusiastic," and, with permission from their superiors, they soon repaired to the prison.

Subsequently, Norman recalled that the prisoners numbering thirty to forty, were composed of "communists, pacifists, Korean nationalists and members of a Shinto sect which did not recognize the claim to the throne of the present ruling family in Japan." Emmerson's recollection, on the other hand, was that the group comprised sixteen—two Koreans, two members of the Shinto sect, and twelve communists. Regardless which figure is correct, one suspicious RCMP officer marginally noted on Norman's explanation of what had occurred at Fuchu prison: "was TSURU in this group?" The answer is no. After compiling a list of names, Norman and Emmerson drove back to Tokyo to make a preliminary report. This was probably on October 5, 1946, one day after General MacArthur's Headquarters had issued the order to release all political prisoners arrested by the Japanese. General Thorpe asked both of them to return to Fuchu prison with others, and to bring back for interrogation "representatives of all the political groups in the prison." Norman claimed that they executed these instructions, probably on October 7. What he did not explain, however, was that he and Emmerson brought Tokuda, Shiga, and a Korean communist from Fuchu prison to headquarters for interrogation. It appears that they questioned only these three which can hardly be regarded as a representative sampling. Although it was later maintained that this action gave the Japanese Communist Party a much needed boost, there is no evidence to support this assertion. Nor was there anything improper in Norman's or Emmerson's actions, in view of the prior permission they had received from their superiors.[39] On the other hand, Norman's enthusiasm, described by Emmerson, to talk to the communist inmates cannot go entirely unnoticed. Did he show similar enthusiasm to interview the non-communist prisoners, specifically those belonging to the Shinto sect, and possibly others who, like the communists, had suffered at the hands of the Japanese military?

Lastly, there was the return to Japan of Sanzo Nosaka, the leader of the Communist Party. One must guardedly view General Willoughby's suspicion that Nosaka, who had returned via China and North Korea, did so with permission obtained for him by Norman.[40] Nosaka is only aware of the role Emmerson and his associate John Stewart Service played in obtaining permission for his return.[41] In fairness to Willoughby, however, it has to be pointed out that United

States Army counterintelligence in Tokyo had accurate information from "local sources" that Norman was a friend of Service who was subsequently dismissed by the State Department on the advice of the Loyalty Review Board because he had been implicated in the *Amerasia* case. The board, therefore, had reasonable doubt as to his loyalty. Although President Truman had declined to review the State Department's decision, on appeal, the Supreme Court unanimously ruled in Service's favor, holding that he had been wrongfully discharged. He returned to active duty with the State Department, retiring in 1962. According to Army counterintelligence, Norman and Service along with Emmerson and others had made an "abortive attempt" to expedite the return to Japan of the Japanese communists from the town of Yenan controlled by the Communist Chinese.[42] Nosaka was one of them, and if the attempt to hasten his return and that of the others was made prior to MacArthur's order of October 4, it does raise some suspicions. If it was made after the order was issued, it can be cogently justified.

The important point, however, is how General Willoughby perceived these different incidents. Collectively, they led him to believe that Norman "was very active and unduly concerned with Communist affairs." This perception was later heightened by reports from military intelligence, connecting him with "Communist leanings."[43] His previous, ideological strolls and associations were now slowly coming home to roost. What had started out as Willoughby's objection to his employment had shifted to doubts about the man himself. As Willoughby's office was to admit to military intelligence in Washington in late November 1950, they had "long held suspicions" about Norman.[44]

It is unclear, however, whether it was because of Willoughby's initial objections or perhaps because of his accumulating suspicions, or both, that he "terminated this extraordinary intimacy"[45] between Norman and American counterintelligence. Suffice it to note, that the general's action may partially explain why Norman served in General Thorpe's unit only from October 1945 to January 1946, despite his knowledge of Japan, his linguistic skill, and obvious intelligence, all of which would have been of considerable value to American military counterintelligence.

There were other problems. During that period in Tokyo many of Norman's old associations were rekindled. No sooner had he arrived in September 1945 than he searched for and discovered in a war-torn Tokyo his old Harvard study group leader Tsuru who later testified that they were to meet many times in the years that followed.[46] Though Owen Lattimore had known Norman "very slightly" when they had been associated with the Institute of Pacific Relations, during that Tokyo period he saw him "quite frequently."[47] According to Senate Subcommittee records, Norman also "closely associated in Japan" with the ubiquitous Chi Ch'ao-ting, and Lattimore, aside from now being close to Norman, was also close to him[48] and, in turn, met Tsuru in Norman's company several times.[49]

It was Tsuru's display of loyalty to the communist cause that initially attracted the attention of the Americans. Whether rightly or wrongly, he was described as an "intellectual Communist and one of the group who would be called upon to run Japan in case of a Communist coup." Moreover, it was held that he was a "member of the Japanese Young Communist League and the Japanese Communist Party."[50] Even if this was not true, it must have raised additional suspicion about Norman in Tokyo quarters, in view of his prewar and postwar association with Tsuru.

Norman's contact with other Japanese also raised suspicions. One was with Matsubei Matsuo, a translator-interpreter for the United States political adviser's office in Tokyo.[51] When the Japanese Council of the Institute of Pacific Relations had to be reorganized in 1946, Matsuo left that position to undertake the task.[52] Norman, however, had also been involved in reorganizing the Institute's Japanese branch which Willoughby allegedly viewed as a Russian spy nest,[53] and which his office described as "heavily weighted with known 'leftists' in control positions."[54]

It is in the nature of intelligence officers to be suspicious. Events in Tokyo had contributed to Willoughby becoming more so than would ordinarily have been the case. He had been directed, at one point, by whom is unclear, to impound a "possibly damaging . . . study on leftist infiltration" into Tokyo's military intelligence headquarters after the commencement of the occupation.[55] As a human being, he was not without fault, but his postwar experiences in Tokyo had sensitized and alerted him to be wary of all things and all people around him.

Following Norman's tour of duty in Tokyo he was appointed alternate Canadian delegate to the Far East Commission, technically in charge of overseeing Japan's occupation. Concurrently, he also became first secretary of the Canadian Legation in Washington. He returned to Japan in the summer of 1946 as Head of the Canadian Liaison Mission to MacArthur's Supreme Command. In 1947 he attended as a member of the Canadian delegation the tenth conference of the Institute of Pacific Relations at Stratford-on-Avon. At that point, as we have seen, he visited Kiernan at Cambridge. Also, as a member of the Canadian delegation, he had attended the Institute's conference in January 1945 at Hot Springs, Georgia and, seemingly on his own initiative, the Institute's 1942 conference at Mont Tremblant, Québec. The Commonwealth Conference at Canberra on the Japanese peace treaty (August 26-September 3, 1947) found him as an adviser to the Canadian delegation.[56]

During the years in Tokyo as Head of the Canadian Liaison Mission, Norman "frequently and quite openly" attended Marxist study group meetings at night. It was, supposedly, because of his desire to escape the accumulated drudgery to which he was exposed at the mission, as well as his attempt to enjoy exchanges with some Japanese intellectuals.[57] Oddly, no one appears to have been aware of these nocturnal forays. If, however, he would have been questioned about them, his perfectly reasonable response would have been that as head of a liaison mission it was his job to keep his hand on the pulse of Japanese left-wing opinion. What better way to do this than by attending these study groups, in view of the leftist current that appeared to be rising in Japan during that period.

Concurrently, Norman's personal relations with MacArthur were "good," although listening to the general's lengthy monologues must have been trying. His rapport with him appears to have been genuine despite Norman's concern with the so-called "reverse course" adopted in 1948. Under it, the establishment of a national police force was recommended, as an initial step toward setting up a defense force. Thousands sympathetic to the Left, including labor leaders, civil servants, and journalists, were dismissed from their jobs. Likewise, economic reforms were postponed to allow an increase in production and investment, at the risk of engendering failure in the breakup of Japan's ubiquitous business oligarchy.

This tack had been adopted by Washington in order to draw Japan, once again, into the global balance of power, now that Soviet Russia was perceived in western capitals as an anti-status–quo power. The struggle was largely political and strategic, although garbed in an ideological cloak. MacArthur's initial reforms, including the release of political prisoners in October 1945—in which Norman had played

a role—led to a strong left-wing upsurge that threatened the establishment of Japan as Asia's industrial and political bulwark against
Soviet Russia. These events led Norman to question MacArthur's
optimism about the occupation. Pessimistically, he warned Ottawa
that Japan's extreme Right was always close at hand.[58]

In late January 1950, Pearson came on an official visit to Japan.
MacArthur accorded him the attention, courtesy, and protocol war-
ranted by his stewardship of Canadian foreign affairs.[59] During the
visit, Pearson broached the subject of Norman's next posting, pro-
posing a possible tour of duty in Moscow. Norman opposed the
suggestion on the grounds that the embassy staff there was limited
and would not allow him to profitably follow Far Eastern events.
Instead, he raised the possibility of serving in Ottawa or somewhere
else. Subsequently he wrote to Pearson that although he would like
a European posting in the future, his choice would exclude Moscow.
London, in the immediate future, made more sense for anyone interested in the Far East, especially if the British capital from time to
time became the hub of conversations about the region. As another
future possibility, he suggested a posting to Peking, if and when
Canada recognized the Communist Chinese. Wherever sent he would
do his best, he assured Pearson.[60]

One would think that any ambitious and discerning senior officer
of the Canadian diplomatic service would have jumped at the opportunity to be assigned to Moscow as chief of mission, despite the
difficulties of living in Stalin's Russia in the early 1950s. Impediments
that might have caused others to balk at such an assignment did not
apply in this case. Norman was now in his early forties, healthy,
without children, and accustomed to the severe weather, likely to
be encountered during a Moscow winter. His argument had ignored
Russia's physical proximity to the Far East, especially its historical
involvement with China, Japan, Korea, and other countries in the
region. Certainly, the impact that postwar Soviet Russia was having
on the politics of the Far East, and Japan in particular, was enormous.
To view the Far East through the Kremlin's prism would have been
a unique opportunity for someone of Norman's expertise. One should,
however, accept him at his word when he said that the Canadian
mission's limited Moscow staff precluded close surveillance of the
Far East. It is not outside the realm of possibility, although there is
no proof of this, that Norman might have been approached by Russian intelligence services for possible recruitment and that he had

fended them off. Accordingly, avoiding Moscow and possible harassment might explain his rejection of the post. On the other hand, if he was being "run" by the Russians he might have been of limited value to them, sitting in Moscow. He would have been of greater use in London or Ottawa, the two cities he seemed to prefer to the Russian capital. Of course, going to Peking at some future point, as he had proposed, once Canada recognized Communist China, would have allowed him to meet his intimate friend Chi Ch'ao-ting. With the communist victory in China, Chi Ch'ao-ting, like the spy coming in from the cold, had dropped his disguise for all to see that he had been a member of the communist apparatus and a secret member of the Chinese Communist Party for close to three decades.

Probably at this juncture, and documentation is far from clear, the proposal was made to assign Norman as liaison officer between American and Canadian intelligence.[61] Since his posting had been a topic of discussion between him and Pearson, and he had expressed a wish to return to Ottawa, it probably had been first raised by Pearson with Norman, rather than the other way round, and then proposed by Pearson to the Americans. Indeed, he may have raised the subject with the Americans without first consulting Norman.

Circumstantial evidence for this exists, for in a communication to Norman on February 22, 1950, External Affairs' Under-Secretary Arnold Heeney noted that he and Pearson had concluded that, after an additional few months' duty in Japan, Norman should return to Ottawa. Accordingly, if he were to depart from Tokyo some time after mid-May he could have home leave and then report for his new External Affairs posting in early autumn.[62] No doubt, the North Korean invasion of South Korea in June of that year obviated these instructions, but it is interesting that Norman's new assignment was not described—an understandable precaution in view of the very sensitive nature of the functional position for which he was being groomed.

Pearson might have approached the Americans about Norman's appointment as liaison officer between American and Canadian intelligence through Glazebrook's Defense Liaison II, a division within External Affairs whose task was the "coordination of intelligence with other government agencies and with foreign governments." Defense Liaison II had "particularly close contact" with the Canadian Defense Department,[63] and Pearson's proposal made through them would have obviated RCMP concurrence or review of Norman's possible appointment.

Since the CIA had expressed to Ottawa a desire to have some sort of liaison arrangement with Canadian intelligence,[64] making Norman liaison officer made a certain amount of sense. This is especially true if one keeps in mind his wartime work as head of a special intelligence section within External Affairs, as well as his Far Eastern research activities with the British and Colonel William Donovan's Office of Strategic Services. In addition, one must not forget his work in General Elliot Thorpe's counterintelligence unit in Tokyo after the war. The proposal to the Americans, however, was the pressing of a lever that would release the gears in the machinery of government.

Chapter 5

Whitewash: First Phase,
October–December 1950

Any proposal to make Norman the liaison officer between American and Canadian intelligence would have entailed the consent of the CIA and of United States military intelligence. Technically, their tasks lay in overseas endeavors, while the FBI's, as the investigatory arm of the Department of Justice, lay within the confines of the United States and its possessions. Accordingly, any assessment of Norman's fitness or worthiness to play the important role the Canadian government wished to assign to him, and subsequent American consent, would have required that he be investigated by the FBI in the United States. Since it could not do so in Canada it would naturally have asked the RCMP for assistance. Direct and indirect evidence clearly shows that the RCMP was never made aware of the fact that Norman was being considered for the liaison post. This buttresses the notion that the proposal might have been conveyed to the Americans through External Affairs' Defense Liaison II. However, due to the long and close association between the FBI and the RCMP, their possible collaboration on this matter should have been foreseen. It obviously was not by those who had channeled Norman's name to Washington. Surely, any proposal of this nature also should have been preceded by an inquiry from External Affairs, the employing department, to the RCMP for information pertaining to Norman. The whole procedure appears to reflect a certain amount of hubris or External Affairs' determination to keep the RCMP out of its business. It also shows its lack of confidence in, if not outright hostility toward the Force.

The FBI's interest in Norman had been aroused well before he was proposed for the job of liaison officer. Following the defection in the autumn of 1945 of Igor Gouzenko, the cipher clerk at the Russian Embassy in Ottawa, the RCMP had made available to the FBI a copy of a notebook belonging to Israel Halperin, Norman's former classmate at Victoria College.[1]

Based on the documentary evidence found in the papers removed from the Russian Embassy by Igor Gouzenko, Halperin, now an associate professor of mathematics at Queen's University in Kingston, Ontario, was arrested in mid-February 1946 on charges of conspiring to convey to unauthorized people classified material. It appeared that in the course of Russian espionage operations directed in Canada by the embassy's military attaché Colonel Nikolai Zabotin, Halperin—ironically code named "Bacon"—had allegedly been asked to supply ballistics and other information. He apparently was considered well qualified for the job because of his wartime research activities as a Canadian Army major, serving at Valcartier, Québec. Indeed, when approached for assistance, he had supposedly shown enthusiasm and, as Zabotin's office was informed in late March 1945, was "politically experienced."[2] His latter quality probably was not unknown to Zabotin, for as the Canadian Royal Commission examining the whole affair had laconically noted, Halperin "was already known at the [Russian] Embassy."[3]

Halperin had refused to testify before the Royal Commission[4] and was acquitted at his subsequent trial. The court ruled that the evidence against him, including testimony that might have been given by Gouzenko, was inadmissible in a conspiracy case, since the defendant's alleged role as a conspirator had not been established. Curiously, a second charge, apparently stronger in law, alleging that Halperin had breached the Canadian Official Secrets Act, was also dropped.[5]

Since Norman's name had appeared in Halperin's notebook about seven times,[6] the FBI had made inquiries about him at Harvard University and at the University of California. However, they had closed the file[7] without reporting the matter to the RCMP.[8]

Lester Pearson assures us that Canada had "turned over all Gouzenko's evidence to the FBI."[9] Therefore, there can be no doubt that the RCMP had given the Bureau copies of documents dealing with Russian espionage in the United States. That material had been removed by Gouzenko from Colonel Zabotin's files at the Russian Embassy in Ottawa. Although most of it has been released for examination at the Public Archives in Ottawa, this documentation pertaining to espionage in the United States is still closed. It is a good example of third-country espionage, that is to say, conducting espionage against one country—the United States—while operating from another, in this case, Canada.[10]

In fact, Halperin's notebook contained not only Norman's name but also Tsuru's[11] and those of 140 to 160 ordinary Americans. As well, there was the name of Klaus Fuchs[12] who, in 1950, a few months before Norman's file was reactivated, was charged under the Official Secrets Act in Great Britain. He pleaded guilty to having conveyed to the Russians highly secret information about nuclear fission and atomic weaponry.[13]

Supposedly, while in Tokyo, Norman's outward tranquility belied his inner *angst*. He claimed to have discovered that he was being investigated by American counterintelligence and that one of its agents had started squiring his secretary. This is, of course, possible but there is no proof to show that any surveillance had been instituted. Indeed, the RCMP's October 17, 1950 report about Norman, in response to the FBI's request of May 23, was not communicated by the FBI to General A. R. Bolling, Military Intelligence's Assistant Chief of Staff, until November 1, 1950[14] and was not forwarded to Tokyo until well after Norman had departed for Ottawa.[15] Accordingly, the agent's dating may have been perfectly innocent. If Norman was uneasy and appeared "deeply worried and almost neurotic in his fears,"[16] and he may well have been, it had nothing to do with counterintelligence in Tokyo, or with any other American agency.

No, something else had occurred to upset him so. What can be suggested is that, at this juncture, Norman became aware of the fact that in early April 1950 his name had been raised in testimony before a subcommittee of the United States Senate Foreign Relations Committee. Under questioning, his former superior in Tokyo General Elliot Thorpe was asked by Senator Bourke Hickenlooper (Republican of Iowa) whether he and Norman had prepared an intelligence report that was subsequently submitted to General Willoughby. According to Senator Hickenlooper, it dealt with the political situation in Asia and contained certain recommendations. Thorpe could not remember it although he correctly identified Norman.[17]

When the press asked Hickenlooper about his reference to Norman he refused to comment. Under-Secretary Arnold Heeney informed Norman of the matter, adding that he thought it would not prove useful to issue a statement. External Affairs was "distressed," he explained, that Hickenlooper should have raised his name in that manner without offering a suitable explanation. Norman responded that he was "completely at a loss to explain Hickenlooper's query," and "disturbed" that the senator should have raised his name. He also was "puzzled" how the senator had got his name, particularly when it was of no relevance. He agreed with Heeney that a public statement at this time would serve no useful purpose.[18]

Norman had lived long enough in the United States, both as a student and as a diplomat attached to the Canadian Embassy in Washington, to be fully aware of Congress' awesome powers to institute committees of investigation. Based on Hickenlooper's comments, something obviously was afoot, as the Senate Subcommittee on Internal Security learned.[19] Exactly what was unclear, however, the exchange that had taken place in the Foreign Relations subcommittee, and any possible leak forewarning Norman that he was being investigated by the RCMP and might be recalled to Ottawa for questioning, would have been enough to keep anyone on edge.

On May 23, about six weeks after Senator Hickenlooper had made his comments, the FBI reactivated Norman's file. Then a new fact was revealed for the first time, namely, that in Norman's Harvard University doctoral dissertation, published by the Institute of Pacific Relations, he had acknowledged Tsuru's assistance in the preface. There was nothing in his FBI file about his association with Halperin,[20] although the FBI was now aware of it. The 1942 incident at Cambridge concerning Tsuru's papers, the fact that both Norman's and Tsuru's names had appeared in Halperin's notebook,[21] and Norman's name in Jaffe's address book acquired when the latter was arrested,[22] were things that help to explain why the FBI attached so much importance to Norman's acknowledgment of Tsuru's assistance. In addition, its request to the RCMP for information about him was repeated in August, it appears, to military intelligence in Washington which, in turn, contacted Willoughby's office in Tokyo. In response to this request, his office related Norman's "connections" with Tsuru,[23] however, this information apparently was not relayed to the RCMP.[24]

The question might be raised why the Norman-Halperin connection had to be brought to the RCMP's attention by the FBI. Why had not the RCMP itself spotted it before conveying the notebook to the FBI? The answer is really quite simple: the notebook was only one of numerous exhibits presented to the Royal Commission, established to investigate Gouzenko's disclosures of Russian espionage in Canada. In fact, a total of 601 exhibits filled twelve filing cabinet drawers, yet an index of all the individuals mentioned in these exhibits was not completed until November 1951. The truth was that the number of RCMP personnel attached to security work at that time was woefully small and the operation underfinanced. As the RCMP cogently pointed out, if they had spotted the Norman-Halperin connection and had joined it with other information they had about Norman, they would have approached External Affairs as early as 1948.[25] Had it done so at that time, its efforts would have coincided with the commencement of External Affairs' own vetting process. It had entailed the extraction of biographical materials from the files of External Affairs personnel and requests to the RCMP for record checks and field investigations. Since Norman was a senior External Affairs official serving overseas, he was in one of the last categories to be vetted. "Wonderful!" was the ironic marginal minute by one RCMP officer to this admission by External Affairs. It was not until April 1950, when Norman's name was raised by Senator Hickenlooper, that a "detailed investigation" of his background commenced.[26]

Erroneously, the RCMP believed that the FBI's renewed interest in him stemmed from Hickenlooper's query, and it was "easy to understand the FBI's interest and desire to get all the facts they could." Indeed the FBI, the RCMP mused, may have felt slightly remiss in not pursuing its first investigation of Norman more vigorously, in the same way as the RCMP felt remiss in not pursuing more quickly the Norman entries in Halperin's notebook.[27]

Based on the "need to know," a prime principle in intelligence management, the FBI had, doubtlessly, not been informed of the American government's interest in Norman as a possible liaison officer between American and Canadian intelligence. Senator Hickenlooper's comment, therefore, appears to have been a timely intervention and explains the RCMP's surmise that it had triggered the FBI's request for information. Even if the FBI had known why the government was interested in Norman, which it probably did not, it would not have conveyed such information to the RCMP on the "need to know" principle. Indispensable as it may be for security reasons, it is not without drawbacks. What the FBI had done was merely to reactivate a file it already had, based on its own indices and the special indices of the Gouzenko materials that the RCMP had no doubt made available. At this juncture, the difference between the two agencies was that the FBI was better staffed and better funded.

"Flagstone" was the code name the RCMP now slapped on the Norman investigation.[28] Its first step, in line with the FBI's request, was to check the Criminal Index which proved as negative as the RCMP's check of the Security Clearance Index, i.e. no request about Norman had been received from External Affairs. On the other hand, the RCMP's check of the "subversive" indices yielded the following information.

Aside from existing data pertaining to Norman's 1942 repatriation from Japan on the *Gripsholm*, the mention of his name in Halperin's notebook, and the recent material supplied by the FBI, additional disquieting information had come to the RCMP's attention in 1948. In May of that year, his name and telephone number had been discovered on the personal desk pad of an employee of the National Council for Canadian-Soviet Friendship, at a time when communist control of the Council was well known. Moreover, the official in question was closely associated with the Canadian Communist Party, and suspected by the RCMP of being a Russian agent. Norman's telephone number on the pad—73481—had been crossed out and a new number—6129—inserted. It proved to be that of External Affairs' Far East Division. This convinced the RCMP, beyond doubt, that the "Herb Norman" referred to on the desk pad and Egerton Herbert Norman were one and the same person. Many other names and telephone numbers or addresses were inscribed on the same desk pad, including those of persons involved in the trials that followed the Royal Commission investigation of Gouzenko's disclosures. Also listed were many names and telephone numbers of known members of the Communist Party, persons suspected as subversives, as well as those of ordinary Canadians.

There was one further interesting piece of information. On February 20, 1940 the RCMP had ascertained from a "reliable source" in Toronto—a euphemism for an agent controlled by the RCMP—that a Professor Norman, formerly at McMaster University in Hamilton, Ontario, and then studying at Harvard University, was a Communist Party member. According to the source, he would prefer to join the faculty of the University of Toronto or Queen's University in Kingston, Ontario upon his return to Canada. The RCMP carried out an investigation but was unsuccessful in locating anyone who fitted the description and had taught at McMaster University. Hamilton families with the surname Norman were contacted, but no one knew a Professor Norman. The RCMP in Toronto was asked to check the information the "reliable source" had offered, to "clarify this point but it appears that a report was never received covering this discrepancy." Since one of Norman's addresses in Halperin's notebook was in Hamilton, the RCMP thought that there was "a possibility that there may be some foundation to that information."[29]

The agent's report invites dissection: Norman was not a professor but did have a doctoral degree from Harvard University; he had never taught at McMaster University, but at Upper Canada College, the prestigious Toronto private school. When the agent's report was given to the RCMP, Norman was already working in External Affairs, though when awarded the Rockefeller Foundation fellowship to study at Harvard, he had expressed a desire to teach Far Eastern history at a college or university. As to Hamilton, Mrs. Norman was a Hamiltonian and the couple had visited there during the university's summer recess.[30] As to his membership in the Canadian Communist Party, there can be no doubt about that, at least until 1939 when he entered External Affairs. It is a point conceded even by someone partial to Norman.[31]

It may well be that the information from the RCMP-controlled source who probably had been insinuated into the Canadian Communist Party, had been supplied by or elicited from other sources within the party. This would explain the collage of facts, near-facts, and errors which is not uncommon when information is filtered through several sources. Also, in view of the accuracy and near-accuracy of the information, it is probable that Norman was the originator of some of it; he had, undoubtedly, spoken to people within the party of his future plans, and may have mentioned possible employment by the two universities. It is even conceivable that he had approached them regarding a position. Whether he actually applied appears to have gone unexplored, and certainly is untraceable now. It would be safe to say that, based on the nature of the comments, they were probably made prior to his appointment to External Affairs in July 1939.

The important point is, however, that an RCMP-controlled source within the Canadian Communist Party had obtained information which coincided with Norman's movements and desires. In general, it is the RCMP's sole role to supply available information to the concerned government department. If External Affairs had desired additional clarification, and if Norman's alleged applications to Toronto and Queen's universities, rather than his assumed employment at McMaster had been pursued, conceivably the errors in the agent's report could have been rectified.

On September 13, 1950 Inspector Robert MacNeil discussed the matter with George Glazebrook, the Director of External Affairs' Defense Liaison II which was responsible for the Department's security.[32] Several weeks later, he sent him a memorandum detailing the information and, parallel to the text received from the RCMP's "reliable source," someone had scribbled into the margin that there was "no means of checking" this information.[33] Whether or not this was true could have been beyond the expertise of the person who wrote it. It reflects, however, a malaise within External Affairs that will become progressively more obvious, namely, the desire to look into the Norman matter as perfunctorily as possible if at all. Indeed, in reporting what had developed to Pearson, who then was at the United Nations General Assembly with the Canadian delegation, Glazebrook had misjudged the FBI's interest in Norman, believing it had developed from the Bureau's study of Halperin's notebook. His impression was that when Pearson saw a copy of it and the references to Norman, he had remarked that these jottings were an example of the names of innocent people cited in a book of addresses and social engagements. Needless to say, Glazebrook observed, the FBI saw them in a different light.[34] It, therefore, becomes obvious that early on, unlike the RCMP, Pearson was aware of a connection between Norman and Halperin, but had not thought it fit to convey this fact to the RCMP. What was jotted in Halperin's notebook was basically a police matter, and Pearson's way of handling it was odd to say the least.

Between September 13 when Inspector MacNeil approached Glazebrook and October 11, the date of the RCMP's next report to Glazebrook, additional investigations were conducted in Hamilton and Toronto. For one, Norman's Hamilton address shown in Halperin's notebook was discovered to be that of his father-in-law. A check at the Department of Vital Statistics in Toronto revealed that when Norman was married on August 31, 1935, one Charles P. H. Holmes was a witness to the ceremony. He and Holmes, as we have seen, had been contemporaries at the Methodist academy at Kobe and also at Victoria College in Toronto. Holmes, employed by the Civil Service Commission, had associated with Norman in Ottawa during the war. Allegedly, according to the RCMP, he was, "a secret member of an underground branch of the [Communist] Party in Ottawa and was very active in the Communist movement." After the war, he also raised the suspicions of American military intelligence in Tokyo.

In reviewing its records, however, the RCMP had come across another intriguing piece of information. Gouzenko, in his testimony before the Royal Commission, had stated that in 1944 Moscow had asked his boss Colonel Zabotin if he knew an individual by the name of "Norman." Zabotin had replied in the negative. Later, on December 16 and also on December 20, 1944, in the thrice-weekly Russian language newspaper *Vestnik* (Herald) which appeared in Toronto, a photograph of Norman Freed, a senior official of the Communist Party, was published. The assistant military attaché Lieutenant Colonel Motinov had asked Zabotin whether or not Freed was the person about whom Moscow had inquired. Zabotin had instructed Motinov to approach their civilian counterpart Vitaly G. Pavlov, the resident officer of what today is the KGB, the Committee for State Security (*Komitet Gosudarstvennoy Bezopasnosti*). When Motinov spoke to Pavlov, whose real work was disguised under the title of second secretary, he was admonished with the remark: " 'He is ours, don't touch him.' " Zabotin then sent Moscow a second message stating that he thought the "Norman" about whom it had inquired, was Norman Freed, a man who was "busy" with Pavlov. Moscow apparently did not respond to that message.

The RCMP speculated that Russian army intelligence whose acronym is GRU (*Glavnoye Razvedyvatelnoye Upravleniye*), had received the name "Norman" from some other branch of the Russian intelligence services. Possibly, that Norman had been cited as a Canadian information source which interested the GRU. The latter, wishing an independent confirmation, then asked its Ottawa representative Zabotin if that Norman was known to him. The RCMP cogently argued that it was unlikely that Moscow would have wanted the Christian name checked of a person previously unknown to Russian army intelligence and thus to Zabotin. Norman Freed and Norman Veall, the latter's name had surfaced during the Royal Commission investigation of 1946, were already known to them. Moreover, Zabotin and Motinov had not asked if Pavlov knew someone called Norman, but had restricted their discussion to Norman Freed. There was no link between Freed and Norman other than Zabotin's assumption that there was, and, significantly, Moscow made no attempt to confirm it. Cautiously, the RCMP concluded that Norman appeared to be the surname of someone in whom the Russian intelligence services were interested. Beyond that it was impossible to definitely identify the individual involved.[35]

Although unidentified and undated notes by someone in External Affairs, perhaps Glazebrook, showed reservations about some of the information conveyed by the RCMP, it was concluded that Norman had to be recalled from Tokyo.[36] On October 14, 1950, Under-Secretary Arnold Heeney wrote to Canadian Ambassador Hume Wrong in Washington explaining what had developed. He pointed out that although the RCMP had held off sending a reply to the FBI, it could no longer be delayed, and would be sent in several days' time. It would be largely biographical, including information the FBI had not yet noted, such as Senator Hickenlooper's mention of Norman's name in early April, Norman's service in General Thorpe's counter–intelligence unit in Tokyo after the war, and his association with the Institute of Pacific Relations before the war. Heeney stated that the situation was such that he had requested Norman to return the week after. This was important, should there be publicity about him in Washington and also to take "reasonable precaution." Once in Ottawa he would be placed on leave and Norman Robertson, now the Secretary to the Cabinet, would query him so he could answer questions arising from the evidence presented by the RCMP.

Heeney's worry was J. Edgar Hoover. Alluding to the FBI Director's attitude toward the "Fuchs incident"—perhaps because Fuchs' name had appeared in Halperin's notebook but the FBI had not been informed of it—he felt that Hoover might "take precipitate action, including, perhaps publicity." Heeney, therefore, wanted the State Department kept informed of what had occurred, suggesting that it be asked for its "cooperation in avoiding a storm" which could only do harm. Accordingly, Wrong was to move quickly.

Heeney thought the State Department would appreciate Norman's international reputation as a scholar and as a man of academic tastes. External Affairs was "*not unaware* that in his younger days, like so many undergraduates, he had associated with a variety of people, and had, again like undergraduates of the '30s, flirted with Leftist ideas." The RCMP, however, now was presenting evidence that was "in part of a different nature." There were the citations in Halperin's notebook, Norman's involvement with Tsuru, his attempt to acquire Tsuru's papers, and his association with different communists which appeared to be more than "casual friendship." The evidence was being carefully sifted, since Norman had "always been entrusted with highly classified work." The hope was that, upon his return, a reasonable explanation would be found for indications which, at first glance, were awkward. Nothing for the moment was being assumed. Hume Wrong, however, would realize the serious nature of having suspicions develop about an External Affairs officer whose work closely associated him with the Americans.

Heeney asked Wrong to burn his letter. (Fortunately the file copy never was destroyed.) He correctly held that it was impossible to communicate by telegraph on the subject and that Wrong might need to make "veiled reference" to it over the telephone. He asked him to send a letter, for his eyes only, by diplomatic courier. Heeney felt he did not need to explain how unhappy he was about the situation, and that he hoped explanations would be found which, at least, would satisfy him.[37] On the same day, October 14, he also wrote to Pearson at the United Nations enclosing a copy of his letter to Hume Wrong. He pessimistically observed that he was "very much afraid that even if we satisfy ourselves of Norman's innocence, we will never be able to satisfy the Americans." He hoped to discuss the question with Pearson later.[38]

Acting on Heeney's instructions, Wrong saw H. Freeman Matthews, the State Department's Under-Secretary, who, it appeared, would talk to Hoover privately. In turn, he wanted to know what External Affairs had discovered about Norman. Believing the request to be "entirely reasonable," Wrong hoped that Heeney would be able to comply. He described the whole affair as "disconcerting and distressing," and shared Heeney's hope that a satisfactory explanation could be found. He was not keeping a copy of his letter, the security-conscious Wrong observed to the equally security-conscious Heeney.[39]

On the morning of October 18, Glazebrook was informed by Norman Robertson that Pearson wanted the RCMP report to the FBI delayed until he had seen Norman's security file. However, when Robertson looked into the matter he discovered that it had, in fact, been sent the day before, and that any attempt to stop it in Washington would be counterproductive. Glazebrook told Pearson that it had been held up for more than a month, and "we have been worried as to the effect of that delay." The RCMP "had been authorized" to submit to the FBI a "full description of the evidence" which had been seen by External Affairs.

Touching on External Affairs' tentative thinking on the question, Glazebrook observed: "We are hopeful with our knowledge of Norman's character and intellectual interests that the various connections which he has had with Communists or near Communists can be explained to our satisfaction." External Affairs, however, was far less confident that the Americans, particularly Hoover, could be persuaded to reach the same conclusion.[40]

As Pearson's concern persisted, he wanted to discuss the Norman case with Robertson when he returned to Ottawa, Wrong informed Robertson on October 23. There also was the question of the RCMP providing information to the FBI, especially the reciprocal aspects of the exchange.[41] If it was Pearson who had suggested Norman to be the liaison officer between American and Canadian intelligence, then his recommendation had come home to roost. The RCMP's response to the FBI, long delayed because of External Affairs' pressure, was not an obsequious appeasement of the Bureau, but an effort to cooperate with it. Understandably, the RCMP had attempted to defend its actions,[42] but one suspects that its words were not appreciated, in view of External Affairs' perception of its own infallibility in all matters, not excluding those concerning the police.

There were, however, two curious omissions in the information amassed about Norman by the RCMP and sent to the FBI on October 17. One, was the fact that in 1934 he had attempted to recruit into the Communist Party his Canadian classmate at Cambridge University Robert Bryce who in 1950 was Assistant Deputy Minister of Finance and Secretary of the Treasury Board; and two, the encounter between Norman and the unpaid RCMP informant, Patrick Walsh, at the February 1936 meeting of the Canadian League Against War and Fascism. At that meeting, as we have seen, Norman was elected to a provisional committee to establish the Canadian Friends of the Chinese People, a communist-front organization; either Jaffe or Chi Ch'ao-ting had urged him to create such a group. During the meeting, MacLeod introduced Norman to Walsh who, in turn, reported all that to John Leopold who was handling the RCMP's surveillance of communist activities in Canada.[43] Since RCMP officers are essentially police officers and thus mesmerized by the written word and the official report, one would think that Leopold would have filed an account about what Walsh had told him. But if such a report was ever written it certainly does not appear to be part of the Norman record. Perhaps, inadvertently, Leopold never filed it or if he did, it may have been lost through some clerical error.

On October 24, 1950, three days after Norman arrived in Ottawa from Tokyo, he was questioned by Arnold Heeney and Norman Robertson. Heeney observed that he had the "unpleasant duty" of informing him that Ottawa and Washington had found in Halperin's notebook a number of entries that concerned him. From the moment Fuchs' name had been discovered in the same notebook, he explained, it had assumed a prominent place in security matters. Heeney was sure Norman would understand the implications of these entries for himself and for External Affairs. This was the reason why he had been recalled from Tokyo, and after making his first reports, Heeney would put the matter to him directly and hear whatever he wished to say.

Norman admitted that he knew Halperin from their days at Victoria College. He claimed that he had seen him six or seven times after his repatriation in the summer of 1942 and prior to his return to Tokyo in 1946.

Once Halperin's name had surfaced in the proceedings of the Royal Commission, Norman had undoubtedly distanced himself from him, in the same way as he had dropped Jaffe and MacLeod. He observed that his association with Halperin was that of former classmates and that their wives had certain common interests and saw each other occasionally. He categorically denied that he was guilty of conveying information of any kind to Halperin, insisting that his conduct from the time he had entered External Affairs "had been meticulously careful and his own conscience was quite clear."

Heeney asked if he had ever been a member of the Communist Party. Norman "categorically replied that he had not." This was a blatant falsehood which was compounded by asserting that as a student, both at Toronto and at Cambridge, he had merely "associated with radical undergraduate groups, some of whose members were Red." He admitted membership in the League for Social Reconstruction when residing in Toronto, and in a "social group" while at Cambridge University. There he had known individual communists who he mentioned. He maintained that these "political interests and activities" had ended with his undergraduate days at Toronto and

Cambridge and that his interests at Harvard had been different. Again, his statement was deceptive. Whether in contact with Halperin or others, once he entered External Affairs, Norman noted, he had been careful not to discuss the secret work in which he was involved.

Heeney emphasized that he was making "no allegations," but Norman had to recognize that the discovery of his name in Halperin's notebook and his association with him and perhaps others, raised very serious questions for External Affairs. If the matter became public knowledge both his position and that of the Department would be very difficult. Heeney questioned him why he had remained silent once Halperin's name had surfaced in the proceedings of the 1946 Kellock-Taschereau Royal Commission. He had "worried about this point a good deal," Norman responded. Based on the assumption that External Affairs would be cognizant of his association with Halperin, he had concluded he "should not himself raise the question." Neither Heeney nor Robertson was willing to accept that explanation. They correctly pointed out that had he admitted knowing Halperin at that time, his position now would be far stronger. Norman conceded that his stance had been wrong, but held that because of his clear conscience, "he had not felt then that to mention the matter would be the wise course."

He recognized the embarrassed position in which events had placed External Affairs and was very anxious not to cause it harm. He offered to resign if this were believed to be the right course. There was no response to the suggestion. Instead, it was explained that after consulting Pearson the next day, Norman would be placed on leave. In the interim, both he and External Affairs would ponder the course that should be adopted. Norman closed the discussion by noting that though "he had known a good many individuals of Leftist views, he had no associations other than those with Halperin, which might give rise to suspicions." He reiterated that his "active interest in Marxist and Communist thinking had been limited to the period of his university career."[44]

Just prior to the talk with Robertson and Heeney on October 24 or shortly thereafter, Norman, it appears, was interviewed by the RCMP. However, there seems to be no record in their files about who questioned him, or exactly when the interview took place. Nor, it seems, was a formal memorandum of the conversation ever written. During that interview, Norman "admitted to an academic interest in Communism but said he had never been a [communist] party member or disloyal to Canada."[45] He had been as disingenuous with the RCMP, acting with the same aplomb, as he had been with Robertson and Heeney.

The important point is that it appears he was interviewed only once by the RCMP during that period. Therefore, Pearson's subsequent contention, echoed by Norman whenever he found it convenient to do so or was in need of sympathy, that the interrogation lasted six to seven weeks, is blatantly untrue.[46] Perhaps Pearson confused the Robertson-Heeney-Norman interview—a discussion among gentlemen of breeding—and the RCMP interview, with the time required to convey a second RCMP report to Washington which was sent on December 1, 1950, six weeks after the initial RCMP report of October 17. Unlike the first one, this report had *not* been solicited by the FBI. In 1957, following Norman's suicide, Pearson wrote a letter to the Montreal *Gazette* stating that the December 1, 1950 report had been distributed by the RCMP "in exactly the same manner as the earlier one."[47] After a photocopy of his letter had been received at FBI Headquarters in Washington, an unknown hand had underlined the words: "in exactly the same manner as the earlier one."[48] Pearson's comment was denied by FBI Director Hoover in a memorandum to Attorney General Herbert Brownell. He observed that the statement that both RCMP reports "were furnished to the appropriate United States security agency in the same manner" . . . was "inaccurate and undoubtedly has created a false impression in Canada of what actually happened in this case."[49] Hoover's further comments were deleted from the pertinent document, but as cryptic as they are one can conclude that he was quite aware that the December 1 report was an unexpected follow-up to the one of October 17. In his letter to the Montreal *Gazette*, Pearson had attempted to disguise that point by maintaining that the December 1 report "covered a number of unrelated matters,"[50] as if the Norman question was merely an aside in a much larger issue. This clearly was not the case as the second report attempted to explain away Norman's prior foibles in a ploy by External Affairs to undercut the impact of the RCMP's first report which had been clearly damaging to Norman. As Pearson had been too late to prevent it from being conveyed to the FBI, the "squeeze" was applied until the RCMP succumbed to External Affairs' pressure by composing, under its direction, a version more favorable to Norman.

The pavan between External Affairs and the RCMP really commenced on November 22 when Inspector George McClellan, in charge of Special Branch, conveyed to George Glazebrook an updated report on Norman. The question was approached evenhandedly, and though McClellan was unaware of certain crucial facts, it contains information which enables the present reader to comprehend Norman's ability to fracture the truth and be less than candid. Though he admitted that he frequently attended meetings sponsored by the leftist Socialist Society while at Cambridge, he claimed that he had kept an open mind. He did acknowledge that he had been under John Cornford's influence. This was, as we know, a fraudulent statement, as he had admitted at that time to having been a member of the Communist Party. When he returned to Canada he had continued his study of communism, he explained, but it had been confined to reading and he "knew no communists or left-wingers during this period." Again he had given a falsified answer. As we have seen, he did know MacLeod, Jaffe, and Chi Ch'ao-ting, and was a member of the Canadian Communist Party at this juncture.

Though he admitted attending several sessions of Tsuru's study group, he denied knowing him as a Marxist. Nor could he recall writing a paper entitled "American Imperialism." McClellan's report pointed out that, by this point, while at Harvard University, Norman had been studying communism for about five years and, "irrespective of the extent, he must have been partially conscious of the object of the study group." To accept anything else would place him in the "category of being politically naive, or worse, a fool." Since Norman was neither, it had to be assumed that he did attend Tsuru's "study group meetings fully conscious of their Marxian character."

In support of his position, Norman held that he had never accepted, without question, any political theories. The world depression had been on and he had been open to any theory that would have ameliorated the situation. He forcibly stated that communism did not supply the answer. Soviet Russia's version of socialism, that is to say, its communism, he explained, "was not to his liking and the purges was (sic) one of the deciding factors." Again, his reply was less than honest. As we have seen, he looked upon the Moscow spy trials as a vindication of Soviet justice and a plot concocted by Trotsky and the fascists against Stalin's Russia.

While at the Institute of Pacific Relations, Norman admitted having been acquainted with individuals, some of whom were communists, but "this acquaintanceship did not develop into close association." He had conveniently forgotten Jaffe and his friend Chi Ch'ao-ting whose political activities, especially after the communist victory in China, were well known. Also unmentioned was his To-kyo meeting with Chi Ch'ao-ting after the war. In his circumspect comments about communist associations at the Institute, he admitted far less than what they actually entailed in the way of ideological commitment, personal endeavor, and sacrifice, as well as friendships with individuals, such as Chi Ch'ao-ting. If one were to accept his statements, McClellan's report observed, then his "academic interest in communism had apparently waned" by the time he was associated with the Institute of Pacific Relations.

In discussing Halperin, Norman rejected the idea that they had talked politics, claiming that "he never knew Halperin as a com-munist." Moreover, he denied knowing that Tsuru had left corre-spondence in his Cambridge apartment. McClellan's report observed that not only had Norman studied communism, but he had associated with many "individuals coloured with various shades of red." Only he could answer whether the study of communist theorists, coupled with his associations, had led him to accept the communist ideology. Many of Norman's explanations "could be accepted as logical and reasonable provided he was politically naive." If this was not the case it could then be assumed that he was "quite conscious of the dubious political aspirations" of his associates. If he had been polit-ically naive, then those closely associated with him should decide this—an obvious allusion to External Affairs. Of course he had as-sociated with a group of people "hardly consistent with his respon-sible public position," however, there was no evidence that he shared the ideology of his acquaintances nor was "there any information to suggest disloyalty." Norman denied having consciously given in-formation to unauthorized persons, stating that "he was not an 'un-conscious' source." He also disclaimed having been approached, either directly or indirectly, for information by an unauthorized person.

As to knowing the personnel at the Russian Embassy, Norman mentioned only Colonel Zabotin, Pavlov, and Belakostokov, the embassy secretary.

Turning to the famous telegram from Moscow that had asked whether Zabotin knew Norman, there was no evidence to suggest who this Norman was, McClellan observed. The conclusion reached was that Herbert's surname could have been sent to Moscow by Pavlov or any one else in the embassy connected with the Russian intelligence services. Indeed, the message to Zabotin merely showed that Norman was someone of interest to Moscow, assuming he was the person referred to. Why the telegram was directed to the GRU's Zabotin, was left unexplained. That Norman had been naive was apparent. He seemed "too willing to accept people at their face value without considering the possible implications," the report concluded.[51]

As fair as McClellan's report may have been, it was obviously unacceptable to External Affairs. It takes no vivid imagination to determine what Pearson's reaction to it must have been. Based on available evidence, it is clear that he had not wanted the RCMP's reply sent to the FBI before he had vetted it. Leaving aside the links that existed between him and Norman,[52] by 1950, Norman had worked under him as his alternate on the Far East Commission in Washington (March–June 1946), and as first secretary to the embassy (March–August 1946) when Pearson was chief of mission. This association, therefore, had produced an additional connection, namely, a senior official's loyalty toward a subordinate. As Pearson put it in later life, by the autumn of 1950 he "had known Herbert Norman for some time."[53] Moreover, he must have found it almost impossible to admit that the very person he had proposed to Washington for the liaison job, was somehow tainted. This, no doubt, explains his desire to discuss the matter with Robertson. Like it or not, he would have had to engage in some "damage control" to make sure that bad did not degenerate to worse. He did, and though documentation is far from plentiful, it is there, despite attempts to expunge it from the record.

In External Affairs' Norman file but, it would appear, not in that of the RCMP, there is a draft of the December 1, 1950 report that was later sent to the FBI. It is unknown whether prior or subsequent drafts were made, however, the available document is slightly over four pages long and single spaced. It is an apologia containing far from convincing explanations about Norman, based on information unearthed either by the RCMP or the FBI.

Falling short of being a hagiography on Norman, the draft certainly is less than analytical and probing. It dwells on his education and stature as a scholar, something that had already been mentioned in the intra-External Affairs correspondence, and emphasizes that his studies and academic endeavors had led him to be "most naive in his relationship with man." One could have argued that such naiveté was a fatal flaw in someone destined to be a senior official of one's country's diplomatic service, in someone who also would further its interests, both at home and abroad. However, that aspect was not examined in the draft report. On the contrary, it goes on to explain that Norman had "consistently failed to properly assess his social acquaintances, but rather accepted all at their face value irrespective of their ideologies and motives." He was inclined to judge a person, the draft contends, based on the criterion of whether or not he was interesting. This "underdeveloped part of Norman's personality" partially explained his leftist associations, especially with those knowledgeable about the Far East.

It was thought that Norman's relationship with Tsuru was a good example of his "naivete." The involvement with his study group was dismissed on the ground that Norman's Harvard classes had consumed all his available time, and that after reading Marx, Lenin, and Trotsky he had concluded that communism was not the way to solve the world's ills. This analysis, childish at best, misleading at worst, is certainly at variance with Norman's comments regarding the Moscow spy trials. He also had written to his brother Howard that life's highest endeavor was not the preaching of the teachings of Christ, but communism which was humanity's and liberty's stan-dardbearer. Perhaps these opinions were unknown when the draft report was written.

As to his attempt to acquire Tsuru's library, the draft believes that any slight variations between the FBI's version and that of Norman were "insignificant" and required "no elaboration." Alluding to his work with Colonel Donovan's Office of Strategic Services, it points out that Tsuru's library "was a valuable asset for this specific task." Indeed, these books were subsequently still valuable to Norman in his work. The draft concludes that it was "completely satisfied" that Norman's attempt to acquire Tsuru's library in no way involved its "communist literature and correspondence."

Turning to his relationship with Halperin, the report states that despite their associations at Victoria College and later at Harvard University, as well as their occasional wartime meetings in Ottawa, the two men had no "common interests and thus nothing drew them together." Therefore, Norman was "quite innocent" of Halperin's hidden political and other activities.

Gouzenko's testimony about the telegram from Moscow to Colonel Zabotin, produced the most interesting gyration. The draft report suggests that the Norman referred to in Moscow's 1944 message was "very probably none other than E. H. Norman." While the man mentioned by Moscow would never be identified, it speculates that it must have been an attempt to cultivate Egerton Herbert Norman for possible recruitment into the Russian intelligence services. This explained why the KGB's Pavlov had approached Norman on several occasions to engage him in conversation. The draft report thought it likely that it was Pavlov who had talent spotted Norman and then had suggested him to Moscow. What the report left unanalyzed is why Moscow would have contacted the GRU's Zabotin about Norman rather than the KGB's Pavlov who had supposedly suggested Norman to begin with. It observes that apparently Moscow knew little of Norman since it had supplied few details to the GRU's Zabotin. Precisely. If Pavlov had suggested Norman's name to Moscow, all the intricate details would have gone with it, and the message sent to Zabotin would have left little doubt in his mind as to the Norman Moscow was seeking. Indeed, the draft goes on to say that Zabotin had actually met Norman at official receptions, but it was "obvious there was no recollection." Although the analysis does not hold water, it asserts the "opinion that Norman was never developed, consciously or unconsciously by the Russians" as an agent, if, in fact, the query to Zabotin did refer to him. The weakness of the argument was manifest. When this paragraph was included in the definitive version of the December 1 report, an unidentified RCMP officer had noted in the margin that it was all a poor assumption, in view of the parallel espionage rings operated by the KGB and the GRU, as well as the fact that Moscow had queried the GRU rather than the KGB about Norman.

Dismissed as "mistaken identity or unfounded rumour by an unidentified sub-source" was the 1940 report about a Professor Norman from Harvard University who was a member of the Communist Party and had formerly taught at McMaster University. The majority of points raised had been "determined to be in error" and the few that remained had "not been confirmed," nor did there appear to be answers to them. The draft report claims that as the source who had supplied the information could not recall the matter, it had been deleted, insofar as Norman was concerned. Also dismissed on grounds of misinformation were his associations with certain other individuals.

Harder to explain away was the mention of his name and telephone number on the personal desk pad of the employee of the National Council for Canadian-Soviet Friendship. Norman had admitted knowing and meeting him several times, but did not know him well, nor was he familiar with his political ideology. The report believes that he was sincere in his explanation.

As to Charles P. H. Holmes, he had correctly identified him as a former classmate at Kobe, Japan, and at Victoria College, admitting to have met him later in Ottawa and seeing him on several occasions. He had explained that since they had been living in widely separate parts of the city their social contacts had been very limited.

The draft concludes that there was "no evidence uncovered which would indicate disloyalty" on Norman's part. The worst that one could say was that he showed "very apparent naivete in his relationship with his fellow man." It then states that External Affairs had been informed of the RCMP's findings.[54]

The document, of which only a photocopy of the original is available for examination, appears to have been produced on the same typewriter as the one Inspector MacNeil had used for his previous communications with External Affairs. Photocopies of these documents were submitted to Donald N. Brown of the Pacific Forensic Science Consultants and Services Ltd. and, after close examination and in-depth comparison, Brown concluded that there was "some evidence to indicate that ALL of the typewriting" on the submitted exhibits "could have been executed by one and the same typewriter."[55] However, unless the originals of that document, and of those sent previously by MacNeil can be examined by an expert such as Brown, it would be unwise to categorically state that all these communications were produced on the same typewriter, but so it does appear.

The phrasing of the draft report is unlike any prior or subsequent RCMP communication dealing with the Norman question. This might be explained by the close vetting it had received for, here and there, are marginal corrections and additions made by External Affairs officials. Of particular interest is an attempt to remove not only any mention of External Affairs, but also references to the aid it had rendered in investigating Norman. This applies especially to the conclusions mutually arrived at by the RCMP and External Affairs. Naturally, any mention of the Department would have raised the FBI's suspicions that it was protecting one of its own. The Department's correct legal stance was that Norman was innocent of any disloyalty to Canada, and that it would be up to the RCMP to produce evidence that would put it in doubt. The fact remains that everything Norman had said had been accepted at face value. No attempt appears to have been made by the RCMP to interview some of the more important individuals who had been identified with him, such as for example, the employee of the National Council for Canadian-Soviet Friendship. The whole procedure lends credence to the view that the draft of the December report was a whitewash, presumably generated by Pearson. No experienced police organization such as the RCMP, would have allowed Norman's contentions to go unchecked, unless it had been hamstrung by some higher political authority.

From this flow of events it becomes clear that External Affairs wished to contain the matter within its bosom so as not to tarnish its image. Asking Norman to resign would have been its prerogative and, no doubt, it could rationalize its decision not to do so, on the grounds that the investigation had been inconclusive. No evidence of criminal offense had been proven, particularly no breach of the Official Secrets Act. Thanks to Pearson, Norman had successfully passed between Scylla and Charybdis.

The smoother version of the RCMP report composed and sent to the FBI on December 1, contains much the same material. Though there were minor differences in terminology and phrasing it reflects the political thrust of the draft. Its key sentence, appearing in the third concluding paragraph, contains the words that no evidence had been "uncovered which would indicate disloyalty on the part of Norman."[56]

Following the dispatch of the December 1 report to the FBI, Under-Secretary Heeney concurred that the RCMP's "findings," suggested by information in their possession, had satisfactorily removed any doubt that Norman was a security risk. Yet the phrasing of his statement to RCMP Commissioner Stuart T. Wood was either erroneously or deliberately misleading, as "findings" would have had to come from External Affairs, the employing department, and not from the RCMP whose responsibility it was to merely present whatever information it had ascertained. One might argue that this is a picayune point, but words are weapons, and in this case they constituted substance. The end result, hastily arrived at, was that Heeney informed Wood that he was assigning Norman to be Head of External Affairs' American and Far Eastern Division.[57] (Norman's Cambridge University contemporary, Donald Maclean, was Head of the American Department in the British Foreign Office.[58]) In a second letter to Wood, dated December 1, 1950, Heeney expressed his appreciation for the "helpful attitude displayed" by the RCMP officers in the "full and detailed examination which was necessary" in this case.[59] Wood's reply was short, cool, and correct. He expressed his pleasure "for all of us concerned that the matter has turned out satisfactorily."[60]

About six weeks later, RCMP Inspector McClellan conveyed to Glazebrook an S.A. (Special Assignment) clearance for Norman, placing him in a security category above "Top Secret" with access to communications intelligence which included code word material.[61]

Yet, despite Pearson's later comments that Norman had regretted his youthful indiscretions there was not the remotest chance that he would be acceptable to the CIA or United States military intelligence. Like Caesar's wife he would have had to be above reproach, but he was clearly tainted.

Chapter 6

Whitewash: Second Phase,
December 1950–March 1952

The public announcement of Norman's appointment as Head of External Affairs' American and Far Eastern Division soon attracted the attention of Alexander George Heakes who had been aware of Norman's involvement with the Communist Party at the time he had obtained for him the teaching position at Upper Canada College.[1] He was upset and, although he did not want to hurt Norman, he felt that with the Korean war in full swing this new position would give him access to important information connected with the conflict. Moreover, Norman had never disguised his communist commitment, and Heakes thought that he was as evangelical about the cause as his missionary parents were about Christianity. He also believed that others who knew about Norman would be less restrained to disclose his background.

After pondering the problem for some weeks, Heakes decided to approach Paul Martin, the Minister of National Health and Welfare who, like himself and Norman, had attended Cambridge University, albeit some years earlier. He told him of his concerns and, several days later, Martin informed him that the FBI had conveyed to the RCMP information similar to his own. The question, therefore, was whether or not Norman was or had been a party member. Heakes' response was that he himself had admitted that fact to him. He also took the opportunity to convey to Martin what other facts he knew, expressing his concern, lest Norman be named in public. That important Washington circles suspected Norman interested him, but he also felt that there was obvious distrust in the United States' capital of Canadian security procedure.[2]

Having called on many other Ottawa officials, Heakes now had a very clear notion of what they knew about Norman. The RCMP, however, informed him that they felt he had acted in an unusual manner by approaching someone like Paul Martin to identify a communist in a key government position, even before that person had been publicly exposed. Most people would approach the RCMP only after public exposure had occurred.

About six months later, on June 8, 1951, Heakes wrote to Martin, pointing out that he had seen press reports about the defections of Guy Burgess and Donald Maclean to Moscow. He noted that Burgess and Norman had been his contemporaries at Cambridge, drawing attention to a number of interrelated facts that might be of significance: Burgess, almost the same age as Norman and also knowledgeable about Far East affairs, had been engaged in communist activities at Cambridge; Maclean, Heakes claimed, had recently been on an official visit to Ottawa; Norman had just been temporarily posted to the United Nations.

Heakes' letter must have had an impact on Martin, for he tried, several days later, to contact him by telephone. He was not successful but soon received a second letter from Heakes in which he reiterated what he had written before, namely that Burgess, Maclean, and Norman could have been in contact with each other on matters associated with their work. Regardless of Norman's present ideological orientation, he thought he might be able to solve the mystery of the Burgess–Maclean disappearances.[3]

Martin dutifully supplied copies of the Heakes letters to Pearson, observing that Pearson would appreciate the great importance of this matter. However, it seems, he neither responded to Martin's missive, nor was apparently any action taken regarding this unusual correspondence.[4]

Nothing further developed during the next seven weeks until Wittfogel identified Norman early in August 1951 in his testimony before the Senate Subcommittee on Internal Security. External Affairs then issued the statement that Norman had been subjected to the normal security clearance, according to the rules which applied to all its officials. Subsequently, the statement continued, reports had reached

External Affairs which adversely reflected on Norman's loyalty to Canada, in that it alleged he had, in the past, been associated with the Communist Party. Having been "very carefully and fully investigated" by the appropriate security authorities "Norman was given a clean bill of health." Accordingly, he remained a "trusted and valuable official" of External Affairs.[5]

At its meeting of August 15, 1951 the Cabinet "noted with approval" Pearson's report concerning the response to Wittfogel's allegations.[6] With respect to Norman, his testimony was erroneous and confused which made it easier for Pearson to explain to the Cabinet what had happened.[7]

Norman had been Head of the American and Far Eastern Division for eight months when Wittfogel had unexpectedly pegged him as a communist. Now the State Department, as well as the CIA, together with United States military intelligence could ill afford to be charitable, as open to attack the German professor's comments may have been. No doubt, there was general concern in the State Department's upper echelon about Norman who now was a key official involved in Canadian-American relations and privy to highly confidential material. Without question, much of this classified material touched on American-Canadian political and security arrangements.

Some people may have criticized the State Department for overreacting, however, the niceties of protocol and diplomacy are always the first casualties whenever it is perceived, rightly or wrongly, that the security of the state might be in jeopardy. The defections to Moscow of the two British Foreign Office officials Donald Maclean and Guy Burgess in late May—only months before the Wittfogel testimony—had left bitter memories in Washington, making the State Department more cautious than ever.

Pearson's riposte to Wittfogel's testimony was to show continued confidence in Norman, maintaining him as Head of the American and Far Eastern Division. He also appointed him chief adviser to the two-man ministerial delegation (one of whom was Pearson), scheduled to proceed to San Francisco to conclude the Japanese peace treaty. After signing for Canada, Pearson supposedly handed him the gold pen, in appreciation of the yeoman service he had rendered to the delegation.

It was reported that outwardly Pearson and Norman treated Wittfogel's testimony with levity, however, some of Norman's close friends have suggested that he was "deeply worried" and in no way reassured by Pearson's public "jovial support."[8] There was good reason for this.

About three weeks after Wittfogel had testified, External Affairs learned that Norman's recall to Ottawa in October 1950 had caused "some comment in military-diplomatic circles in Tokyo." Apparently, a long message, meant only for senior American military personnel, had reached Tokyo "connecting Norman with Communist and Communist-front organizations." Thus, at least some information about him was known to American military intelligence and had been circulated confidentially through MacArthur's Headquarters some time during the previous year.

This was reflected in a comment made by the wife of MacArthur's former chief of staff that Norman "was or had been a communist or fellow traveller." Indeed, at a party, a senior State Department official with a "reputation for brilliance and unbalance" had "openly charged Norman with being a Communist or fellow traveller." He had apparently responded that he did not know what the American was talking about.

In a memorandum dated August 31, 1951, Heeney now warned Glazebrook, that "Norman's alleged Communist association was a matter of gossip in upper military-diplomatic circles in Tokyo before Norman's own departure for Canada." As the minister responsible, Heeney conveyed this information to Pearson[9] who, in turn raised the matter with Norman. What was said is unknown, obviously, however, such talk at the senior level of the American government was the very thing Pearson had tried to prevent.

Norman blamed the State Department official's hostility toward him, he explained to Glazebrook, on a disagreement they had had over former Prime Minister Prince Fuminaro Konoye's responsibility for getting Japan on the Axis side during the war. This had been followed by another difference of opinion regarding the Tokyo war trials. The American had insisted that they had been a mistake, especially the hanging of General Hideki Tojo, Konoye's successor. The execution, he had maintained, had made him a martyr. Norman had disagreed, alleging that the American, "apparently not sober and in an argumentative mood," had criticized the British judge and argued that the war trials had been very badly handled. Norman had found those remarks inappropriate, retorting that the American prosecutor had not presented the best case. He also had been informed that the particular State Department official was not liked, had intrigued against his chief, and later was recalled from Tokyo. He claimed that no one in Tokyo had ever hinted that "he was regarded as a fellow traveller," nor had the question ever been raised in conversation with him. Certainly, the Americans he had met in San Francisco during the signing of the Japanese peace treaty, had gone "out of their way to be friendly."[10]

During that period, Norman's own reaction was to refuse all interviews. He assured his brother and sister that he had never broken his secrecy oath,[11] and, furthermore, he fended off anyone who tried to offer him solace about Wittfogel's testimony. One such person was the social worker Bessie Touzel who Ferns described as "politically someone like myself." Today, this description can probably be fairly applied to any person who had meandered politically, and finally had settled on democratic pluralism, as well as on social and economic justice. Touzel had known the Normans well. When, prior to the outbreak of hostilities in the Pacific, Mrs. Norman was evacuated from Japan, along with other legation wives, she had stayed with Touzel until Norman was repatriated from Japan in the late summer of 1942. In fact, in the summer of 1945, Touzel spent some time with the Normans at their cottage in Ontario, prior to Herbert's assignment to the Far East immediately after the war.[12] By 1951, however, it was no secret in Ottawa that Bessie Touzel had been mentioned in testimony before the Kellock-Taschereau Royal Commission investigating Gouzenko's disclosures, as someone who allegedly had attended a prewar communist study group.[13]

Re-establishing contact with Touzel, therefore, had its risks for Norman. So when she phoned to offer him her support she "encountered," according to Ferns, the "same distancing" as Ferns had experienced. Generously, she took no offence and "refused to be bitter or to criticize."[14] Bessie Touzel, however, can recall no such phone call nor Norman's alleged reaction.[15]

September 1951 proved to be a bad month for Norman. At the very moment he was attending the San Francisco Japanese peace treaty meeting with Pearson, he was the subject of a telephone discussion in London between MI5 and J. P. Sigvaldason, Administrative Officer of the Canadian High Commission. It was explained that in going through some old documentation, MI5 had stumbled on the "name of E. Norman." Because of this, it was anxious to know whether he had attended Cambridge University in 1934–1935. Informed by Sigvaldason that he had indeed studied at Trinity

College from 1933 to 1935, having taken a bachelor's degree in History, MI5 divulged that it "held a compromising letter involving 'E. Norman' who had apparently been at Cambridge in 1934 and 1935." Following established procedure, MI5 observed it would furnish the information to the RCMP, and that this would be "done by diplomatic bag and with appropriate discretion." Sigvaldason wrote to Glazebrook that he had not intended to report the matter to him, but after thinking it over he had felt that he should know about the conversation, especially since the person with whom he had spoken, obviously a senior MI5 official, "seemed to think that the letter in their possession was of very considerable significance." Sigvaldason cautioned, however, that the documentation merely dealt with an "E. Norman" which could well be a case of mistaken identity.[16] The latter comment was a whistle in the dark because MI5 had pinpointed the right Norman. Its explanation, however, about the discovery of the name in old documentation was, no doubt, a smoke screen, as Wittfogel had testified almost a month before Sigvaldason had been approached by MI5. It would be safe to assume that, based either on an RCMP or FBI request, MI5 had checked that old standby: the indices. In doing so it had come up with the name "E. Norman."

Some days later, more difficulties developed for Norman when his October 1945 activities with Emmerson at Tokyo's Fuchu prison surfaced in testimony before the Senate Subcommittee on Internal Security. He immediately supplied to External Affairs his version of the events which, as we have seen,[17] obfuscated the fact that he and Emmerson had interviewed only the communist prison inmates. In a ploy to fend off Hoover and the FBI, Glazebrook conveyed Norman's explanation to the RCMP Commissioner, believing it would be appropriate to transmit the "gist" of it to the RCMP liaison officer in Washington. In doing so, however, he was not to put it in the "form of a statement by Mr. Norman." Likewise, the Canadian Embassy in Washington had been instructed to convey to the State Department similar information, in view of the fact that Emmerson, a State Department officer, was also involved.[18]

During that autumn additional information about Norman was conveyed to Ottawa. The exact date, by whom, and its substantive nature, are unknown. It would, however, be fair to assume that the data deleted from the pertinent documentation had come from MI5.[19]

Finally, in late December 1951, Alexander George Heakes once more stepped forward, this time to inform the RCMP of what he had told Paul Martin so many months before. He made it clear that he had not seen Norman since the mid-1930s, and was "unable to offer any additional information." In transmitting a synopsis of the conversation to Glazebrook, RCMP Inspector Terence Guernsey of Special Branch's "B" Section which dealt with counterespionage, observed that taking "into consideration the lapse of time, we are of the opinion that the information offered by [Heakes] is reasonably accurate."[20]

At this point it must have been obvious to the RCMP, if not to External Affairs, that a formal questioning of Norman by the RCMP would have to take place. Perhaps, with Pearson's help, the RCMP's desire could have been fended off, but eventually could have developed into a major irritant if not carried out. Moreover, there was an element of danger in taking an intransigent line toward the RCMP. Intelligence bureaucracies do "talk" to each other, and the discovery, especially by London, that Ottawa had not acted on information MI5 had supplied, might have raised some eyebrows within British intelligence services. During that period, and probably even now, Canada's intelligence information largely flowed south to north and east to west, rather than in the opposite directions. Since intelligence bureaucracies, in turn, communicate with their political counterparts, additional suspicions might have been raised in those quarters and, in extremis, the flow of political information to External Affairs might have been very closely regulated, especially about Far Eastern affairs.

Unlike the situation in the autumn of 1950, External Affairs, like it or not, had to subject Norman to a formal RCMP interrogation. Exactly when it took place has not been recorded, though it probably occurred some time between January 4 and January 18, 1952.[21] Nor is there any information as to exactly where it occurred, though it probably was in Ottawa. What one can say is that, without Norman's knowledge and at Glazebrook's request, the interrogation was tape recorded.[22] Aside from Herbert Norman, present were McClellan, now an RCMP Superintendent, Inspector Terence Guernsey, and George Glazebrook. The latter's presence was certainly odd, in view of the fact that the interrogation was to be conducted not by External Affairs, but by the RCMP, who were responsible for security, counterespionage and subversion. Of the three interrogators, some comments about Guernsey might be in order. Born in Penticton, British Columbia, he was by this point an experienced RCMP officer. He has been described as "quiet," with a thoughtful countenance and a "mind that absorbed detail without sacrificing imagination." Trained for intelligence work in Great Britain, he was an outstanding and innovative officer who had left his mark on the RCMP's counterespionage service. Years later, when he had retired on medical grounds, he received several offers to join the ranks of the British intelligence services, but declined the invitations.[23]

The January 1952 meeting was the only formal interrogation to which Norman was ever subjected. Even so, it had taken the RCMP almost fourteen months before facing him across the table. Based on an oral reading of the tape–recorded verbatim text, the interview could not have lasted more than one hour. From the questions posed it is obvious that MI5 had supplied the RCMP with an enormous amount of information. Unless cited otherwise, what follows is drawn from the interrogation which was largely, but not exclusively, conducted by Inspector Guernsey.[24]

In his opening gambit he asked for Norman's opinion about a number of former classmates at Cambridge University. Exactly to whom he referred is difficult to assess since their names, as required by Canadian law, have been deleted from the pertinent document. Norman assured him that none of them had been communists. Then Guernsey inquired if he had ever heard of the Indian Students' Secret Communist group at Cambridge University. "No, I never did," was his response. Obviously, Guernsey was dissatisfied with this reply, for he later returned to Norman's role in, and association with, the group. What would you say, Guernsey noted, "if a high executive of the British Communist Party stated that you, and none other than you," were in charge of recruiting Indians and other Asian students into the Communist Party? Norman retorted that he did not know where that person would have gotten such an idea. Perhaps someone might have said that he was the likely person for the task, Norman suggested, but he denied having participated in such an activity. Naturally, he had known some Indian students in the Socialist Society of which he had been a member. Cornford, Norman continued, had hinted several times that he should become interested in the Asians, but nothing had developed. Since he was interested in them he certainly saw them, but he denied that Cornford had proposed he "should engage in secret work, go to India or get connected with the Indian Communist Party and [he] didn't have any doings with it at all." If someone had got the idea that he was involved with Indian and other

Asian students he could not "help that." He had "never volunteered to do any such work—I certainly didn't do it," he insisted.

Norman certainly knew of this group and had proposed that the Communist Party attempt to acquire control of the Majlis, the long-established Indian society on campus, by recruiting Indian students into the party. He had been selected to do the actual recruitment, a task he had successfully executed, and which had led to communist control of the Majlis.[25]

Guernsey then slowly shifted the conversation to the Canadian League Against War and Fascism. Was he a member of the League? Norman replied that he had had only a "slight connection" with it "for a few weeks." This had entailed some speechmaking to the youth group or something like that in Toronto. He admitted knowing, at that time, that it was a communist organization. In the External Affairs copy of the transcript the text was changed in ink to read that Norman *"didn't then"*[26] know that the Canadian League Against War and Fascism was a communist organization.

He had learned of the League, Norman thought, through someone at the University of Toronto. Guernsey queried why he had left it, and Norman claimed that during that period he was doing some postgraduate work at the University of Toronto,[27] and was also teaching—an allusion to Upper Canada College. He recalled having been told that he had the reputation of being on the Left. Since he could not have maintained this posture if he wished to go on teaching, he had discontinued his association with the League. In fact, he had felt that he was too busy to get further involved with it. He had won the Rockefeller grant in the spring of 1936 and wanted to get on with his studies.

The answer did not satisfy Guernsey for he subsequently asked whether Norman's departure from the League had been motivated more by financial than by political considerations. Norman thought it was due to his maturing and becoming more responsible. But did he think this change had occurred during the few weeks he was with the League? No, it was probably by late 1935, and he did not know whether it extended into 1936. It certainly was a very short period. He had not enjoyed giving speeches, anyway, though he had made some on foreign affairs. It did not appeal to him and he wanted to commence his studies.

As we have seen, it was after his return from Cambridge in the summer of 1935 that he and Jaffe met through Chi Ch'ao-ting. The following year, Jaffe or perhaps Chi Ch'ao-ting, urged Norman to organize a Canadian counterpart to the American Friends of the Chinese People. This was arranged in February 1936 at a meeting of the Canadian League Against War and Fascism, chaired by Jaffe's longtime friend Alexander A. MacLeod, a veteran communist. Subsequently, MacLeod admitted that during that period he had attended secret Communist Party meetings in Norman's lodgings. This corroborates information acquired by the RCMP in the late 1960s, alleging that Norman had had a secret party affiliation. His comments to Guernsey, therefore, were untrue. If he did depart from the League in 1935 or early 1936, it had more to do with going off to Harvard than the maturing process he claimed.[28]

Guernsey then shifted the conversation to Norman's teaching at Upper Canada College. Using the information provided by Heakes, he asked him whether he had been warned by Headmaster Mac-Dermot that he would be given the job only if he kept to himself "any Communist feelings" as they were not wanted at the college. Norman admitted that this was so. "Were you at that time, Mr. Norman, a member of the Communist Party"? Guernsey asked. "No," was his predictable reply. Based on what he had admitted to Heakes, he had again deceived his interrogator.[29] "You never have been a member of the Communist Party"? Guernsey repeated. "No," Norman responded a second time. As we know he certainly had been a member while at Cambridge University.[30]

Was he ever approached or had he been associated with the party or its affiliates? Again the predictable no. Then how about the Canadian League Against War and Fascism? Norman admitted that he had certainly been interested in Marxism, but had not engaged in what one could call "political activities." Had he ever been in touch with anyone in the British Communist Party? "Not wittingly, or consciously," was Norman's reply.

He admitted that prior to his appointment at Upper Canada College, he had been unemployed. Did he ever admit to anyone that he was a member of the Communist Party, just prior to his discussion with MacDermot? "No," was Norman's response. Then who would he suggest had brought the matter to MacDermot's attention? Heakes might have, Norman correctly responded. Why would he have done that? Because Heakes had recommended him for the post, observing that if Norman got into difficulties for his "political thoughts" he did not want to be admonished for having recommended him. If that was the case, Heakes must have known something of his then communist views, Guernsey retorted. Well, in so far as they pertained to his days at Cambridge, Norman explained, he may have had some notion of his views. He did not "hob-nob" with Heakes very much. Norman was willing to admit that he had "talked quite recklessly in those years and in a way I was very carefree and did not weigh my words." Guernsey then returned to Heakes' "photographic recollections."[31] Without exposing him as his source, he inquired if Norman, while living in Toronto, had ever distributed "leaflets or pamphlets for the League Against War and Fascism." He could not recall. Could he have distributed them on the grounds of the Canadian National Exhibition? He could not stand doing anything like that, Norman explained, though he might have "casually passed something to someone, but [I] didn't go out on the street."

Guernsey then moved to other topics. Had Norman ever been a member of the Young Communist League, now known as the National Federation of Labour Youth? No, Norman replied. Returning to the question, he pointed out that the RCMP had a report that in 1939 he was a member of the National Federation of Labour Youth. Norman denied it. Guernsey retorted that it was during the period Norman was in Ottawa. The discussion led nowhere.

In the mid-1930s, did Norman think he could have identified a communist or a socialist? Yes, in any conversation. Guernsey immediately followed up by asking what his response would be if he, Guernsey, had, in the mid-1930s, said that a number of the people just mentioned were known as active communists at Cambridge. Well, based on his knowledge, Norman answered, he could not affirm or deny it; he could only attempt to characterize their political views.

The discussions moved to Norman's days at Harvard and his association with Tsuru who had told him that he was a Marxist. Norman interpreted this to mean that Tsuru had no interest in any political activities, nor in following the policies of the Communist Party. Guernsey thought this was not reflected in the documentation the FBI had found in Tsuru's papers. Most of his activities, Norman claimed, were unknown to him. He was the only non-economist in a study group, composed of economists, that met a few times and was academic. He did not think there was any attempt made during discussions to reconcile Marx's economic theories. Norman did not believe that it was a "Communist study group in the sense that everything had to be in party lines."

Focusing on the mass of material supplied by MI5, Guernsey next dealt with the anti-war march and wreath-laying ceremony at the Cambridge War Memorial on November 11, 1933. Norman described the event and the fracas that followed, but failed to mention that the march had been organized by Guy Burgess.[32]

He then ruminated about his interest in politics, in Asian students and their views. He had maintained what he considered was "a discreet and loyal attitude" and had tried to use his knowledge of things oriental to assist the government. If he had entered university teaching as he had intended, he would have ended up doing research and writing. He had published with External Affairs' permission, and before entering the Department, if he had known certain Indians, Chinese, or someone considered left wing, he would not "necessarily have liked him for being left-wing." Then again he would not "have been afraid to know him because he was." He denied, however, knowing any Chinese during the period he was a student. Flying in the face of facts, he had conveniently forgotten his intimate friendship with Chi Ch'ao-ting. In keeping with the civilized nature of the "interrogation," the group then adjourned for tea.

When it reconvened, Guernsey again raised the question of Norman's membership in the Communist Party or whether or not he was a communist. The point he wished to make appears to have been that even if he had been a member in the past, it would be wise for him to admit it now. Despite the dispensation that seemed to have been offered to him, his revealing response showed the depth of his ideological commitment: *In my Cambridge time I came close to [being a member of the Communist Party] and if I had stayed there another year I might have.*[33] The facial expression he may have maintained when speaking these words can only be imagined, but the enormity of his falsehood leaps at you from the verbatim text of the interrogation. Even when offered a way out of the predicament that faced him, Norman had rejected it.

Inevitably, the group examined the testimony Wittfogel had given to the Senate Subcommittee on Internal Security in August 1951. Wittfogel, Norman explained, had merely been a name to him when he was a student in the United States. He was not sure, at that time, whether or not he was a communist. "I never said are you a Communist—I didn't say to him I was a Communist because I wasn't."

Wittfogel had been a Nazi prisoner because of his political stance, and after being released from prison, had secured refuge in the United States. Norman had heard about him from various people and, since he was in the last year of his Rockefeller fellowship and in New York, had called on him. He claimed they had met three or four times at his Columbia University office. Their discussions had been always academic, and he could not recall delving into the subject of contemporary China, about which he conceivably might have expressed views which Wittfogel might have interpreted as being communist in nature. Wittfogel who was something of a pedant and loquacious, according to Norman, did most of the talking and he most of the listening. He treated Wittfogel with deference because of his experience with the Nazis and because of his reputation as a great scholar. He was Germanic, thorough, and well organized, and though he might have asked him several things pertaining to Japan, since he knew he was specializing in the subject, Wittfogel really did not ask for information, he merely gave it.

Guernsey asked what Wittfogel's motive might have been for making such statements under oath and thereby perjuring himself. Norman's response was made easier by the erroneous facets in the testimony. He pointed out that if, in their conversations, Wittfogel had interpreted anything said by him as communist, which was not the case, it could have been justified. But what he had said was factually wrong. He had never been to Cape Cod, nor had he attended any communist study group at the home of Finkelstein, a man whose name he had never heard before. He thought it was all a "curious business," observing that he was not attempting to say that Wittfogel held any animus against him, but that there was "such a thing as being an obliging witness."

Oddly, Glazebrook had said nothing during this discussion. Perhaps he had forgotten the memorandum Norman had sent to him soon after Wittfogel had testified (the pertinent document is to be found in Pearson's papers). In it he had admitted having known Wittfogel, and having talked to him. He was an eminent Sinologue who had suffered at the hands of the Nazis and had "recently" been released from a concentration camp. However, as this had occurred in January 1934, the adverb "recently" was the salient word, for Norman had admitted to Guernsey that he had met Wittfogel in New York, some time between 1938 and 1939. He probably had met him at Cambridge, some time between May and July 1934 when

Wittfogel had stayed with Maurice Dobb and Roy Pascal.[34] If he had admitted that they had met at the home of these two men who had played a role in the Cambridge communist movement in the mid-1930s, Guernsey would have been off and running. The last thing in the world Pearson and External Affairs wanted, would have been an intelligent interrogation of Wittfogel conducted by someone as skilled as Guernsey. For if this had occurred the confusion in his mind about when he had first met Norman would have been straightened out. This partially explains why he was never asked by External Affairs to come north of the border to be questioned by the RCMP, or why the FBI, it appears, was not asked by the RCMP to question him in depth about his alleged association with Norman.

At this point the questioning was assumed by Superintendent McClellan. Educated at the Royal Military College at Kingston, Ontario, he later was trained in police work. By experience and deportment he was not the subtle type.[35] His questions covered much the same ground as Guernsey's had done, until he succinctly put it to Norman: "Some of the accusations [against you] are of a pretty concrete nature and are from sources which we have no reason to believe are other than reliable. We have this thing at Cambridge . . . We have these things in the States; we have the question of Toronto." He was willing to admit that he did not "believe that where there is smoke there is necessarily fire." Again he asked him whether he had ever been a member of the Communist Party. "*No, I considered myself very close to it [for] about a year but I didn't accept any posts or responsibilities,*" Norman repeated.[36] Would it be fair to categorize him at that period as a "fellow traveller?" Yes, Norman agreed. Well, McClellan observed, if he had concluded that communism was not for him, when had he decided this? Certainly it had not come suddenly, Norman ruminated, like St. Paul's conversion on the road to Damascus. His had been a "slow process" during which he had acquired "intellect from maturity." He had found Stalin's purges "very distasteful, to say the least," he falsely maintained. He thought life was "getting too complex to just take a theory and superimpose . . . it and say 'now you [have] it.' " McClellan observed that his views at that time would have led some to consider him a communist. Having come to that conclusion "it would seem reasonable that approaches would be made to you to continue your affiliation with the [Communist] Party if you had any, since you said you had." For instance, once back in Canada, because his Cambridge associates believed him to be a "fellow traveller," it was only reasonable that they would have directed their Canadian communist associates to approach him. "Do you remember," McClellan queried, "being approached in any way like that?"

Norman denied that there had been any approaches. On the contrary, he had made the mistake of contacting the Canadian League Against War and Fascism on his own initiative. This indeed may have been the case but Norman, in a manner unknown, appears to have made contact with Chi Ch'ao-ting soon after his return from Cambridge.[37]

Glazebrook now injected himself into the discussion by trying to differentiate between Norman's long–held scholarly interest in Marxism and his political beliefs. In his disjointed reply, Norman noted that while at the University of Toronto he had been "on the side of being rather hermetical," except that he had attended to his studies. Though he "didn't have any particular interest in politics" when at the university, there had been a leftist group on campus he had heard of, though he had had no interest in them. Although it is unclear whether he was associated with any such group, he certainly was deeply involved in studying Marx as an undergraduate and before.[38] He recounted meeting Cornford at Cambridge, and went on to discuss the rise of Hitler's Germany. The atmosphere on campus, he correctly observed, was politically charged. He had definitely been influenced by all of this, but it had not made him "overwhelmingly non-critically pro-Soviet." Soviet Russia appeared to be the only state standing up to Nazi Germany. The Cambridge reaction had been very Marxist, but had not followed the Communist Party line. His "intellectual interests were influenced somewhat by political views." He "wanted to get the political views of oriental students on that," he continued, "so naturally politics came into it."

Then he did discover, to a certain extent, Glazebrook observed, the answer in communism. Well, not in communism exactly, but in Marxism as the instrument of analysis, Norman explained. Then, as he had already noted, he had outgrown this position. He had not consciously thought about what living in a communist state would entail. Had he done so it "would have been a sobering thought." His approach had reflected the "irresponsibility of such views." All this explained his association with the Canadian League Against War and Fascism, a "carry-over" from his interest in Marxism. The conversation meandered. Understandably, Glazebrook's questions, coming from a colleague in External Affairs, appear sympathetic.

Guernsey then re-entered the discussion. Had Norman ever heard of The Apostles? No, he replied, wanting to know who they were. A Cambridge group that went by that name. What Guernsey did not explain was that it was a secret society of "cultural élitists," long established in Cambridge. Its membership consisted of such luminaries as historian G. M. Trevelyan, economist John Maynard Keynes, novelist E. M. Forster, and others. By the mid-1930s it had shifted to the "far left" and included Anthony Blunt and Guy Burgess.[39]

The discussion soon led to Norman's association with the employee of the National Council for Canadian-Soviet Friendship on whose personal desk pad Norman's name and telephone number had been inscribed. The RCMP suspected him of being a Russian agent,[40] and Guernsey wanted to know how he had become associated with a man who was both a "rabid" and "dangerous Communist." He had met him in Ottawa two or three times during the war years, Norman explained. When Guernsey interjected that no guilt by association was implied, he responded that he had met him at a party. He denied having been close to him or having had politically significant conversations with him, either in private or in a larger group. He did not know whether he was a communist, nor had it been indicated. Aside from meeting him a few times, he had had no dealings with him that would interest Guernsey. Be that as it may, the underlying suggestion was, Guernsey retorted, that Norman was "still carrying on" with the left-wing crowd, in which the employee was involved. Norman denied that he had met him at a left-wing gathering. Then Guernsey noted that his telephone numbers were on the employee's personal desk pad on which he was referred to as "Herb." It was as though he was practically in his house. Norman denied that they had mutually visited each other's homes, or had met anywhere to conclude questionable deals. That the employee had selected the first-person use of names after only a short acquaintance was something he could not have controlled; he was not an intimate friend of his. The fact that he had encountered him several times was just bad luck. After additional conversation the meeting adjourned *sine die*.

Reading the verbatim text of the interrogation, even after thirty-odd years, Norman's responses are astonishing. If he could fabricate such falsehoods without the slightest qualms, what value could be placed on anything he would say in the future? A testimony can only be measured against a person's past performance, and in this encounter Norman had spun a web of deception. According to one of the individuals who interrogated him, he had taken the questioning quite well. However, any such experience can be a trauma, and those who knew him contend that, years later, he could still recount and would still talk about this wrenching episode.[41]

Neither McClellan nor Guernsey was satisfied and both had their doubts about Norman. Indeed, his was the initial file opened by Guernsey in what later became known as "Featherbed"—the coded file for a collection of names and information that would help uncover the activities of those Canadian civil servants whose recruitment into the communist apparatus was based on ideological fanaticism.[42]

Following the interview, the RCMP concluded that despite Norman's denial of "all the serious implications directed against him, it would seem there [were] far too many from various sources to entirely discount them all." Norman had admitted that in the mid-1930s "he could have been identified as a communist . . . but had rejected that ideology. Whether or not this is true remains unanswered. In fact there are numerous points to which no answers have been found."[43]

Did these RCMP comments reflect the hope that the interrogation would, at some point, recommence, or that an attempt would be made to check out through systematic field investigation—with or without FBI and MI5 assistance—some of the comments Norman had made? It was not to be, despite the fact that a sustained effort by the RCMP in conjunction with others might have uncovered additional information. Just as in the initial 1950 investigation, External Affairs seemed disinterested in having the RCMP probe the Norman matter any further. Although it was forced to make certain admissions, it absolved Norman, based on largely personal and subjective criteria, without considering the possibility that he might have misled all concerned.

Glazebrook took the plunge on January 18, 1952 soon after the interrogation ended. He pointed out to Under-Secretary Heeney that, in general, the new evidence presented by the RCMP, coupled with Norman's interrogation, showed that at one period Norman "was, in effect, a Communist in opinion" and "an active member of the [Communist] Party with a particular job." The new evidence had also introduced "new Communists who were alleged associates," and had extended the period of "Communist belief to some undefined point after he left Cambridge for Toronto."

Accordingly, External Affairs was considering an employee who "was a Communist or fellow traveller in 1935 with no certainty on when this belief changed." It was thus necessary to examine both the new as well as the previous evidence because the latter was directly affected by the new and thereby had assumed new importance.

Various problems had to be considered. First, Pearson's position since he would "presumably continue to be responsible for the decision" as to whether External Affairs would still employ Norman. There also was the possibility that the question might be raised in the House of Commons and, indeed, the Department had been warned that this might occur. A press interview, some months earlier, with General George Pearkes had suggested that the parliamentary opposition might do so. Then Glazebrook alluded to Pearson's August 1951 declaration about Norman, following Wittfogel's testimony. Was Washington's apparent acceptance of that statement "based on a real agreement or simply on a readiness to take our decision?" What would be Washington's attitude, he asked, based on the "new evidence if it became known to them?" As to the Senate Subcommittee on Internal Security, he thought it "unlikely to pick up either the old or the new evidence." However, he correctly and prophetically observed, the subcommittee would not display the FBI's or the State Department's reticence in dealing with the Norman question. What would be Washington's attitude if Norman's duties required that he work with the Americans "on highly sensitive material?" Whether this comment was an allusion to Norman being the liaison between American and Canadian intelligence, is unclear.

Glazebrook then turned to an examination of the British evidence. On being questioned, the British "were satisfied with the validity of the evidence on the Cambridge period." He presumed that this material had surfaced as a result of the publicity that had arisen from the Senate Subcommittee's inquiry, ignoring the possibility that either the RCMP or the FBI might have contacted MI5 about Norman. Likewise, he disregarded the enormous British effort, following Burgess' and Maclean's defections to Moscow in late May of 1951 to investigate events in Cambridge in the mid-1930s. The Americans, Glazebrook perhaps incorrectly assumed, had none of the British evidence, and it was impossible to forecast what their view would be if they had.

Finally, he came to analyze the position of External Affairs. At no time, he observed, had there been any suggestion of disloyalty by Norman during the period he had been in the Department. Interestingly, he observed that External Affairs "should consider whether Norman [had] attempted to influence policy to the left in the period before this case broke." It was a wise suggestion to examine the possibility that he may have used his influence and position to misdirect and misinform his political superiors about policy that should be adopted. Unfortunately, Heeney did not see the point, and his bizarre marginal comment was that he saw "no need for [an] exhaustive enquiry." Glazebrook again touched upon the problem of whether Norman could be "freely posted," especially to England or to the United States. This problem, Heeney marginally noted, could be tackled. Even if he left the Department and accepted a teaching appointment, Glazebrook wondered what a university's position would be, in view of the preceding publicity and his departure from External Affairs. Would the public assume he had been asked to resign on security grounds? The immediate problem, he believed, was to decide whether Norman "effectively broke with Communist thinking before he entered the Department." Even if the answer was positive, External still had to consider whether it was in Norman's as well as in the Department's best interests that he should continue as one of its officers.

Heeney's response, to say the least, was naive. The immediate and essential question concerning Norman was whether he had shown either by "direct evidence" or "indirect 'evidence' " that he had been, or was likely to be *"unreliable* (disloyal)." Since it was government policy not to employ communists in classified work, the indirect evidence might be manifested by close association with "Communist elements" during service in the Department, or by membership in the Communist Party. If the Department was satisfied that Norman was "trustworthy" then what had to be considered was whether or not he could continue to be an effective officer when dealing with the British and the Americans.[44] Heeney's analysis, however, could not really be fully and successfully implemented, except by asking the RCMP to conduct a full field investigation, in cooperation, perhaps, with the FBI and MI5. This was exactly what External Affairs appeared unwilling to do.

Several days later, Glazebrook sent a memorandum to Heeney to which he attached excerpts from the case's pertinent documentation, observing that he had shown it to the RCMP. With its agreement he had dropped those items which now seemed insignificant.

There was, however, cause for worry. Heakes, it was discovered, was "talking." The FBI liaison in Ottawa had approached the RCMP "with some sketchy remarks that [Heakes] had made to someone, perhaps in the [American] Embassy." Glazebrook did not believe that "any great harm" had as yet occurred, but Heakes' action was unhelpful, and he hoped that some tentative conclusions about the Norman question could be reached before Heeney and Pearson left Ottawa. He enclosed an extra copy of the documentation for Pearson and had already made one available to Robertson.

Using Norman's responses to Inspector Guernsey's questions, Glazebrook attempted to trace his connection with communism and the Communist Party, his distinction between Marxism and communism, and his contention that he had changed his opinions as he had matured. From these responses it was clear that Norman "had associated to a marked degree with Communists," although in most cases he had claimed that he had not known then that these people were communists. Although his association with them "was over a protracted period," how much value was to be given to this evidence? It was difficult to say, Glazebrook observed, but had "some significance when examined in the light of other evidence." He suggested that "an attempt be made to study the case on other and more definite grounds." Heeney's marginal comment was that dates were of considerable importance in this matter. "We sh'd 'cross-examine' MI5" was his astonishing proposal. His next scribbled remark was more to the point: "The main difficulty I have here is why did N[orman] not tell us of his Communist associations and inclinations when the case was first gone into?"

Glazebrook then turned to Norman's connection with the employee of the National Council for Canadian-Soviet Friendship who he described as "a well known Communist." He recounted that Norman's telephone numbers had been found on his personal desk pad and that Norman had acknowledged knowing the man but only slightly. Heeney marginally commented that the information was "not in itself of much help, either way." He assumed the same stance when Glazebrook related Gouzenko's testimony about Moscow's message to Zabotin, inquiring whether he knew "Norman." Glazebrook noted that it "seems pretty clear [that Norman] . . . was a surname," although it did not necessarily follow that it referred to

Egerton Herbert Norman. He surmised that Moscow was "either enquiring about a prospect or checking on a man who was already assisting them." Likewise, Heeney was not moved by Glazebrook's detailed review of Norman's connection with Tsuru. Though Glazebrook was willing to buy his story that he "may well have been unconscious of the purpose of this [study] group," he found it "less easy to understand that he did not realize its nature." On the other hand, someone who had been a member of the study group confirmed that it "was not obviously Communist." As to Norman's attempt to acquire Tsuru's library, Glazebrook asserted that this had been "satisfactorily explained." Whether the FBI or, indeed, the RCMP would have agreed with that assertion is open to discussion.

Neither did Heeney see any significance in the appearance of Norman's name in Halperin's notebook. Then there was the information that the American military in Tokyo had received a message from Washington "connecting Norman with Communist and Communist front organizations." The message which ran to two pages suggested that it was "more than a listing and that it would be desirable to know the grounds for making these charges." In response to these comments Heeney had scribbled that if the Norman "case was to be taken up in Washington we sh'd get after this." To which someone, probably Glazebrook, replied, "Can we?"

Glazebrook then analyzed Heakes' testimony. His comment that it proved "very little," moved Heeney to jot down marginally that it proved "Nothing!" After recounting the Heakes-Norman-MacDermot exchanges before Norman was hired to teach classics at Upper Canada College and what he called his "slight connection" with the Canadian League Against War and Fascism, Glazebrook observed that Norman did not know during that period that an individual connected with the League, probably Alexander A. MacLeod, was a communist. In the RCMP copy of Glazebrook's memorandum someone has written the ironic marginal comment that "N[orman] didn't seem to know *anybody* was a communist." Glazebrook's conclusion was that after returning from Cambridge "Norman was still far to the left," pointing out that he had not volunteered "evidence on his membership in the League when he was questioned" by Heeney and Robertson in October 1950.

"This doesn't seem to me very significant—any of it," Heeney had scribbled, querying what sort of person Heakes was. This comment was the first step in an attempt to place Heakes rather than

Norman under the microscope. Heeney's recollection was that "there were a good many non-Communis[ts]" in the Canadian League Against War and Fascism. Although that was certainly true it showed Heeney's appalling lack of knowledge about how communist-front organizations are established and run. The purpose was and still is to place in visible positions reputable members of the community, while the Communist Party manipulates the organization from the wings. Heeney, trained in the law, had strayed into the arcane and murky world of subversion, espionage, and counterintelligence. He was no more fit to comment on what Glazebrook had been discussing than the RCMP was able to comment on the dispatch of diplomatic notes to the Russian Embassy in Ottawa.

Lastly, Glazebrook closely examined the Norman testimony given in the Senate Subcommittee on Internal Security, in particular, Wittfogel's confused statements. He did not dismiss the possibility that they might have been invented and Wittfogel, therefore, should not be regarded as a "good witness." Why he might have perjured himself, Glazebrook did not tackle, however, he thought Norman had answered the testimony, to which Heeney's marginal comment was a short, "I agree."

Certainly, Glazebrook's memorandum to Heeney was food for thought, but it was returned to him with Heeney's minutes on the very day he had presented it, January 22, 1952. In a busy schedule he had probably pondered it with less time than it deserved. Based on the material, and on his prior contact with the case, Heeney had scribbled, "from my knowledge of Norman," he would say, "Norman had been, is and is likely to continue to be a trustworthy officer of the Department and that we sh'd reaffirm our confidence in him on the basis of the evidence." Moreover, Ottawa should be frank with London and Washington, and inform them fully and at the highest level that if either was, despite Ottawa's conclusions, "unwilling, or even reluctant" to deal with Norman in "full confidence" Ottawa was "bound to reconsider the position."[45]

Like Norman and Pearson, Heeney was also the son of a member of the cloth. Perhaps, deep down he may have been bothered by the amateurish manner in which the Norman case had been handled by External Affairs, and by his role, in particular. Years later, following Norman's suicide, he wrote that, based on the evidence "so exhaustively and painfully assembled," he had given his "private recommendation" to Pearson that Norman be unreservedly supported.

At the same time, he admitted that it "was not possible to produce irrefutable proof" of his loyalty to Canada.[46]

Surely, in situations like this, "irrefutable proof" is the rarity. If there is serious doubt, perhaps unavoidably, it must always be resolved in favor of the state. Public service is a privilege that citizens enjoy. The survival of the state and its value system is the basis of any political order; the stakes are too high for it to be otherwise. The exoneration Heeney had given Norman was subjective and based on personal acquaintanceship. This was inadequate as long as a margin of doubt existed. Further investigation by the RCMP was called for, a possibility not even raised by Heeney. Clearly, the evidence uncovered by the RCMP, the FBI, and MI5 contained grains of truth. Moreover, there were enough contradictions in Norman's testimony to have raised doubts in the minds of some External Affairs officials, Heeney in particular. Norman should have been placed on indefinite leave and the investigation continued. It was not done.

In late January, Glazebrook had another discussion with Norman, following a conversation he and Heeney had had with Pearson. He queried him about his 1947 Cambridge visit, information that could only have been supplied by MI5. Norman explained that he had gone to Trinity College to examine the list of Fellows and to see if he knew any of them. He had recognized Kiernan's name and had had a talk with him about books and other matters which could not affect the present inquiry. This was patently false; Norman had transferred to Kiernan the task of recruiting their Indian classmates into the Communist Party, at a time when Kiernan was still a member. From Kiernan's description of this conversation it must have touched on political questions.

Asked by Glazebrook about his Trinity College contemporary Guy Burgess, Norman claimed he knew the name but had not been acquainted with the man. This was possible, but as he had admitted to Inspector Guernsey, he had participated in the anti-war march and wreath-laying ceremony organized by Burgess at the Cambridge War Memorial. Since they had attended the same college, had shared the same friends and ideological orientation, and Burgess had organized the march, the probability that he knew Burgess was excellent. Moreover, Norman's track record on veracity does not inspire confidence in the answer he gave Glazebrook. He also claimed that he never knew Donald Maclean and had never met him. Again this was possible, but, as in the case of Burgess, they had shared the friends and ideological orientation. In addition, when Norman was Head of External's American and Far Eastern Division, Maclean was Director of the Foreign Office's American Department. It is difficult to believe that they were unaware of each other or had never communicated officially, either directly or indirectly. Norman admitted being in London in May 1951, just before Maclean defected, to discuss the Japanese peace treaty with Foreign Office officials. It stretches credulity that they did not meet at that time.

When the discussion turned to Wittfogel, Norman observed that he had been informed by a senior official of the Institute of Pacific Relations that Wittfogel had uttered at least one lie relating to the Institute. Norman, however, does not appear to have ruminated on the testimony.

A week later, there was another conversation between Norman and Glazebrook. This time Norman admitted visiting the Foreign Office in May 1951, as well as Oxford and Paris. He had not gone to Cambridge as he had done in 1947. Glazebrook explained External Affairs' "difficulty in reconciling [MI5] evidence concerning his active work for the Communist Party." Norman responded "it would be accurate to describe him as a Communist during his second year at Cambridge." He had been under Cornford's influence and, on one occasion, he had hinted that Norman should join the party. He did not do so and the matter was never raised again. He admitted that he often saw his Indian classmates, some of whom were to the Right and others to the Left. Accordingly, he could "have been regarded as an 'unconscious agent,' but [was] convinced that he went no further." In the RCMP copy of the transcript of this conversation someone had scribbled in the margin the word "mole?" after the phrase "unconscious agent."

When he returned to Canada from Cambridge in the summer of 1935, Norman had felt he might still have been considered a communist; the influence had lasted for about a year, and it was during that period that he had joined the Canadian League Against War and Fascism. He denied Heakes' allegations of having seen him distribute leaflets or pamphlets at the Canadian National Exhibition in Toronto, maintaining that he had not been on the exhibition grounds since he was a child. Anyway, he got married in late August 1935 and was not in Toronto for several weeks. "This appears to dispose of the idea," Glazebrook intoned, that Norman was at the Canadian National Exhibition at that time. Not exactly, for the exhibition opened on August 23, and Norman was married on August 31, 1935. It is both possible and probable that Heakes saw him there. This exchange about whether Norman was or was not at the exhibition ground was an excellent example of the futility of discussing anything with him. The only way to have gotten to the bottom of all this was through a thorough RCMP-directed field investigation. Again, as so often in the past, there was a discussion about Tsuru's study group. Norman held that it had reflected various opinions and he did not feel that it was "obviously communist."[47]

In view of Heeney's remark about Heakes, Glazebrook asked Inspector Guernsey to inform Heakes that he would be pleased to talk with him. Guernsey understood, however, "that not too much [was] to be made of this."[48] Glazebrook's meeting with Heakes did not occur until late February 1952, when Heakes recounted what he had told Paul Martin and Inspector Guernsey. Glazebrook observed that External Affairs "never took such matters lightly," but that, in principle, they were handled "quietly." He wrote to Heeney that Heakes' information did not really shed further light on the matter, since what he had said about Norman at Cambridge had dovetailed with Norman's own admissions. Regarding his denial of distributing material at the Canadian National Exhibition, an "examination of his activities" during that period—what examination was not explained—suggested that he had not done so. However, whether he did or did not distribute such material seemed unimportant since he had admitted that, for a time, he had been a member of the Canadian League Against War and Fascism.

As to Heakes himself, Glazebrook did not know what to make of him. He strongly maintained that he was "intellectually honest" and had "no desire to harm Norman." He was a "great talker," Glazebrook observed, "and did not make a very good impression on me." It had been a useful conversation, and apart from the point about Norman distributing material, everything mentioned by Heakes had dovetailed with what Norman had admitted.[49]

It was probably at this point, the exact date is unrecorded, that Norman sent Glazebrook a handwritten note discussing his association with the Canadian Friends of the Chinese People. He described the initial attempt to organize the group in Toronto, and if he had been selected as its secretary, he certainly could not recollect it. He did not know whether the organization ever met again or operated at all, which he very much doubted, surmising that the lack of political consensus among the members of the Chinese community in Toronto had caused the group's demise. In effect he did not believe that it had had any existence beyond the initial meeting that he attended.[50] This may have been true, but the fact that he had acted as either Jaffe's or Chi Ch'ao-ting's surrogate in establishing it was unmentioned.[51] That it folded could more likely be traced to the fact that Norman departed for Harvard University in the summer of 1936, and thus never had the opportunity to develop and structure it as the Communist Party would have desired.

On March 10, 1952, Glazebrook recapitulated for Heeney what had been ascertained, so far. Since the last meeting, presumably with Pearson and Heeney, he noted that attempts had been made to "follow the leads." How this was done and by whom, and what leads were followed is unclear. Both at Cambridge and upon his return to Toronto, Glazebrook continued, Norman had been a "convinced Communist," and it was likely that he knew that the Canadian League Against War and Fascism was communist dominated. Whether, as Heakes had claimed, Norman had distributed communist material, mattered little. If Wittfogel's evidence, relating to 1938, were to be dismissed, Norman's assertions that he had changed his views as he had matured, might well be accepted. Certainly, there was nothing to indicate that he had been a disloyal employee.

On the question whether he was a Communist Party member with a specific task there was conflicting evidence. MI5 was satisfied "with the validity of their evidence." On the other hand, Norman had maintained that while Cornford had hinted he should join the party he never did. If the MI5 evidence had been dismissed, External had done so only because of its "confidence in Norman's integrity." Glazebrook thought that everyone shared this confidence, despite "what might be interpreted as concealment in the early questioning." There was no question that the RCMP would accept External's decision since it was External's responsibility to determine whether Norman did or did not continue as an employee. The Department's confidence in him, however, would not "answer all items on the file as we were able to do in 1950," Glazebrook admitted. If the Americans had additional evidence about Norman, he saw no way of obtaining it. The message sent to the American military in Tokyo may have contained no more than the information initially conveyed by the FBI to the RCMP in the spring of 1950. "Unless they get the

[MI5] evidence (which they may not like) it is a reasonable guess that they would not hesitate to work with Norman."

As to the British they had their own evidence on Norman's Cambridge period; MI5 did not regard a Cambridge undergraduate's communism as necessarily an ongoing risk. What American or British security officials would say, Glazebrook pointed out to Heeney, "if they had all the evidence that is in our possession probably must remain a speculation." Then he offered one last thought. It was likely that more of the Norman case would be heard in the future and that echoes may be produced in the House of Commons, in the American Senate, or in public opinion. This "will embarrass both Norman and ourselves," and although this should not be an important consideration in External's decision, it had to be "borne in mind."[52]

Even after thirty years one is left speechless when reading these admissions, especially about the intelligence services of countries allied with and friendly to Canada. The long and the short of it was that External Affairs, based on the flimsy consideration of personal acquaintance and collegial solidarity, was intent on giving Norman clearance, despite the fact that answers could not be found to many of the items uncovered by the RCMP, the FBI, and MI5. Also, despite the fact that in his initial discussions with Robertson and Heeney and with the RCMP in the autumn of 1950, his responses, as Glazebrook admitted to Heeney, "might be interpreted as concealment."

The potential fly in the proverbial ointment on any decision whether or not to clear Norman was, of course, Alexander George Heakes. It appears that he had mumbled something to the Americans in Ottawa and also had contacted Paul Martin. The possibility was there that he might go "public" to the press; what else he might do could not be predicted. He had, however, undermined his favorable position by writing a series of letters to the Minister of National Revenue, James J. McCann, bitterly complaining about the way he had been treated in relation to his income tax. Copies of these letters were sent to Paul Martin who, in turn, showed them to Lester Pearson. "The letters are violent to such a degree," Glazebrook observed in a memorandum for the file, "that they might easily suggest either a person of unbalanced mind or at least one who could not control his temper." In one of them Heakes had stated that the ministry's action was sufficient to destroy whatever sense he had of being a law-abiding Canadian, and definitely made him regret the trouble he had taken during the previous year to avoid embarrassing publicly

McCann's cabinet colleagues and their officials. It was probable, Glazebrook pointed out, that Heakes was alluding to the "Flagstone case" and that the letters certainly reflected on his character.[53]

The denouement occurred on March 31, 1952, when, at Pearson's request, RCMP Commissioner Leonard Nicholson who had replaced Wood and Superintendent McClellan, came to External Affairs. Heeney and Glazebrook were also present. Pearson went through the civilities of thanking Nicholson for the "understanding and helpful way" with which the RCMP had handled the Norman inquiry, explaining that all the evidence had been carefully sifted by External Affairs. He, Pearson, had decided that while Norman had been a communist when he was at Cambridge, he had subsequently changed his opinion, and he now regarded him "as a loyal Canadian and an efficient and trustworthy member of the Department." He proposed that the case be closed, that the inquiry be considered ended, and that Norman be cleared. If new evidence were to surface the RCMP should bring it to External's attention. If necessary, as in the past, he would make a statement either in or outside the House of Commons.

Nicholson, described as a "man of integrity and convictions," also maintained the civilities. He thanked Pearson for his remarks, observing that "in his view it was the duty of the RCMP to bring forward and, if requested, to discuss the security evidence concerning a member of the Department." He correctly noted that the "decision, however, was for the Department and not for the RCMP" to make.[54] He had neatly made his point: the RCMP had brought forward evidence but had not been asked to discuss it with External Affairs who, in turn, had made its own decision for which the RCMP carried no responsibility.

Chapter 7

The Road to Cairo

What happened between autumn 1950 and the early spring of 1952 must surely put to rest any notion that Norman had undergone close security vetting, as the term is understood. Pearson, in his memoirs asserts that he had reviewed the evidence with the responsible security officer and had "concluded that [Norman] had a clean bill of health." If he was referring to Glazebrook or Heeney as the person responsible for the check he was correct; if he was implying that he had gone over the evidence with the RCMP, he was decidedly in error, as he had reviewed nothing with the Force.[1]

As in previous encounters, Norman had again escaped unscathed. It is, however, important that the absence of an RCMP-directed field investigation put the lie to Pearson's statement of April 12, 1957 when he told the House of Commons that Norman's record had been "thoroughly rechecked in the light of all information available, including, of course, information from confidential sources."[2] Nor can one give credence to his statement published in the Montreal *Gazette* of April 18 that the RCMP had made a "meticulous examination" of all available evidence regarding Norman's "association with Communists during his university days," as well as any possible communist associations before he entered External Affairs.[3] Equally hard to swallow are Pearson's pique with the Senate Subcommittee on Internal Security for taking testimony about Norman in 1951, and his comment, at that time, that "we have our own methods of security in Ottawa which may not be the same as those employed in Washington, but which we consider to be fair and effective."[4] All these pronouncements may lead any prudent and reasonable person to wonder whether Pearson was protecting Norman, seemingly beyond their strong personal links.

Based on the "need to know," the exchanges that had taken place about Norman among the different security and intelligence agencies—FBI, CIA, American military intelligence, MI5, and the RCMP—were obviously unknown to most senior officials of the United States State Department, the British Foreign Office, and the Canadian Department of External Affairs.

In mid-1952, Norman relinquished his directorship of the American and Far Eastern Division which he had headed for the comparatively short period of about a year and a half. He then was appointed Head of External Affairs' Information Division. This transfer from one of its most important functional positions to one of lesser political significance signaled that he was under somewhat of a cloud.[5] During intra-External Affairs discussions, it had been proposed that if Norman were cleared by the Department, the Americans and the British should be asked if they too would work with him. Whether Pearson ever made such approaches to both Washington and London cannot be verified at the present time. If he did, one may suspect that Norman's demotion was the result of either a negative response from the State Department and the Foreign Office or, at the minimum, an ambiguous one.

In view of Pearson's public support of Norman, his transfer to the Information Division was a convenient way for Pearson to disengage himself from what can only be described as an awkward situation. His public bravado now had to take a back seat to the realities of American-Canadian relations, namely that Washington would be cautious indeed, especially on matters of national security and continental defense. There can never be confident exchange between two allied and friendly powers if one side harbors suspicions about an important participant on the other side, however unwarranted, misperceived, or exaggerated they may be. They can only be dispelled if the individual concerned is removed or replaced.

Norman served as Head of the Information Division until early 1953 when he was named High Commissioner to New Zealand.[6] An External Affairs assignment to Wellington was regarded as a kind of Siberian exile for those who had transgressed, or as a dignified post for someone who was about to retire. In early 1940, Prime Minister Mackenzie King sent Walter A. Riddell to open the diplomatic mission in Wellington. The appointment followed Riddell's earlier pro-sanctionist initiatives at the League of Nations in Geneva during the Italo-Ethiopian War—a stance that had not been to the Prime Minister's liking.[7]

Wellington in the early 1950s was not a diplomatic posting that would tax anyone's stamina. Norman's colleagues probably considered it as the place that would give him the necessary time to relax and unwind from the events of the previous two and a half years.[8] By 1953 the Senate Subcommittee on Internal Security also appeared to have forgotten him and, doubtlessly, his friends and supporters thought that, with time, his star would again be on the ascent. Indeed, Pearson told him that he considered Wellington a less active posting than Tokyo and less tiring than External Affairs, but possibly one that he would find satisfying and rewarding. Equally important, Pearson observed, it would keep him in the Pacific rim, and give him the time to maintain his interests in Far East problems and thereby to pursue his scholarly endeavors in this regard. Lastly, he hoped that Norman would interpret the Wellington assignment as an expression of renewed confidence in him and in his service to Canada, both by Prime Minister Louis St. Laurent and himself.[9]

Norman warmly responded to Pearson's letter, recording his appreciation for having been able to serve under him, an experience which, he insisted, had sustained and encouraged him during the previous years' difficulties.[10]

The banalities and formalities over, Norman left for the Southwest Pacific. What Ottawa did not know, however, was that the State Department had conveyed his biographic background to the American Embassy in Wellington. What was in these reports is unknown, since the relevant documents are still considered secret by the American government and not open for examination at the National Archives in Washington, D.C.[11] However, no matter how generous to Norman they might have been, they would have alerted even the most somnambulant embassy official in Wellington to be cautious when dealing with his Canadian counterpart.

It would also be safe to assume that similar information was conveyed to the American Embassy in Cairo when, in the spring of 1956, Ottawa decided to switch him to Cairo and Ambassador Kenneth Kirkwood from there to Wellington. Norman looked forward to the Cairo challenge, he wrote Pearson.[12] His new ambassadorial posting was a clear sign that his career was once more on the rise. The embassy was an important mission at that time, in view of the fact that Nasser's Egypt was the keystone of Arab and Middle East politics.

Kenneth Kirkwood, the new High Commissioner in Wellington, joined External Affairs in 1928, the same year as Pearson. From 1929 to 1939 he served in Japan, and his long sojourn there had, no doubt, brought him into contact with the Norman family. This may explain why the salutations in the Kirkwood-Norman correspondence commence with "Dear Ken" and "Dear Herb." In 1954 Kirkwood was appointed as the first Canadian Ambassador to Egypt and, concurrently, Minister to Lebanon.

Before leaving Wellington, Norman had spoken highly of the domestic staff he had employed at Stadacona, the High Commissioner's official residence outside Wellington. However, what Kirkwood found there was sufficiently odd to call into question Norman's judgment, as he considered the domestic staff unsuitable in all respects. In addition, Norman apparently had breached security regulations by leaving the key to the study's filing cabinet with a member of the staff rather than with an official at the High Commission. From then on, Kirkwood made it a point to keep all official papers in his office at the High Commission instead of in the study. This decision showed prescience of apparently subsequent staff forays into the study filing cabinet. In the residence itself, the doors were devoid of keys, although there was a Yale lock on the door to the staff's quarters which were kept locked at all times. On the other hand, staff members demanded that the doors in the residence be left open and, if by chance, one was found closed, they would soon open it. They also appeared to have other talents, including the unusual ability to open safes; they demonstrated it when the domestic staff of a neighbor asked for assistance in unlocking their employer's. Superfluous inspections of the residence occurred at all hours, and staff members eavesdropped on conversations in both English and French, including those conducted on the telephone.

The domestic staff also showed great interest in Kirkwood's private life and in his career, insisting that Mr. Norman had shared such information with them. Along these lines, they consistently kept in touch with members of the High Commission, and thus were privy to both confidential as well as unclassified information. Likewise, they maintained contact, it appears, with New Zealand's Secretary of External Affairs Sir Alister McIntosh, as well as with the United Kingdom High Commissioner Major General Sir Geoffrey Scoones. McIntosh who was a close friend of Norman, must have heard about Kirkwood's frustration with the Stadacona staff; although he conceded that they were difficult to handle, he felt they should remain at the High Commission. It would appear that the minister's interest in the matter certainly was at variance with diplomatic protocol.

Kirkwood watched and tolerated the situation for eight months. Finally, on April 10, 1957, within a week after Norman had committed suicide in Cairo, he informed External Affairs and McIntosh of his intention to dismiss the domestic staff. However, the New Zealander persuaded Kirkwood to first ask for Ottawa's permission to terminate their employment. He agreed, and an appropriate message was sent on April 12. Permission was granted but on April 18, before Kirkwood could give them notice, he was instructed by External Affairs to immediately return to Ottawa for consultation. This he did, although no consultation ever took place. His reports about the situation in Wellington were ignored. He was not allowed to return to New Zealand, and was given a post in Ottawa. In 1959, several years before the mandatory date, he was retired during the Diefenbaker government's term of office.

In view of his twenty-nine years of faithful service to Canada, especially to External Affairs, the treatment he had received can only be described as deplorable. One possible explanation for it may be that McIntosh, egged on perhaps by the domestic staff's kitchen gossip, by others, or indeed by External Affairs, could have taken a dim view of the fact that Kirkwood's private secretary Mrs. Christine Christians resided in the High Commissioner's residence. The lady, who was of Polish nationality, occupied a separate self-contained apartment in the house, just as Kirkwood's sister had also stayed there for a period of time. This might explain McIntosh's insistence that the staff stay on, the open door policy, the eavesdropping, and so on. Victorian prissiness, no doubt, was strong in Wellington during that period. Since Mrs. Christians had been Kirkwood's private secretary in Cairo and they had resided in separate apartments there— an accepted custom in diplomatic circles, especially among bachelor diplomats—their employer–employee association must have been known to External Affairs. In 1960, after Kirkwood had retired, he married her, following the death of her husband in Poland from whom she had been canonically separated.

There is, however, a second possible, if unconvincing explanation for Kirkwood's recall. Conceivably, Mrs. Christians' Polish nationality and her presence in the High Commissioner's residence might have raised security considerations, although if that had been the case she also must have been considered a security risk in Cairo, an issue that had never been raised previously. Moreover, she belonged to that social class in Polish society which had suffered a great deal under the communist government in Warsaw. She also was a devoted Roman Catholic who for many years had worked for the American, Canadian, and French diplomatic missions in the Polish capital. Her record was exemplary, as attested to in her letters of recommendations. In fact, she was only able to acquire a passport and an exit visa through the intervention with the Polish authorities by two successive French ambassadors; later, the French even supplied her with travel documents to replace her Polish passport. She also obtained a Swiss visa which allowed her to visit relatives in Switzerland. Without proper security clearance, it would have been virtually impossible for residents of eastern Europe to acquire such visas at that time.

There is one last plausible explanation for what happened to Kirkwood. His message to Ottawa regarding the dismissal of the High Commission's domestic staff, may have arrived at the same time as a possible missive from McIntosh and at the height of the House of Commons debate on Norman's suicide which led to some startling admissions by Pearson. Since Norman had employed the staff in Wellington, their dismissal by Kirkwood, at that point, might have necessitated an investigation into how they had been hired in the first place. To reopen the Norman security file was the last thing Pearson or External Affairs would have wanted to do. If Kirkwood had to be sacrificed, so be it.

Early in 1963, Mrs. Kirkwood, with her husband's approval, approached the RCMP to report in detail the situation that had existed at the High Commissioner's residence in Wellington. Several weeks later, Kenneth J. Burbridge, Kirkwood's second successor, terminated the staff's employment with a great sense of relief. By then the Liberals—and Pearson—were out of office, replaced by the Progressive Conservatives under John Diefenbaker. At that point, of course, the dismissal action entailed no risk, as memories of

Norman's suicide had faded, and he no longer was front-page news. Thanks to a less than discerning media, in their place the myth arose of a Norman who had been hounded to death by the Senate Sub-committee on Internal Security.

In August 1963, Kirkwood attempted to redress the injustice that he thought had been done to him, by writing to his old friend Lester Pearson, then the new Canadian Prime Minister. Beginning the letter with "Dear Mike," he recounted what he considered to have been an "illegal separation" from External Affairs under the Diefenbaker government, as a result of the April 1957 events in Wellington. At that time Pearson was External Affairs Minister and Jules Léger (the future Governor General), the under-secretary. Kirkwood touched upon the subjects of the domestic staff at Stadacona, his recall to Ottawa, and his premature retirement. It all had been done without investigation, nor had anyone consulted with him. He considered the whole course of events a "denial of justice" by the Diefenbaker government, and in gross violation of the regulations meant to pro-tect civil servants, as well as of the Bill of Rights enacted by the Diefenbaker government. He believed that Pearson, as a longtime colleague, would be willing to re-examine the case with a "sense of fairness and justice." Kirkwood was confident that the Prime Min-ister would wish to undo the injustice that had been done by the previous government. The case had led to "unjustified personal dis-honour" for himself and his wife and also reflected, he believed, on External Affairs. He asked for an interview, offering to provide documentation which, he was sure, Pearson would find "shocking and discreditable." Kirkwood ended by stating that he had refrained from making the issue public because this was not his style, and because he had hoped justice would inevitably prevail. Although he had written a long and moving letter to an old friend and colleague, it seems no interview was ever arranged. Nor is there any indication that Pearson ever asked for whatever documents Kirkwood had in his possession. What followed instead was a long silence.

It was not until early December 1963 — almost five months later — that Pearson responded. He attributed the delay to his desire to thor-oughly investigate what had occurred. He owed this to Kirkwood, he explained, as a longtime friend and associate in External Affairs. His investigation had forced him to conclude, however, that it would be unwise and undesirable to re-examine the case. The information he had received confirmed the legality of Kirkwood's early retirement; he also denied that his recall from Wellington had been based on the comments made by the domestic staff. The letter was polite but not as forthcoming as may have been expected from an old friend. Kirkwood certainly never received due process on this issue nor did he have an opportunity to defend himself.

This denial of procedural justice should be contrasted with Pearson's action a few years later when he telephoned the terminally-ill postal clerk George Victor Spencer, to inquire whether he wanted a judicial investigation into his dismissal by the postal authorities after it was discovered that he had spied for the Russians; by then Pearson was under political pressure. The Kirkwood episode which is only one small aspect of the Norman story, is admittedly based on the perceptions of one of the participants and, therefore, less than impartial. However, like the Norman story, it invites a thorough investigation if for no other reason than to set the record straight about Kenneth Kirkwood who had served his country long and faithfully. [13]

Norman's arrival in the Middle East coincided with the momentous events in the autumn of 1956—the Suez war and the Anglo-French and Israeli attack on Egypt. In fact, Norman was in Beirut presenting his credentials to the President of Lebanon when the fighting erupted and, for a period of time, was marooned in the Lebanese capital, until he was able to take up his post in Cairo.

There was one oddity, however, during these hectic days that cannot go unrecorded. When Egypt severed diplomatic relations with Great Britain the Swiss Legation was asked to represent British interests in Egypt. Concurrently, when Egypt severed diplomatic relations with Australia, the Canadian Embassy was asked to represent Australian interests there. One would have thought that the British, like the Australians, would have asked the Canadians to look after their affairs. However, Commonwealth solidarity appears to have fallen by the wayside, as Ottawa's stance during those days was as critical of London as it was of Canberra. Why did the British pick the Swiss over the Canadians? One plausible, but speculative answer is that MI5, sensitized to Norman, may have warned the Foreign Office. The Australians, lacking similar intelligence information, picked the Canadians.

In the weeks and months that followed, because of concurrent events in Europe—the Russian invasion and suppression of the Hungarian revolution—there were long workdays, tense conditions, and serpentine negotiations with Egyptian authorities about the Canadian military contribution to the United Nations Emergency Force in the Sinai.[14] At that moment, the Senate Subcommittee on Internal Security again focused its attention on Norman. The witness this time was the State Department's John K. Emmerson, Counsellor of the American Embassy in Beirut, who had first met Norman in prewar Tokyo and again after the war when they both served in General MacArthur's Headquarters.

Prior to appearing before the subcommittee, Emmerson was warned by the State Department's Deputy Under-Secretary Loy Henderson that the subcommittee's chief counsel Judge Robert Morris had mentioned in a telephone conversation that "one of the interests in the hearing" would be Emmerson's relations with Norman. That interest had undoubtedly arisen because of its "inquiry into faulty intelligence reports in the Far East by American diplomats" who then were transferred to missions in the Middle East.[15] The experienced Henderson had pointed out to Morris that it would be inappropriate for an American foreign service officer, such as Emmerson, to testify in open session about the activities of another country's diplomat. Indeed, although Henderson had not mentioned it, when General Willoughby was similarly queried about Norman in August 1951, he had been "reluctant" to discuss him and did not do so. Morris had assured Henderson that this would not be the case, since the hearing would be in executive session. Under the American congressional committee system this means that it is in secret and confidential and, as in public session, testimony is given under oath.[16]

The hearing was scheduled for March 12, 1957, however when Emmerson asked for a short delay on March 11, so he could refresh his memory, Judge Morris refused the request without explanation.

On the morning of March 12, prior to his appearance, Emmerson perused the transcripts of the previous hearings. However, that same morning, in conversation with his attorney, he neglected to mention that Norman was now Canadian Ambassador to Egypt, concurrently accredited as Minister to Lebanon. That the Normans had lunched with the Emmersons in Beirut—something that Emmerson viewed as a social occasion devoid of "professional intent or purpose"—did not cause him to consider it "significant to the matter at hand."

He was wrong and, in fact, compounded his mistake during his testimony in the afternoon of March 12. To the question whether he thought Norman was a communist he responded that he had no reason to believe so. He then let it slip that Norman now was Canadian

Ambassador to Egypt. That remark caused great consternation among the members of the subcommittee. Here was a man overseeing Canada's relations with two of the most important countries in the volatile Middle East while, at the same time, maintaining political contact with his American counterpart.

The fact that the subcommittee's staff had not kept track of Norman's diplomatic postings was inexcusable, considering the suspicions it had had about him since 1951. Though there is no documentary evidence, it is possible that the discovery of his presence in Cairo provided an opportunity to investigate his associations with American colleagues. By doing so, the subcommittee could come to grips with Pearson who had successfully avoided its public scrutiny since Elizabeth Bentley's executive session testimony in August 1951.

Bentley became a member of the communist apparatus in 1940, under the tutelage of her lover Jacob Rasin. Born in Russia but having acquired American nationality, he was a Russian intelligence agent who used the code name "Golos" which means "voice" in Russian. Bentley, under the alias Helen Johnson, became a courier for Rasin, and made weekly trips to Washington to collect information from well over thirty employees of American government departments, agencies, and wartime boards. However, in July 1945 she approached the FBI to confess her espionage activities and, for one year after that, worked under the Bureau's control as a double agent.

Bentley's uncorroborated testimony, however, was insufficient to bring indictments for espionage against any of these American government employees. She did testify that she collected William Remington's party dues for two years, and he was charged and convicted of perjury having denied to the Grand Jury that he had ever been a member of the Communist Party. Her disclosures also had aided in the 1949 conviction of eleven top American communist leaders. Under the Smith Act they had been charged with conspiring to overthrow the American government, and their convictions had been sustained by the Supreme Court. In addition, Bentley had testified at the trial of Julius and Ethel Rosenberg who were executed for conveying atomic energy secrets to Soviet Russia.

In her 1951 executive session testimony to the subcommittee, and in a subsequent interrogation by the FBI, (see Parts A and B of the Appendices), Bentley had asserted that Lester Pearson had been the source of secret information passed on by her agent Hazen Sise who was a communist and an employee of the Canadian National Film

Board. She had stated that she had been running him while he was attached to the Canadian Legation in Washington, adding that her assertion about Pearson had been based on Sise's alleged comments to her.

Elizabeth Bentley died in December 1963. There is no doubt that she had escaped American government prosecution for espionage because of her cooperation as a witness in several cases. In view of her testimony involving Pearson and because of his inordinate protection of Norman, political wisdom must have dictated that he rather than Pearson be the target of the subcommittee's March 1957 investigation.

During his questioning of Emmerson on March 12, Judge Morris read a security report about Norman which apparently was an amalgam of FBI and RCMP information, first collected in 1950 when Norman was being considered for the post of liaison officer between American and Canadian intelligence. Then Emmerson mentioned that he and his wife had met the Normans, who had travelled from Egypt by ship, upon their arrival in Beirut. Because of what he subsequently called a "mental block," he could not recall how they had contacted each other. Nor could he remember the substantive details of their conversation, except that they had discussed the deepening Middle East crisis. He stated that there had been nothing in Norman's comments which had struck him as either odd or procommunist.

In closing the session, William Jenner, the Republican senator from Indiana, reminded everyone that Emmerson's testimony had been taken in executive session, making it clear that his comments were not to be repeated outside the confines of the subcommittee's hearing room.

Then a State Department security officer who had been present at the executive session criticized Emmerson for having been "less than forthcoming" in his remarks about the Normans. Realizing that he should, perhaps, have given a fuller account of their meeting in Beirut, Emmerson contacted Judge Morris, asking if he could provide the subcommittee with a more detailed report about it. A second executive session was arranged for March 21[17] and, on Judge Morris' instructions, Emmerson's prior testimony was closely scrutinized by a member of the subcommittee's staff.[18] It was at this point also (see Part C of the Appendices) that Judge Morris and William Rusher, his associate counsel, discussed with members of the State Department Bentley's testimony and the American government's security aspects involving Herbert Norman, Lester Pearson, and others.

During the March 21 session, Emmerson, in an attempt to elaborate on the Beirut meeting, described how it had been arranged. The subcommittee further scrutinized every one of his associations with Norman, investigating the claim that the Canadian was a communist.[19]

Understandably, the Norman reference in Emmerson's testimony made the State Department feel uneasy, as the Canadian government had already protested against prior references to him. Acting Secretary of State Christian A. Herter then pointed out to Senator James O. Eastland, Chairman of the Senate Judiciary Committee, that additional "publicity in this connection would, in our opinion, render further serious damage to our relations with the Canadian Government." He hoped that the subcommittee would "not feel it necessary to release publicly" that portion of the testimony which referred to Norman. Eastland was not receptive to the idea, claiming that the subcommittee had an obligation to present to the "Senate the whole picture of subversion as it relates to the security of the United States." Emmerson's comments, he wrote to Herter, contained references that corroborated previous statements before the subcommittee. Deletions would present a partial picture and be unfair both to Emmerson "whose version of his meeting with Dr. Norman has now been changed from what it was in the public record," and also "to the integrity of the Subcommittee's record."[20]

A third encounter between Emmerson and the subcommittee took place on March 23, also in executive session. He was asked to identify over one hundred people, as to whether or not they were communists. Though his testimony of March 12 was corrected and expanded in the March 21 and 23 executive sessions, the subcommittee in its 1957 report was far from convinced of his performance.[21] Of the three sessions only the one of March 23 was not released to the press, in fact, it was not published until 1970.[22]

However, the release of his March 12 testimony on March 14 provoked a public furor in Canada. Why it was released is unclear, although it can be suggested that Judge Morris' assurances that it would never be made public had been sincerely given. He had had some experience in these matters as a young lawyer having first served on the Rapp-Coudert Subcommittee established by the New York State Legislature to investigate and subsequently uncover communist infiltration of New York City's school system. In addition, he had served during the war as a Naval Intelligence Officer.[23]

What was discovered about Norman was as clearly unacceptable to the subcommittee in 1957 as it probably had been to the State Department by 1952 when he was Head of External Affairs' American and Far Eastern Division. Release of the Emmerson testimony, therefore, might have been seen as a way of exposing Norman to embarrass the Canadian government into removing him from the sensitive Cairo and Beirut posts. That such a step would be contrary to Morris' promise to Henderson, that it would cause difficulties with the Canadians, and bring about the release of secret FBI and RCMP information, was probably viewed as a necessary move. Moreover, the subcommittee undoubtedly had the darkest suspicions about what they perceived to be Norman's charmed existence and his ever-ascending importance in the bureaucracy of External Affairs.

J. Edgar Hoover pointed out to Attorney General William Rogers that the hasty release of the Emmerson testimony had been executed by the subcommittee in agreement with the State Department's Security Division. Unfortunately, that division had never cleared it with the Diplomatic Division and, accordingly, "it did not appear that either the Committee or Morris was to blame."[24] Despite Hoover's comment, it is not unreasonable to suggest that perhaps elements within the State Department's Security Division had seen eye to eye with the subcommittee in its urgent desire to expose Norman publicly.

If the release of the testimony caused public furor in Canada, it provoked private rage in J. Edgar Hoover who, less than amused by the release of secret intelligence information, publicly denied that the FBI had furnished it to the subcommittee. Despite this, Judge Morris points out that Hoover's good relations with it were not affected.[25] Inquiries by the FBI to the American military had ascertained that the information it had shared with them in the autumn of 1950, when Norman was being considered for the liaison post, had been circulated only to the army's Far East Headquarters.[26] An investigation was ordered and it was soon discovered that the document from which Judge Morris had quoted was a Summary of Information prepared on Norman in mid-April 1951 by the army's Far East Command. It was an enclosure to a special report dealing with the Japanese Council of the Institute of Pacific Relations, and prepared for General Willoughby who was scheduled to testify in Washington.

Some of the general's footlockers containing pertinent material for this 1951 inquiry had then been sent to Judge Morris. The army concluded that the "presumption" appeared justified that the Summary of Information on Norman had reached the subcommittee via Willoughby "on a personal basis."[27] When General Willoughby was subsequently subjected to a close and less than friendly interrogation by the army's Counterintelligence Corps, it led nowhere,[28] no doubt because the report, as Judge Morris notes, had not reached the subcommittee, either through the FBI or General Willoughby.[29]

The Canadian reaction to these developments was best reflected in the House of Commons debates. If the subcommittee thought that the members would rise in anger against the government for having posted Norman to Cairo and Beirut, it was sadly disappointed. American–bashing is an old and honorable tradition in Canada and often politically lucrative to boot. The release of Emmerson's testimony, as well as Judge Morris' citation of secret FBI and RCMP intelligence information was a veritable Klondike gold rush. John Diefenbaker, Progressive Conservative leader of the official Opposition, rose to take the initial swing. He was no political novice, and the dim view taken in Canada of American congressional committees of inquiry, presented him with an excellent opportunity to hitch his wagon to the public outcry. He asked Pearson if the subcommittee's allegations were unjustified. If so, would the strongest possible protest be raised with the Americans against its attack which was "detrimental not only to the Canadian diplomat but to Canadian international relations."

Angered by what had occurred, Pearson pointed out that the released testimony had been given to the Washington press before reaching the Canadian government, and that the press and radio had, in turn, presented it as "evidence" which it was not. The best commentary on the whole procedure, he thought, was mirrored in Senator Jenner's concluding remark when he had admonished everyone to remember that Emmerson's testimony had been taken in executive session. The government, Pearson informed the House, would strongly protest to Washington about this matter. The released testimony, he continued, contained "a great many innuendoes and insinuations that Mr. Norman was a communist." These charges, raised by Washington in 1951, resulted in Norman being "subjected, in his own interests and in the public interest and with his own approval and co-operation, to a special and exhaustive security check." In view of what we now know about this so-called "exhaustive security check," the only comment that can be made is that Pearson was misleading the House of Commons. He then assured the members that confidence in Norman's loyalty was unaffected, on the contrary, everyone was even more convinced of his devotion, efficiency, and loyalty to the government. He was doing extremely important work in Cairo, Pearson observed, in a manner which "commanded" his "whole-hearted admiration" and deserved his "full support." The subcommittee's "slanders and unsupported insinuations" against Norman could be treated "with the contempt they deserve."[30]

The Canadian protest to the Americans was made several days later, on March 18. Pearson's comments to the House of Commons were repeated, unmentioned however was the initial and unsatisfactory questioning of Norman in autumn of 1950. One would have thought that greater care would have been taken in composing this protest, since the FBI was not uninformed about the RCMP scrutiny to which Norman had been subjected. In the note, the subcommittee was lambasted, and its action was described as "inconsistent with the long-standing and friendly co-operation characterizing" Canadian-American relations.

At about the same time as the protest note was sent to Washington Pearson received two interesting messages. The first one was from Norman, expressing gratitude for his "generous and forthright" remarks concerning the subcommittee's allegations against him. While he felt that the repetition of these old charges had had a "vexing and discouraging effect," the reaction to them by the House had increased his "pride in and devotion" to Canadian institutions and to "our sense of fair play." He asked Pearson to convey to Diefenbaker his "sincere appreciation for the thoughtful and considerate manner" with which he had introduced the question in the House of Commons.[31] Ten days later, Pearson passed on these remarks to John Diefenbaker.[32]

At about the same time, probably on March 25, 1957, Pearson's office received a telephone call from Patrick Walsh, the former unpaid RCMP informant who had first identified Norman in 1936. Although he sought an opportunity to present to Pearson a brief on Norman's communist background, no interview to do so was ever granted.[33]

It was probably at this point, and possibly in reaction to Walsh's message, that Pearson, it appears, sent Norman what was probably a handwritten note, telling him that he didn't "believe a word of any of this," asking him to pay "no attention to it, that he himself certainly wouldn't."[34]

Concurrently in Washington, Norman's Japanese friend Tsuru was appearing before the Senate Subcommittee on Internal Security, and his testimony must have been brought to Norman's attention. Tsuru, having returned to the United States was now teaching at Harvard.[35] Considering the suspicions about him in certain official American circles, it is unclear how he had managed to obtain permission to enter the United States. Perhaps by this point any suspicions that might have existed had been resolved to Washington's satisfaction.

With Norman making front-page news, Alexander George Heakes again surfaced. Having kept his peace for over five years, he once more contacted Paul Martin to remind him of their previous discussions and of his concern, lest Norman be identified publicly. That had now occurred. Noting that Washington obviously distrusted Ottawa's security procedures, he quoted a remark which he had seen in the press. It had been made by an External Affairs official who had stated that Canada was handling subversion questions with "dignity."[36]

Curiously, the American response to the Canadian protest note was not given for over three weeks. It finally did arrive on April 10, six days after Norman had committed suicide. Condolences were now offered to the Canadian government and to Mrs. Norman. In addition, Pearson was given a civics lesson on the peculiarities of the American constitutional system, to wit that the executive branch— White House and State Department—had "no jurisdiction over the views or opinions expressed by members or committees of the United States congress," and that the subcommittee's investigation lay completely within its own control. Washington desired the continuance of the friendliest relations with Canada, and deplored any development, whether American or Canadian, which might damage these relations. The note was short, polite and—it would not be unfair to say—distinctly cool.[37]

Despite the public and private support from Pearson, Diefenbaker's published statements, and the sympathetic letters received from Ottawa friends, Egerton Herbert Norman committed suicide on April 4, 1957. Heakes, now throwing caution to the wind, sent an open telegram to Paul Martin on the same day. Couched in Aesopian language to fend off the curious, he stated that he was "shocked and upset" by the unnecessary "tragedy" which could have been avoided if Martin's efforts, supplemented by his own, had been successful. He felt that Martin must have shared his feelings of frustration and helplessness as he had watched this awful tragedy unfold.[38]

The next day, April 5, Heakes admitted to Martin that he had drunk himself to sleep on the previous night. He could not remember a similar experience, and had not wanted to talk to anyone, adding that he hoped Norman would rest in peace. Because of his public silhouette, it had only been a matter of time before he would be identified, seeing that he was at the end of the hook. Someone should have taken him off, and frankly, Heakes observed, those in charge of External's security arrangements should be sacked. He reserved comments on Pearson, but expressed a wish to see Martin.[39]

Since Heakes could be compared to a ticking time bomb, and therefore was politically dangerous, Glazebrook, acting no doubt on either Under-Secretary Jules Léger's or Pearson's instructions, drafted a reply for Martin. It stated that he fully shared Pearson's sentiments which had been expressed in the House of Commons on April 4. As Heakes knew, Norman had had the government's "full confidence" which had been thoroughly established by his prior investigation. Martin also "fully shared that confidence" and believed that everything that could have been done was done. The activities of the Senate Subcommittee on Internal Security lay beyond Canadian control, the draft note continued, and even vigorous protests to Washington had proved ineffective. Heakes had conveyed to Martin certain information about Norman which, in line with other data, had been carefully analyzed at the time. Martin believed the government had been "fully justified in maintaining their confidence in [Norman's] integrity."[40] However, when Glazebrook took this draft letter to Martin, he decided not to reply to Heakes.

The arrival of the news that Norman had committed suicide set off another round of American-bashing in the House of Commons. Pearson cited a press release he had issued that morning, blaming Norman's tragic self-destruction on a "nervous collapse" caused by a combination of "overwork, overstrain, and the feeling of renewed persecution on a sensitive mind and a not very robust body." Not to be outdone, Diefenbaker was soon on his feet to object that Norman's "good name was filched from him by indiscriminately branding him as an enemy, trying him by suspicion and, in the public mind to a great extent, convicting him by innuendo." He had been a "devoted public servant" who was a "victim of witch-hunting proclivities." Diefenbaker proposed that the Canadian flag flying over Parliament Hill be flown at half-mast "for one who served well and died in the service of his country." Others added their voices of dismay.[41]

At first, Diefenbaker felt comfortable supporting Pearson and the government.[42] Then, on April 12, he unexpectedly reversed his position. What had caused this change? Solon Low, Leader of the Social Credit Party, had read reports about Norman in a rabidly anti-communist newsletter published by one Ronald Gostick. He asked him for his complete file on Norman, including any official documentation that may have originated in Washington. Gostick obliged by sending the requested material, however, what it was cannot be ascertained at this time. After examining it and apparently agreeing with its contents, Low felt it would have greater impact if Diefenbaker, as the leader of the official opposition, rather than he who headed the second minority party, were to use it to question Pearson. Low, therefore, passed it on the Diefenbaker, asking him to check it carefully and to take whatever step he felt was necessary. Seemingly, two hours later, without questioning its nature, Diefenbaker walked into the House, Gostick's material in hand, and proceeded to pose his question:[43] Would the government confirm that the "allegations and statements" made before the Senate Subcommittee on Internal Security on March 12 and 21 when Emmerson had testified, "specifically were untrue, unjustified and had no basis in fact?"

Pearson avoided a direct response. Instead, he admitted that Norman, during his university days, had "associated quite openly . . . with persons who were thought to be communists or who appeared to behave like communists." Unsatisfied, Diefenbaker repeated his question. He was not going to say, Pearson retorted, "whether any single statement made in a United States [Senate] Subcommittee is accurate or not." His answer was "equivocal," Diefenbaker maintained, and he wanted it made clear whether the statements made before the subcommittee "had no basis in fact in order to assure that Mr. Norman's memory will not be subjected to the stigma of statements such as were made there."

Diefenbaker never really got his answer. Solon Low then jumped into the fray. Norman's university associations, he pointed out, were something Pearson had held back since 1951. He wanted to know what had been his security check in 1951. From Pearson's comments he had understood that there had been a "double check." Who had done this "double check?" Pearson: the RCMP. With this answer he misled the House, as he obviously was unwilling to admit that after Wittfogel's testimony, additional information, especially from MI5, had led to Norman's interrogation in January 1952. Nor was he willing to mention that MI5, more than the FBI, had conveyed to the RCMP some of the most damaging evidence. In the Canadian setting, then and now, what the British cousins say is trusted more and has greater influence than anything that might be said by the American neighbors. Therefore, such an admission was to be avoided. It is possible that in dividing the field of attack against Pearson, Diefenbaker assigned to Low the task of concentrating his questioning on the "double check" that Norman supposedly had received.

So the RCMP had done the checking, Low continued. Then who had cleared him? The government, Pearson responded. Then it had not been the security people? With these questions, Low had made several telling points but, unfortunately, their value was not appreciated by the House. Its members were unaware of what had occurred, commencing with the Robertson-Heeney-Norman conversation in October 1950 to the RCMP interrogation of January 1952, and subsequent intra–External Affairs discussions. Nor were they aware of the way Pearson had protected Norman from an inquisitive RCMP. Low then wanted to know whether checks had been made after 1951. Yes, Pearson correctly replied. Again his response was deceptive; there had not been a "check" but an interrogation—a substantive difference in semantics. Pearson then assured the House that he bore no share in Norman's tragic death. He had been "convinced of his loyalty and decency as a Canadian from the first day" he had entered External Affairs.[44]

The most interesting aspect of these debates was not so much Pearson's ability to fracture the truth but the continuing silence of Prime Minister St. Laurent who said virtually nothing, and when he did speak it was anodyne in the extreme. Moreover, the name Egerton Herbert Norman never passed his lips, as though it were repugnant to him. In fairness it must be said that, as early as 1954, St. Laurent began to show signs of exhaustion which led to depressions and an inability to firmly direct government affairs.[45] The Norman debate may have been one of these occasions.

In Washington, six days after the House of Commons debate on Norman, the FBI's J. Edgar Hoover succinctly summed up the case in one of his rare, marginally scribbled notes: What had occurred "certainly shows the hypocrisy & self serving expediency of the Canadian Gov't."[46] Pearson's performance, in particular, was appalling and deceitful, an insult to the Canadian House of Commons, and a denial of everything it stands for: honesty in open parliamentary debate and respect for the House. Some of this was acknowledged by Pearson several days after the debates were over. In a private letter he solemnly noted what had occurred, and that the admissions he had made about Norman in the House of Commons could not be expanded upon. To go further in this matter, he explained, would raise so many problems that it might create more harm than good to Norman's reputation and to External Affairs' security procedures.[47] Though he did not say it, it would also have done more harm than good to his own reputation. The letter was a damaging admission.

Equally damaging was a report submitted over a week later by George Glazebrook. He dismissed the publication of any book of documents on the Norman case, composed largely of materials found in public print, as a gesture that would add nothing of value and probably would be criticized for that very reason. He also rejected a proposal to issue a general statement concerning security procedures within External Affairs. His objections were that it would not apply to Norman prior to 1950, and only would demonstrate the lack of established procedures before 1946. It would also invite additional questions and perhaps controversy, and American critics, in particular, could argue that Canadian security was not up to snuff. To rebut the Senate Subcommittee on Internal Security had its dangers. Some of the evidence about Norman was true, and most of it had been given under oath. To recapitulate the adverse testimony about him would highlight for those who had not read it, in fact most Canadians, the number of references to his alleged communist associations. Ottawa's objections had been directed against release and publication of this testimony, and against Judge Morris' leading questions. Yet, there was one real danger; what additional information was there in the hands of the subcommittee? That was something which, we shall see, probably also had worried Norman in Cairo before he committed suicide. Then again, what evidence might surface which was not yet in the subcommittee's possession?

Glazebrook examined a combination of possibilities. He then rejected them, since there were certain aspects to the question which should not be brought out into the open. They included the weak security arrangements in External Affairs before 1946; the absence of a security clearance for Norman prior to 1950 as well as earlier RCMP practices—an allusion, no doubt, to its efforts to exchange information with the FBI. Lastly, and most importantly, there was the massive evidence that had been accumulated against Norman as well as his own admissions.

While Glazebrook thought there would be clear advantages to issuing a statement to clarify a confused situation, no procedure was discovered which would not make the situation worse. The wise thing to keep in mind, he observed, was not that Americans and Canadians would be satisfied with a fair explanation, but rather that there were elements in both countries "who would pick holes in any statement, demand further information, and generally welcome the statement as an opening to new controversy."[48] Any comments about Glazebrook's memorandum are bound to be anti-climactic.

For obscure reasons it was not until well after Norman's suicide that Pearson asked for a note about what had occurred in Cambridge, Massachusetts in November 1942 when Norman had encountered the FBI in an attempt to acquire Tsuru's possessions. Glazebrook gave it to him on May 13, 1957.[49]

Chapter 8

Unraveling a Thread

It can now be said with reasonable certainty that, prior to entering the Department of External Affairs in July 1939, Egerton Herbert Norman was a member in good standing of the Canadian Communist Party. Understandably, most Canadians would not be able to accept the notion that a Canadian mandarin, like his British cousins or his American neighbors, could be suborned into serving in the Russian intelligence services, either for reasons of ideology, money, flattery, or because of sexual entrapment. However, the trials following the Gouzenko revelations and the more recent example of Hugh Hambleton[1] show the fallacy of such a notion. In Norman's case the reason was ideological, as it was for his Cambridge contemporaries, but judging by recent disclosures in the West, it would appear that, today, the ideological factor has been largely replaced by mercenary considerations.

What has remained unclear, however, is whether Norman's association with the Communist Party continued after he entered External Affairs and, if it did, did he furnish secret and privy information to Russian intelligence?

Fortunately, skeptics are ever present in pluralistic societies and in functioning democracies such as Canada. They and Norman supporters may contend that there is no evidence to sustain either proposition. Norman's membership in the Communist Party was unknown in 1957, and in the years that followed proof of association between him and the Russian intelligence services could not be established. In the past such contentions were easily made and defended, however, access to recently released archival materials and availability of other sources make this defense untenable. In the interim, a greater understanding has been reached of long-term Russian intelligence objectives, as well as of the tradecraft of Moscow's secret services. Accordingly, what was previously ignored in the Norman case or explained away is now recognized for what it is: a distinctive marker on a familiar jungle trail of deceit and subornation.

Certainly, those who maintain that Norman was loyal to his country after entering External Affairs, would be positing someone who was truly unique among that small group of Cambridge University students who joined the Communist Party in the 1930s. Other party members who, like Norman, entered government service, did not discard their ideological loyalty and fanaticism at the portals of the British Foreign Office (Burgess and Maclean), MI6 (Philby), MI5 (Blunt), or the British Treasury (John Cairncross). Indeed, the same applied, at least initially, to Michael Straight, Norman's American contemporary and fellow Communist Party cell member.[2]

Norman's moves, soon after arriving in Toronto from Cambridge University, were clearly in line with this commitment. His quest for a position within External Affairs and his persistence to acquire such a position[3] were in keeping with the instructions issued to Norman's contemporary ideological neophytes by "Otto," their Russian control officer. When they departed from Cambridge University, according to Otto, they were to reject their "open Communism go 'underground', and get [themselves] into the Foreign Office instead of pursuing an academic career."[4]

There is no evidence that Norman knew Otto, but the very low profile he maintained within the Canadian Communist Party was in compliance with these instructions. It was probably done with relative ease, bearing in mind his prior experience at Cambridge when he was admonished to conceal his party commitment and, in general, eschew the activities of the university's left wing while he was recruiting his Indian classmates.[5] Naturally, his target of penetration would have been External Affairs, the Foreign Office's Canadian counterpart. Though he had expressed to representatives of the Rockefeller Foundation a desire to teach Far Eastern history in a college or university setting[6] and, on several occasions, was offered senior professorial appointments (Yale University and the University of British

Columbia), he invariably rejected such offers. As his friend Ferns, who was close to him in Ottawa during the war, tells us, "there was no doubt that the attractions of being 'in the know' were too great. . . . [he was] committed . . . to the bureaucracy, and . . . he remained *en poste* to his bitter end."[7]

One of those who Otto ran early on was Norman's Cambridge University contemporary, the aesthete Anthony Blunt. A confessed homosexual, he was one of the last of the group to be publicly exposed as a longtime Russian intelligence agent. When interrogated by MI5 in 1964 he was clearly in a position to allege that Norman had been recruited, claiming that " 'Herb was one of us.' "[8] Chapman Pincher, the 1981 source for Blunt's alleged statement, is a veteran Fleet Street journalist who has excellent contacts with former and perhaps present members of the British and other western intelligence services. In a more recent publication, he informs us that Blunt's comment which was made "reluctantly," meant nothing more and nothing less than that Norman was a member of the Russian intelligence apparatus.[9] It is exceedingly difficult to believe that Pincher, even if he had initially erred in reporting the alleged comment, would now compound his error, especially in view of the brouhaha his 1981 disclosure generated in the Canadian press. Nevertheless, the same skeptics and those partial to Norman may correctly claim that what Pincher had reported was nothing but hearsay.

Far more difficult to explain away is the alleged disclosure of KGB defector Anatoly Golitsyn who had stated that Norman was a "long-term communist and KGB agent."[10] Is Anatoly Golitsyn worthy of credence? A major and long-serving officer in the KGB until his defection to the West, he appeared unannounced in December 1961, together with his wife and daughter on the doorstep of the CIA's Station Chief in Helsinki. Since he had planned to defect for some time, he had previously searched the KGB's "intelligence reports for clues to the identities of the KGB's sources," and had memorized the "contents of documents pilfered from NATO files." In Moscow he had served in the KGB's First Chief Directorate which conducts espionage activities in Canada, Great Britain, and the United States. Subsequently, he was transferred to a unit that "processed reports from the KGB's spies inside NATO." Accordingly, he was in the KGB long enough, holding sufficiently important functional positions, to have gained access to the information he cited about Norman.

The CIA's initial fear appears to have been that Golitsyn might not be a legitimate defector. However, the information he conveyed convinced them, within days of his defection, that this was not the case. Subsequently, to test his claim that Moscow possessed an enormous amount of NATO's most secret documents, the CIA showed Golitsyn sensitive NATO files, intermingled with spurious ones. In this litmus test of credibility the documents that he claimed to have read in Moscow were indeed authentic NATO materials.[11]

Regarding Golitsyn or any other defector, one Soviet Russian specialist has rightly pointed out that "it is vital to distinguish between what he knows from first-hand experience, what is the result of careful analysis of available sources" and what is, as in Golitsyn's later writings, "sheer guesswork" about Moscow's pantomimes in the international political arena. Like Gouzenko and other defectors, Golitsyn was difficult to handle and produced problems for the CIA. But vintage Golitsyn was very good indeed, and the information he conveyed about the KGB and its agents "proved to be of the highest value at the time."[12] Understandably fearful of KGB assassination, he and his family now live with a new identity, under the protection of the CIA, presumably somewhere in the United States.

As to the first part of Golitsyn's alleged statement that Norman was "a long-term communist," it neatly dovetails with the material on Norman's association with the Canadian Communist Party prior to his admission to External Affairs. Even more importantly, it supports the argument that his commitment to the party did not lapse once he entered the Department but continued even after 1939. His World War II comments to Ferns, once the government had outlawed the Canadian Communist Party, are grist for the mill.[13] Moreover, his wartime fears of being arrested, together with his classmate Charles P. H. Holmes, seem to reflect an unreasonable anxiety if, as Norman claimed, they both had left behind them their earlier party associations.[14]

In line with Golitsyn's statement and Otto's advice,[15] the other markers dotting Norman's jungle trail appear to assume new significance and, therefore, cannot be dismissed as easily today as in the past. His avoidance, for example, of the Jaffes and of Alexander MacLeod, once he had entered External Affairs, attracts as much attention[16] as the comments he made to Alexander George Heakes in the summer of 1935.[17] He also distanced himself from Ferns once Norman Robertson, alerted to his left-wing orientation, decided to force him out of External Affairs.[18] The same applies to Norman's shunning of Bessie Touzel—though she can neither remember contacting him nor his alleged reaction—following Wittfogel's testimony. The fact that Touzel's name had been raised in the Kellock-Taschereau Royal Commission was known in Ottawa and was something of which Norman could not have been unaware, in view of his prior close association with her.[19] Nor must we forget his thwarted attempt in November 1942 to acquire Tsuru's papers at Cambridge, Massachusetts. What was there in those papers to conceivably justify such a high-risk operation? One answer may have been to remove the evidence that tended to show Tsuru's Marxist orientation, but more likely, to remove documents that could have put in doubt Norman's own loyalty to Canada.[20]

Certainly by October 1945, only an unbroken Communist Party association could explain Norman's enthusiastic interest in interrogating only the communists incarcerated in Tokyo's Fuchu prison. The same applies to the role he appears to have played in repatriating Sanzo Nosaka, the leader of Japan's Communist Party.[21]

Also of interest is his attendance at nocturnal Marxist study group meetings while serving in Japan prior to the outbreak of the Korean War. These meetings which he apparently never reported to External Affairs, could easily be explained away, had he been questioned about them.[22] To all this must be added Kiernan's diary entries, following Norman's 1947 visit to his Cambridge University digs, that Herbert's "heart still was in the right place," but it appeared that "he had no organized contact with the Communist party."[23] Lastly, what of Norman's disingenuous remarks to Messrs. Robertson and Heeney during discussions in October 1950, magnified by him when interrogated by Guernsey, McClellan, and Glazebrook, and repeated in subsequent dialogues with Glazebrook? His denial that he knew any Chinese, thereby delegating Chi Ch'ao-ting to the status of an Orwellian "unperson," is understandable, in view of Chi Ch'ao-ting's sinister reputation by the time Norman was interrogated in January 1952. Singularly, these disparate occurrences appear meaningless, but collectively they form a pattern of behavior which lends credence to the first part of Anatoly Golitsyn's alleged statement.

The second part of the statement contends that Norman was a "KGB agent." The techniques of modern espionage, combined with modern technology, can make it extremely difficult to apprehend anyone who supplies secret and privy information to the intelligence services of a foreign state. Persons found working for them and especially for Russian intelligence, can generally be uncovered in three ways:

1. If caught *in flagrante delicto*—although being apprehended in the middle of the act is most unlikely.
2. If caught because of defection, possibly from within one's own immediate family or from within the highest level of the local Communist Party, especially if party leaders were used to "talent spot" potential recruits. In the era of the ideological recruit the tactic was common but had its risks and, therefore, was discontinued.[24] Suspensions of such operations were dictated by defections from different national communist parties, and by western counterintelligence agencies' successful utilization of the information revealed by the defectors. Most importantly, Moscow discovered that agents had been planted inside local communist parties by host security services, and that the meetings of local party members were being kept under surveillance. The most important defections, generally, are from within the ranks of Russian intelligence or from within those of the satellite states. These are less significant because the satellite "defector" is less likely to be aware of a Russian agent's identity. Moscow insists that in these countries the intelligence services surrender to it both their operations, as well as the agents who are engaged in lucrative adventures.
3. Agents working for the intelligence services of a foreign state also can be unmasked by intercepting and decyphering the opponent's codes. That is exactly what led to the exposure of the Foreign Office's Donald Maclean.[25] Breaking the Russian code was the initial step toward rolling up the Cambridge University apparatus which already was in place by the time Norman arrived there. It was subsequently staffed by his contemporaries who, like him, had first been recruited into the Communist Party.

The difficulty with Golitsyn's alleged statement that Norman was a KGB agent, arises from the conventional perception that an agent is someone who just passes secret and privy information to the intelligence services of a foreign state. Certainly, this is one of his or her most important tasks. For example, whatever Burgess, Blunt, and Maclean did convey to Moscow appears to have been formidable;

in the case of Philby it led to important policy failures and probably to the deaths of a great many people.[26]

Yet based on the greater understanding we now have of the workings of Russian intelligence, this perception of how an agent may be used is quite simplistic. Although acquiring secret and privy information is important, equally important if not more so, is his or her value as an agent of influence and/or his or her role as a conduit for disinformation, especially if he or she climbs up the bureaucratic ladder. The three activities are not mutually exclusive and at any given time, agents may be engaged in one or two of them or in all three simultaneously. The worth of agents of influence and of disinformation is that they are more elusive than those who merely provide secret and privy information. Their activities can be low keyed, less intrusive, and thus harder to spot. Contacts with control officers are rare, but their actions are capable of affecting the policy decisions and choices their immediate political superiors will make. Consequently, they can go further to advance the cause of their true political masters than the secret or privy information they might convey. Two students on the subject tell us that an agent of influence "is a person who uses his or her position, influence, power, and credibility to promote the objectives of a foreign power in ways unattributable to that power." This can be achieved through controlled agents, that is to say, people who have been recruited and are directed by a foreign intelligence service through specific orders conveyed to them by their control officers.

There also are agents of influence "who consciously collaborate to advance the objectives of a foreign power, but who are not formally recruited and controlled." They can be held to be "unwitting but manipulated individuals;" Norman would clearly fall into that category. The other activity in which an agent of influence may engage is disinformation (*dezinformatsia*)—"a non-attributed or falsely attributed communication, written or oral, containing intentionally false, incomplete, or misleading information (frequently combined with true information), which seeks to deceive, misinform and/or mislead the target." The target may comprise either governmental and non-governmental élites or public opinion. The avowed purpose of such disinformation is "to lead the target to believe in the veracity of the message" and thus to act in a manner that would further the interests of the nation which the agent is serving. Agents of influence and disinformation fall under the category that Moscow euphemist-ically refers to as "active measures" (*aktivnyye meropriatia*).

Agents of influence, however, are merely one component in a synchronized effort labeled *kombinatsia*—a phrase that came into greater use by Moscow in the late 1950s. It "refers to the skill of relating, linking, and combining various agents of influence (at various times and in various places) with special operational undertakings, in such a way as to enhance effectiveness." One might add that it can be a complex linking, blending, and amplifying of *dezinformatsia* through the coordinated use of various channels. The information imparted can be false, partly false, or completely true, derived from a variety of methods and sources, overt or covert. Since even honest civil servants often interpret the same facts in different ways and can offer divergent advice to their political superiors, agents of influence "may be the most complex and difficult to document. . . . [and] even skilled counterintelligence officers find it very difficult to follow and unravel orchestrated agents-of-influence operations."[27]

In line with the above, Ferns' disclosure that Norman "liked to be 'on the inside' and close to the centres of power and authority" among Ottawa's ruling élite takes on new and greater significance. He writes that he is "not sure that [Norman] had any taste for power and authority in his own hands, but he did have an insatiable interest in people who had power: how they behaved, what motivated them, how skilful they were, and so on." He "can well imagine the tre-mendous satisfaction [Norman] must have derived from his close connection with General Douglas MacArthur and his relationship with the Japanese imperial family,"[28] a relationship which MacArthur had fostered.[29]

Norman's expertise on all things Japanese gave him a unique entrée to MacArthur's office which he used assiduously. His "influence was also enhanced by his personal friendships with leading [Japanese] intellectuals." Supposedly, his historical writing about Japan "clearly influenced" MacArthur's "early directives, especially those relating to land reform, the new constitution and the proposed dissolution of the zaibatsu business complexes." It, therefore, can be suggested that Norman's talks and interviews, official and unoffical, may have given him the opportunity to tender advice on other aspects of Japan's occupation and governance.

Certainly, his private talks with MacArthur offered such possi-bilities, just as his well-written dispatches to Ottawa about these

talks offered an opportunity to place the general in a less than favorable light, especially since he must have had an opportunity to
observe first hand, his particular foibles and inadequacies.[30] Thus,
any examination of Norman's role or involvement in Moscow's
"active measures" would require not only an analysis of the corpus
of his reports, but also of the advice he offered, especially about
Japan, during the period he was with External Affairs. Indeed, he
wanted to be "judged" on the development of Canada's Far Eastern
policy while serving as head of External's American and Far Eastern
Division.[31] The recommendations he tendered during those years
would have to be juxtaposed with Russian desires as they were then
perceived by the West, just as their impact, if any, on Canadian
policy decisions would have to be examined. Assuming he was involved in a disinformation maneuver, the veracity of the information
he was conveying would require very close scrutiny. The feasibility
of such a difficult and complicated task would be virtually nil as even
the most accomplished counterintelligence officers would be hard
pressed when it comes to unraveling orchestrated operations by agents
of influence. However, there is one well–documented Canadian case
where this type of analysis was attempted. Based on information
supplied by a number of KGB defectors, the RCMP concluded in 1964
that John Watkins, the former Canadian Ambassador in Moscow,
had been entrapped by the KGB in a homosexual operation and might
have been blackmailed. Watkins denied that he had harmed Canada's
interests. With his assistance every dispatch he had sent from Moscow
was analyzed to see if he had attempted to direct Canadian policy
along pro-Russian lines, just as his actions as Assistant Under-Secretary were carefully scrutinized. On the last day of the interrogation
Watkins died of a heart attack. His RCMP interrogators who were
not experts on Soviet Russia, concluded that he had not been an
"agent of influence." Whether they had the necessary training and
background to appreciate and analyze correctly his diplomatic reports
can be argued.[32]

   In Norman's case, tips of the iceberg seemed to appear here and
there. In his dispatch number 461 of October 15, 1948, for example,
he paid inordinate attention to the postwar career and political pros-
pects of the elderly Japanese General Ugaki Kazushige. Indeed, it
can be suggested that someone in Ottawa must have felt uneasy about
it, as the Canadian High Commission asked the Far Eastern Department of the British Foreign Office for its views on the dispatch.

To request the foreign ministry of another power to pass judgment on a report written by someone who supposedly is an expert in one's own foreign ministry is not standard practice in international relations, even among friendly and allied nations.

Norman's judgment about the general's political importance was questioned and considered "far-fetched" by one officer of the Foreign Office's Far Eastern Department. He called his analysis a " 'Hindenburg' analogy," comparing the aging Japanese general with the Weimar Republic's Field Marshal Hindenburg who Hitler had succeeded as president of the Reich. Norman's dispatch was, therefore, dismissed as lacking in substance, not only by the Far Eastern Department but also by the British Ambassador in Tokyo to whom Norman had given a copy.[33]

How could this experienced diplomat and vaunted Japanologist have gone so far astray in assessing General Ugaki Kazushige's possible role in and potential danger to Japan's nascent democracy? To properly evaluate this odd episode one would have to be an expert in Japan's postwar democratic development and in Soviet Russia's foreign policy desires in Japan and the Far East during that period.

If Norman was a KGB agent, as Golitsyn had alleged, the immediate question would be, who was his control officer? To convey secret and privy information to Moscow requires a conduit. A search for the person who might have controlled him leads us to those who might be called his gallery of friends and acquaintances. Among them was Chi Ch'ao-ting with whom he was "intimate" and who had introduced him to Philip J. Jaffe.[34]

Trained at Peking's Tsinghua College, the University of Chicago, and Columbia University, Chi Ch'ao-ting was recruited into the American Communist Party in 1926. A fine public speaker, he was considered in party circles as a talented theoretician and able supporter of the Chinese communist cause. From 1926 until 1941 he was a member of the American Communist Party's China Bureau. In early 1927 he attended the first congress of the Anti-Imperialist League in Brussels and in January 1929 the second congress in Frankfurt-am-Main; the League, of course, was a communist-front organization. From mid-1927 until mid-1929 he resided in Moscow where he acted as interpreter for those who had fled to Soviet Russia, following the schism between General Chiang Kai-shek's Kuomintang and the Chinese Communist Party. He was a member of the Chinese delegation to the Comintern's Sixth Congress (1928), and also worked with the Chinese delegation associated with the Red Trade Union International.

He returned to the United States in 1929 and until 1941 when he departed for China, he frequently wrote articles on China under the pseudonyms Hansu Chan, R. Doonping, Huang Lowe, and Futien Wang. He also worked for the *Daily Worker*, was involved with *Amerasia*, and associated with the American Friends of the Chinese People.[35] Naturally, some of his activities were conducted covertly. In 1941, as has already been pointed out,[36] he was recruited into Chiang Kai-shek's Ministry of Finance, while he continued his secret commitment to the Chinese Communist Party. He served as an agent for Chou En-lai, and with the communist victory in 1949, joined the Chinese government, in which he held high positions, especially in the economic field. When he died of natural causes in 1963, his funeral was attended by Chou En-lai and other luminaries, including V. Frank Coe who also was "close" to Norman.[37]

It was during the eulogy that Chi Ch'ao-ting's "underground work" and his long and secret association with the Chinese Communist Party were officially acknowledged.[38] By training, longtime ideological commitment, experience, and conduct, he easily fills the bill as Norman's initial control officer until July 1939 when he entered External Affairs. Possibly, Chi Ch'ao-ting might have been merely a "cut-out" between Norman and his real control officer, who may have been someone who belonged to the Russian intelligence services, or was a high–ranking member of the Canadian or American Communist parties. In turn, that person may have been the contact for a Russian intelligence officer. Norman may not necessarily have known about this arrangement as, in most cases, the agent is kept in the dark about the fact that his seeming control officer is really a cut-out. Based on the experience of Michael Straight, Norman's Cambridge University contemporary and communist cell associate, it would not be unfair to suggest that after leaving England he was assigned to Chi Ch'ao-ting in the same way as Straight was assigned to "Michael Green," his Russian controller who has never been publicly identified.[39] The fact that Chi Ch'ao-ting was Chinese rather than Russian is of no importance. During the 1930s, many control officers were non-Russian as, for example, "Otto" who was probably a Czech. Theodore Maly who ran Philby for a time prior to the Second World War, was a Hungarian.[40]

After his temporary leave of absence from External Affairs to finish his doctoral dissertation at Harvard University (October 7 to December 17, 1939), Norman was ensconced in Ottawa. During that time, he would have had to come under the direction of a new control officer. With Chi Ch'ao-ting in New York, and keeping in mind the vagaries of transportation and hotel accommodations during the war, it would have been difficult for them to meet. Moreover, as an oriental, Chi Ch'ao-ting's comings and goings in the staid society of the Ottawa of the day with its small oriental community, might have attracted some attention. Since a Russian legation was not established there until 1942, and visits by Russian diplomatic personnel from the embassy in Washington would have been too conspicuous, it would be fair to assume that, at this point, Norman was passed on to someone within Canada. That person would have been in a position to contact him unobtrusively, either directly or indirectly, to convey to Moscow whatever secret and privy information he may have had to offer.

It is possible, of course, that this was achieved through an "illegal," that is to say someone without diplomatic immunity, a person who had entered Canada with false documents appearing to be, to all intents and purposes, a respected member of the community. Or, contact might have been achieved through someone involved in clandestine operations but who was attached to a trade mission or some other legitimate Russian agency whose presence in Canada was sanctioned by the Canadian authorities. There is the further possibility of an amalgam: Norman's association with an illegal who had some support from a legitimate Canadian resident attached to an authorized Russian enterprise. These are possible scenarios but the risk involved for so low level an official as Norman was in 1939-40, does not make them too probable. It should be pointed out that, starting in 1938 at the latest until the autumn of 1942 when the Russian Legation was established in Ottawa, Dmitri Stepanovich Chuvakhin resided in Canada and was involved in clandestine operations. He was Soviet Ambassador to Canada from 1953 to 1958 and Ambassador to Israel between 1964 and 1967.[41] Whether or not Norman knew him is unknown.

The above analysis is not unreasonable, since it was not until late in the war, as the 1946 Royal Commission claimed, that Moscow began to think of planting "illegals" in Canada. It had already planted them in the United States as "Canadians" equipped with false documentation which included a Canadian passport acquired in Spain from a Canadian who had fought on the Loyalist side in the Spanish Civil War.[42]

If all the above scenarios were to be discarded, the only one that would remain is that Norman was passed on to the espionage apparatus which, as the Royal Commission pointed out, had been established in Canada as early as 1924. That apparatus which was directed from Moscow, operated with the assistance of communist sympathizers.[43] Norman may have been passed on to someone associated with that particular group, such as the employee of the National Council for Canadian-Soviet Friendship who the RCMP suspected of being a member of the communist apparatus. As Norman himself admitted to Inspector Guernsey during his interrogation of January 1952, they had met, at the earliest, during the war years.[44]

Assuming such an arrangement actually existed, the question that might be raised is how any secret and privy information imparted by Norman to his control officer may have been conveyed to Moscow. One answer is, by whatever direct or indirect links the Canadian Communist Party had with Moscow. It is also possible that it might have been channeled through senior officials of the Canadian Communist Party to senior officials of the American Communist Party and, in turn, or perhaps directly, either to Russian "illegals" operating in the United States or to the Russian Embassy in Washington; that there was close contact over the border during the war years is well documented.[45]

Once transferred to Tokyo in the spring of 1940, another control officer may have been assigned to Norman. At first glance, it is unlikely that this was someone from the suppressed Japanese Communist Party or an "illegal," in view of the brutal efficiency of the Japanese political police. Yet, in the middle of the war, J. Edgar Hoover wrote to Assistant Secretary of State Adolf A. Berle that, based on information imparted by a "generally reliable confidential source," Soviet Russia possessed the "best available inside information on Japan, which it has received through the Japanese Communist Party." According to Hoover's source, the party was an "efficient underground organization which has capable representatives in all the principal cities and towns of Japan," as well as in the armed forces.[46] In light of this, there is a possibility that Norman conveyed information through Japanese Communist Party contacts. However, those Japanese with whom he may have dealt, even on rare occasions, would have had to be under police scrutiny. The fact that he spoke fluent Japanese and represented a nation that the Japanese authorities regarded as a probable hostile power should war erupt in the Pacific, makes it more likely that his new control officer was operating out of the Russian Embassy. Any perusal of the list of its personnel in Tokyo, circa 1940, would prove of little value, since the identities of such control officers are frequently changed. This practice leads to a veritable maze of subterfuge in which, for instance, a Vasili Usmanski in Tokyo would resurface as a Dmitri Shatov in Cairo. Consequently, any contacts in Tokyo between Norman and whoever was assigned to him, would have been difficult and potentially dangerous, in view of the surveillance to which Russian Embassy personnel and that from other diplomatic missions were subjected by the Japanese political police. However, running a fellow diplomat, such as Norman, is considerably less difficult than running other types of agents; encounters at diplomatic receptions and quasi-official functions often lead to contacts, if only of a fleeting nature.

The outbreak of the Pacific war (in which Russia was neutral almost until the end) and Norman's internment by the Japanese, must have led to a break with his control officer. It, therefore, would be safe to say that when he was repatriated to Canada in the summer of 1942 he may not have been under "control," at first. Once back in Ottawa, he might have looked upon his Tokyo experience as having been unique, and a grander version than anything he had accomplished for the cause at Cambridge University. If so, that attitude may have soon undergone a quick revision, probably because of his work in the special intelligence section he was directing in External Affairs. Since that unit had access to decyphered enemy codes, especially those of the Japanese, he must have become aware of the activities of Richard Sorge, Stalin's master spy in Japan. He was a German who had been a member of the communist apparatus for a very long time. Sent to Tokyo in 1933 by Russian military intelligence, he had disguised his covert activities by working there as a journalist, insinuating himself into the German Embassy. Through his position there and because of his well-placed sources in Japan's ruling circle, he was able to convey a formidable range of information to the Russians. It included the Japanese army order of battle, the location, number, and enumeration of divisions, as well as the names of divisional commanders and important officers. In addition, he had warned Russian military intelligence of the impending German attack on Moscow, assuring them that Japan would strike against the United States rather than against Soviet Russia. All this made it possible for the Russians to shift their Far Eastern forces westward to check the German advance.[47] If Wellington was right when he said that the Battle of Waterloo was won on the playing fields of Eton, it is equally true that the Battle of Moscow was won by Richard Sorge from Tokyo. He was unmasked by the Japanese in October 1941 and later executed. By issuing a postage stamp to honor his memory, Moscow publicly acknowledged his self-sacrifice and the important service he had rendered.[48]

Although Norman and Sorge were living in Tokyo at the same time, there is no evidence that they ever met. Yet, his fascination with him and his ceaseless talk and speculation about how he must have conducted his spy activities, seem to go beyond the reaction of someone who merely admired the communist German's "bravery and resourcefulness." Nor is it just his regard for someone "who had outwitted the enemy," honoring him for having "died in doing so." According to Ferns, Norman's admiration stemmed from his "great respect for the competence of the Japanese police and therefore [he] knew what Sorge was up against." Ferns, therefore, invokes that interest in Sorge as an excellent example of why Norman was not an agent of Russian intelligence. If he had been, he would not have talked so much about him and his methods.[49] Had he been involved in the same deadly game at virtually the same time as Sorge, he and his Russian control officer, unlike Sorge, would have enjoyed diplomatic immunity, without experiencing the vengeance of the Japanese police. There but for the grace of God went Norman, though in his case there would have been a price to pay under the strictures of Canada's Official Secrets Act.

As a conventional agent, Norman's value to Russian intelligence, at least initially, would have been limited. He was only the language officer of the Canadian Legation and, keeping in mind Canada's limited role in world affairs when he was serving in Tokyo, any secret and privy information he might have conveyed must have been "low grade." However, things improved, at least as far as Moscow was concerned, once he was promoted to third secretary. This gave him access to far more valuable information, especially whatever he would have been able to ascertain from his British, American, and other colleagues. At all times, of course, his knowledge of Japanese and the wide contacts he had in Japanese society, led him to information that might have proved valuable to Moscow. Whatever its accrued value may have been, it immediately ceased once the Pacific war erupted. Yet, his appointment as director of the special intelligence unit within External Affairs as well as his role as liaison officer on Far Eastern research with Colonel Donovan's Office of Strategic Services and British intelligence, must have enormously raised his value to Moscow. The problem that now presented itself was how to re-establish in Ottawa the contact that must have been severed in Tokyo.

At this point, Igor Gouzenko furnishes us with another marker. According to statements he made to the RCMP soon after his defection, his superior Colonel Zabotin had received, probably in the autumn of 1944, the cryptic message from Moscow asking him if he knew someone named Norman. As we have seen, Zabotin replied in the negative, and together with the Assistant Military Attaché Motinov, identified the Norman referred to as Norman Freed, the senior Communist Party official in Toronto. When Motinov spoke with the KGB resident Pavlov about Norman Freed he was admonished with the remark: " 'He is ours, don't touch him.' "[50] As the 1946 Royal Commission report pointed out, the Russian attitude toward " 'developed' " Communist Party members such as Norman Freed, was summed up with the Russian possessive pronoun *nash* which, literally translated, means "he is ours," or "ours."[51]

Zabotin then sent Moscow Center (GRU) a second message explaining that he thought the "Norman" about whom they had inquired was Norman Freed, who was "busy" with Pavlov. According to Gouzenko, Moscow did not respond to Zabotin's message, although it is conceivable that, unknown to Gouzenko, a reply did arrive earmarked only for Zabotin's attention. From this exchange it becomes obvious that a code name was not involved. Based on a choice whether the name Norman was a first or a surname, and in view of the fact that Moscow had ignored Zabotin's second message, the RCMP's moderate assumption was, as it informed the FBI, that Norman was the surname of a person in whom Russian intelligence was interested. There was no proof for this, but even External Affairs in analyzing this episode opined that the Norman referred to was "very probably none other than E. H. Norman." It speculated that it was an attempt by Russian intelligence services to cultivate him for possible recruitment, and that he had probably been talent spotted by Pavlov. If Pavlov had contacted Moscow about Norman he certainly would have supplied his first names as well as his occupation. The message to Zabotin, therefore, would not have been as obfuscated as it was.[52] Moreover, why would the KGB in Moscow have conveyed his name to the GRU? If Norman was a potential and valuable recruit, the KGB would have monopolized him, and it is unlikely that it would have shared information about him with the GRU. In fact, during that period, KGB-GRU relations were not at their best. By the late 1930s the KGB had achieved control over the GRU, and many GRU officers were consumed by the vortex of the Great Purge.

It is, of course, possible that Norman's name was passed on to the KGB by someone within the Canadian Communist Party. But here again it is not too likely that the KGB would have passed to the GRU any potential recruit as valuable as Norman. If it did, it certainly would have furnished his first and last names, including his occupation. Another possibility is that he was recommended to the GRU by someone in the American or British Communist parties. Here again, his names or occupation would probably have been known. Perhaps a clerical error had occurred at GRU Center in Moscow that was later rectified. It might explain why no one had replied to Zabotin's second message.

If, however, Norman's name was in the GRU records and the exchange of telegrams between Moscow and Zabotin was an attempt to re–establish the contact that had been broken in Tokyo, it reflects a prior association between Norman and the GRU. Based on published evidence, it would appear that breaks in contact between agents controlled by the Russian intelligence services and Moscow have occurred on other occasions.[53]

It is also possible that the cryptic query to Zabotin was sent to ascertain whether or not Norman had maintained his cover. Zabotin had arrived in Ottawa after Norman's repatriation from Japan. If Norman's past activities and affiliations were known to him then any GRU dealings with him would present a distinct risk. Zabotin's negative response to Moscow's query would have removed anxieties and might help explain why Moscow apparently never responded to his subsequent message about Norman Freed.

Another scenario may be that if Norman's name had been given to the GRU, the lack of first names and occupation might have been rectified by approaching the KGB in Moscow. Any knowledge of Norman by the KGB would have raised the same considerations already discussed and also might explain why GRU Moscow never replied to Zabotin. However, in view of the tension between KGB and GRU, this scenario is not very likely.

Could it be that Zabotin was completely unaware that information might have been furnished by Norman to the Technical Bureau of the GRU in Moscow through a GRU espionage operation in Ottawa? Fearing a deception operation and to ease its anxieties, the GRU in Moscow may have asked Zabotin if he knew Norman, to see if another GRU source, in this case its resident in Ottawa, could confirm his bona fides. This would explain why only the bare surname was furnished to Zabotin; the less he knew the better. The fact that neither he nor Pavlov were aware of Norman, may dovetail with this scenario and with the notion that, early on, Norman may have been associated with the Moscow-directed espionage apparatus established in Canada in 1924. Upon his return from Tokyo, he was probably recoupled with it and, in turn, placed in the service of the GRU's Technical Bureau in Moscow.

The question that develops is of what interest Norman would have been to the Technical Bureau of Russian military intelligence. The answer is quite simple. Since the special intelligence section that Norman directed in External Affairs had access to deciphered Japanese and other enemy codes,[54] he could have supplied information about which codes had been broken, and how quickly this might have been done. This would have been of enormous importance to the Russian military, not only to be able to read these codes, especially the military ones, but also to obtain an insight into the technology of their allies' cryptography.

The 1944 incident involving Zabotin, Pavlov, and Moscow was not the only time Norman crossed the path of the GRU. The eventual contact was with Major Vsevolod Sokolov who ostensibly was attached to the commercial section of the Russian Legation in Ottawa but was, in fact, one of Colonel Zabotin's assistants. In the early summer of that year he recruited into the GRU's espionage operations the External Affairs code clerk Emma Woikin, a young, lonely, and naive Doukhobor girl from Saskatchewan. She had had a hard life, did, however, love to cook for friends and had a flair for it. Subsequently exposed by Gouzenko's disclosures, she pleaded guilty and was sentenced to two years and six months at the federal penitentiary for women in Kingston, Ontario. After her release she became a legal secretary in a respected Saskatoon law firm.

Before her death she spoke to David Beaubier, one of the firm's attorneys. With tears in her eyes she described a Doukhobor meal she prepared after her recruitment. The guests were Herbert Norman, Lester Pearson, and others.[55] Since she did not have suitable accommodation to host a gathering of this nature, the dinner would have had to be at someone else's home. Although Woikin's circle of friends in Ottawa was limited, she did see much of the Sokolovs who, it seems, had taken advantage of her loneliness by cleverly orchestrating various moves to suborn her.[56] Thus, the cooking of any meal for so illustrious a group might have had to be done with the Sokolovs as hosts.

As was brought out by Gouzenko in testimony before the Royal Commission, though Moscow believed in inviting potential agents to restaurants, Colonel Zabotin appears to have preferred entertaining them at home. Indeed, it was at a dinner in a private home when Emma Woikin first met Major Sokolov.[57]

In view of the tight and centralized control that is part and parcel of Russian intelligence operations, it is inconceivable that the dinner had been planned at the spur of the moment. Undoubtedly, it had been carefully discussed, examined, and cleared with Moscow before being allowed to go ahead. One or more of those present had probably been instructed to make it as relaxed and as comfortable as possible for the targeted candidate. One GRU defector who paid with his life for the information he had conveyed to the West, wrote that meals of this nature at one's home were permissible "provided that the foreigner is of some interest, from the intelligence viewpoint, or is already being developed and prepared for recruitment."[58] The question can be asked, was it Norman or Pearson who was being scrutinized?

Since Woikin was recruited in early summer 1944, and Norman left Ottawa for the Far East in August 1945 (Gouzenko defected in September of that year), any dinner party would have had to take place within that time span. Pearson was in Washington as Minister-Counsellor of the Legation from June 1942 to June 1944, and as Minister from July 1944 until August 1945. However, because of Canada's important role during the war, he made "frequent visits to Ottawa for discussions" with Prime Minister Mackenzie King, as he tells us in his memoirs.[59] Therefore, the dinner, supposedly cooked by Woikin with Norman, Pearson and others as guests is well within the realm of possibility. Was Woikin fantasizing perhaps? Not according to Attorney David Beaubier.[60] Of all the personnel in

External Affairs how could she have picked the combination of Norman and Pearson? Norman Robertson and Pearson, perhaps; Hume Wrong and Pearson, possibly. Her biographer tells us her story "strains credulity."[61] In the past, it would have, but in view of the cumulative evidence presented in these pages, it might not. The purported meal which Woikin had cooked and probably also had attended as a guest, was certainly a gross breach of the compartmentalization demanded in all intelligence operations, including those of the West. The conventional wisdom is that Russian intelligence officers are ten feet tall. As in this case, however, not all of Moscow's intelligence operations are examples of perfection as to how they should be conducted.

As Norman was promoted to ever higher positions within External Affairs his value to Russian intelligence would have increased. Certainly, his appointment to General Elliot Thorpe's counterintelligence unit in Tokyo offered a cornucopia of possibilities. Although his assigned task was that of Chief of Research and Analysis, involving interrogating and classifying large numbers of Japanese, he strayed into areas far beyond his allotted responsibility. These wanderings, as we have seen, had initially raised General Willoughby's suspicions. What interest did Norman have in acquiring the files of the Hungarian diplomatic mission in Tokyo except to act as a conduit for the Russians? His actions at Fuchu prison together with the American diplomat Emmerson have already been discussed, as well as his apparent role in arranging the return from communist-controlled China's Yenan of Japanese Communist Party leader Sanzo Nosaka.

It is during this period in Tokyo that he again meets Chi Ch'ao-ting and others, reorganizes the Japanese branch of the Institute of Pacific Relations, and attends unreported Marxist study group meetings. In the past, one would have argued that these were innocent gatherings and activities, but they take on new meaning in light of other information we now have about Norman, how Russian intelligence works, and the alleged comments by Blunt and Golitsyn.

In this context we also must closely scrutinize Pearson's trip to Tokyo in February 1950. During that visit General MacArthur explained to him and to Norman that Washington's policy in Asia and its defense perimeter in the region did not include Korea, as it was not vital to America's security.[62] MacArthur's comments were in line with Dean Acheson's speech a month earlier when he told the National Press Club that America's defense perimeter in Asia ran from the Aleutian Islands to Japan and from there to the Ryukyu and

Philippine Islands.[63] Korea had been excluded which was in line with the desires of the Joint Chiefs of Staff who held that the "strategic value of [South] Korea was negligible and that any commitment of U.S. military force in [South] Korea would be ill-advised and impracticable."[64] Acheson's public comments could not have gone unnoticed in Moscow. Keeping in mind MacArthur's military role in Asia, his February remarks to Norman and to Pearson, the foreign secretary of a friendly and allied country, would have stimulated Moscow to favor a possibly low-risk North Korean invasion of South Korea. In other words, in addition to other information available to Moscow, MacArthur's comments, if conveyed to the Soviets by Norman—which might have been done—could have led to the assumption that such a scenario would evoke no American response.

The Pearson visit is also important because not only was Korea discussed but also the question of Norman's new posting.[65] What is one to make of his desire to avoid an ambassadorial position in Moscow? Obviously, having him in London or Ottawa as an agent of influence and/or disinformation would have been far better for Russian intelligence than having him sit in Moscow as an agent of information.

The last question regarding Golitsyn's alleged statement that Norman was "a long-term communist and KGB agent," is to examine the source that furnished that statement. Nigel West is younger than Chapman Pincher but, like him, a journalist interested in the world of intelligence. He is the author of a number of well-received books on the activities of the British intelligence services.[66] He also co-edits a thoughtful newsletter appropriately titled *The Intelligence Quarterly*, which is "devoted to the review of books and events in the intelligence field," its masthead informs us. Like Pincher, West is reputed to have excellent contacts with former and perhaps present members of British and other western intelligence services. Despite these apparently gilt-edged credentials, skeptics and those partial to Norman can rightly raise a hue and cry that Golitsyn's alleged comment reported by West is like Blunt's, reported by Pincher—nothing more than hearsay. There is one small difference, however, and that is that unlike Blunt, Golitsyn is alive and well, living under the protection of the CIA. More importantly, he can be contacted and was.

When I approached him through his publisher—the old and reputable company of Dodd, Mead—I was assured that any letter sent to him would be immediately forwarded and that he would respond quickly. Any reply, I was warned, that might necessitate security clearance would naturally take somewhat longer.[67] In the letter I sent in mid-September 1984, I asked him to "enlarge and expand" on the alleged statement he had made about Norman and that was cited in Nigel West's book. I enclosed a photocopy of the page from Pincher's book showing the alleged statement Blunt had made about Norman.[68]

Contrary to his publisher's assurance which, no doubt, had been sincerely given, there was a long silence. Obviously, Golitsyn's reply on this matter fell under the heading of "security clearance." Finally, almost two and a half months after I had posted my letter, I received a reply. He explained that he was writing a book on KGB operations against the West and, therefore, was not in a position to heed my request.[69]

Golitsyn's letter was interesting, both for its brevity and its attempt to avoid a direct response. It would be safe to say, that it had been vetted by the CIA before being signed by him. But if West's statement was untrue and had been concocted either by him or his "source," then a simple denial by Golitsyn would have been easy enough. This was not done. The suspicion, therefore, develops that the alleged statement cited by West might be true, and that Golitsyn was man enough not to deny it. The CIA, on the other hand, might have been incapable of drafting a letter deflecting the request, and one that Golitsyn would have signed. We should all look forward to his promised book, assuming that CIA interference on grounds of "security" is not attempted with regard to the Norman question.

The scenario least damaging to Norman might be that the Russian intelligence services had considered or actually had attempted to recruit him, but he had fended them off. This also would explain why he would have been unwilling to serve in Moscow. It might have exposed him to constant recruitment attempts, a kind of harassment he would have wanted to avoid. If he was approached, he certainly never reported it which, in itself, would have been a serious security breach.

Perhaps, at this point, it might be appropriate to examine with which of the Russian intelligence services Norman may have been involved. The three most plausible possibilities are:

1. He was, from the beginning, a GRU agent.
2. He was a KGB agent.

3. Though initially a GRU agent, he was switched in 1944 to the KGB or, if initially a KGB agent, from the KGB to the GRU.

In 1933 no talent spotter at Cambridge could have failed to notice Norman's desirable qualities and talents: commitment to the new secular faith, intelligence, sensitivity, knowledge of Japanese, and an appreciation of Asian culture and history, especially Japan's.[70] There were many during that period at Cambridge and elsewhere who were just as committed, equally intelligent, as well as sensitive. But rare indeed was an occidental who knew Japanese and Japan, and who was so familiar with the culture and history of the area. Any induction into the Russian intelligence services of someone with these qualities would, therefore, have been into a branch that was particularly interested in Japan and the Far East. During Norman's Cambridge days that service was the GRU, the intelligence branch of the Russian military. We now know, and MI5 had long suspected it,[71] that during the mid-1930s the GRU, like its "principal competitor"[72] the KGB, was actively recruiting on the Cambridge University campus. Moreover, during that period it was the GRU, rather than the KGB which was involved in Far East espionage. GRU agents in China, Manchuria, and Southeast Asia have been identified since the early 1920s, and major networks have been documented in Shanghai (Lehman Net, 1929–1930; Froelich Net, circa 1930–1931; Sorge Net, 1930–1932, and "Paul"– Funakoshi Net, 1932–1942); Harbin ("Ott-Glemberg" Net, 1929?–1932); and Tokyo (Sorge Net, 1933–1941). From the data now available other GRU operations appear in only the sketchiest form, yet they undoubtedly existed in China, Japan, and Outer Mongolia. Indeed, special efforts, not always successful, were made to penetrate Japan.[73] For the GRU, discovering and recruiting someone like Norman would have been manna from heaven.

Norman's possible connection with the GRU would also explain his sudden reversal of academic interests. Whereas at Victoria College he had studied the classics, and at Trinity College, Cambridge, medieval history which requires a good grounding in Latin and Greek, suddenly, in 1935 he expressed a wish to switch to Japanese, Chinese, Japanese history and a study of the Far East. These were fields in which he did not appear to have shown any previous interest. However, thanks to the Rockefeller fellowship he was able to pursue these studies at Harvard and Columbia universities.

To this might be added Norman's "intimate" association with Chi

Ch'ao-ting. One would have to look hard indeed to find someone better fitted to play the role of his GRU control officer. A longtime member of the American Communist Party's China Bureau, Chi Ch'ao-ting also played his own clandestine role during the war in the Chinese National Government's Ministry of Finance. In addition, there was V. Frank Coe with whom Norman was "close." He escaped from American jurisdiction by establishing residence in Communist China. Then there was Jaffe who had been introduced to Norman by Chi Ch'ao-ting. Although he never was a member of the Communist Party, he was as close to it as one can get without actually belonging. He, too, was interested in China, Japan, and the Far East. Lastly, there was Norman's election to the provisional committee to establish the Canadian Friends of the Chinese People.

The "fingerprints" on his file appear to have been more GRU- than KGB-oriented while he was in External Affairs. If he was GRU why was he never exposed either by Gouzenko or by the documents he had removed from Colonel Zabotin's files at the Russian Legation? The answer is that although Zabotin and his assistants were involved in espionage, the GRU ran a network unknown to him. Called "The Parallel Military System" by the 1946 Royal Commission, it was directed by the Chief of the GRU's Technical Bureau in Moscow. Based on Gouzenko's testimony, Zabotin learned of it only accidentally, as the Royal Commission has pointed out.[74]

But what technical information did Norman have that would have been of value to the Chief of the GRU's Technical Bureau in Moscow? The answer, discussed previously, points to his knowledge of Japanese and other enemy codes. This would have given the GRU an important insight into the cryptography of its allies. His liaison on Far Eastern research with Donovan's Office of Strategic Services and British intelligence would have been of additional importance, not to mention whatever other information he might have been able to offer.

The next question is how he might have conveyed this information to "the parallel network." The answer again is easy enough: through "dead drops" in and around Ottawa—hiding places "where an agent can leave a packet to be later recovered by another agent without the need of direct human contact."[75] The material gathered might then have been forwarded to Moscow by diplomatic pouch by whoever handled this kind of work in the Russian Legation for the Chief of the GRU's Technical Bureau in Moscow. Based on security considerations, such intelligence activity would have been tightly "compartmentalized," without the knowledge of the GRU's Zabotin, the KGB's Pavlov, or the embassy's diplomatic staff.

The notion, therefore, that Norman initially may have been involved with the KGB can safely be put aside, and with it the suggestion that, at some point, he was switched from KGB to GRU control. Even if he had been KGB, it is "rare," although not unknown to shift an agent from one control to the other, and there are, in fact, wartime Canadian and other cases on record where this did occur.[76]

The other possibility, of course, exists that Norman was not recruited into the Russian intelligence services until 1944, following the now famous "do you know Norman?" message. However, it is more likely that he was shifted from GRU to KGB control in 1944, after Zabotin received the cryptic message from Moscow. The exchange between him and Pavlov as to who this Norman was could not have gone unreported by Pavlov to KGB Moscow, in view of the tight centralized control, already noted, that is part and parcel of the Russian intelligence services.

This scenario would dovetail with Golitsyn's alleged statement that Norman was a "KGB agent." Even if he had not been co-opted by the KGB in 1944 but would have continued to be run by the GRU, Golitsyn's comment would still make sense as by the mid-1950s the KGB enjoyed "a one-way window on the activities of the GRU."[77] Norman's reports and/or activities, therefore, could have filtered back from the one to the other. They could have been seen by Golitsyn and misconstrued by him as having come from a KGB agent. It can, therefore, be said with reasonable certainty that, regardless of who ran Norman, he was enmeshed in Russian intelligence work.

Chapter 9

Suicide

The suggestion that Norman's tragic death on April 4, 1957 was due to the actions of the Senate Subcommittee on Internal Security now raises some doubts that this was what drove him to take his own life. A close examination of events before and after he committed suicide shows that the reasons for it are far more complex than would appear at first glance.

The Senate Subcommittee's release on March 14, 1957 of Emmerson's testimony of March 12 included the excerpts from the Summary of Information prepared for General Willoughby in mid-April 1951. This Summary of Information was an amalgam of FBI and RCMP information.[1] The release of the testimony led to a defense of Norman by Pearson which was as forceful as it had been six years earlier. Indeed, in March-April 1957, Pearson was fully supported, at least initially, by the parliamentary opposition leader and future prime minister John Diefenbaker. The opinions of an aroused Canadian public and a press sympathetic to Norman were echoed across the border, although some of the American reaction may have been politically motivated. Ottawa quickly lodged an official protest. Washington was seemingly embarrassed, and though Norman, at first, was "upset," as his deputy Arthur Kilgour subsequently told Ottawa, he was also "somewhat detached."

Morally and politically, Norman's position appeared to be virtually unassailable as the confident tone of his March 19 messages of thanks to both Pearson and Diefenbaker seemed to indicate. Pearson then wrote a personal letter of support in return, which appears to show that he had not only won the government's endorsement but also that of his colleagues and friends. In fact, Pearson's initial comments in the House of Commons had led the embassy staff in Cairo, as well as others, to consider the Norman matter closed. What more could anyone have asked for?

Norman's work habits appeared normal. He never mentioned the Senate Subcommittee to Kilgour, and later inquiries by the embassy staff led to the reasonable conviction that there had been "no sudden and drastic change" in his behavior. Then about March 21, a week after Emmerson's testimony was released, he showed "signs that he was preoccupied." His secretary "found him somewhat tense," he appeared to lose interest in important matters, yet still adhered to the usual daily schedule. The first recorded occasion when his conduct attracted attention was a reception on March 22, for the Director General of the Food and Agriculture Organization. Norman "appeared to several people to be quite upset."

It was not until several days later, on March 25, when he broached the subject of the subcommittee's activities to Kilgour who, much later informed External Affairs that he thought that day had "marked perhaps a turning point" in Norman's demeanor. Complaining that the people in Washington were still after him, he produced a newspaper clipping dealing with a statement by the subcommittee's counsel Judge Morris. Referring to Pearson's protest to Washington, the judge had declared that he would press ahead and present, through reputable witnesses and reliable evidence and documentation, those underlying facts that impinged on the United States' security. Kilgour tried to assure Norman the statement was in character with the judge's attitude, and that he saw no reason to believe that his name would resurface. Norman then noted that when Emmerson had previously been investigated in Washington, he had written an affidavit attesting to Emmerson's character. This was not so, as the particular affidavit dealt only with the events that took place at Fuchu prison in October 1945.[2] He reasoned that when the subcommittee had reopened the case, it must have been angered by the affidavit it had found in Emmerson's file. He also maintained that although his acquaintanceship with various individuals—Owen Lattimore especially—had been raised during his own "investigation" in Ottawa, it had not come up in the subcommittee's previous hearings. There is no documentary evidence to support the fact that Norman was ever questioned about Owen Lattimore in Ottawa. While it is true that the subcommittee was not aware of most of his acquaintances, it did know about his relationship with Lattimore during the postwar period when they were both in Tokyo.[3] Norman then observed that the thought that the subcommittee "might be able to reveal apparently *new information disturbed him very much.*"[4] He added that he found it discouraging to work so hard and then to have something like this develop.

For the next several days he continued to work in his office. Then on March 28, during an informal luncheon at the Young Women's Christian Association, "a decisive change" was noted. Though all the Canadians were seated at a single small table, it did not go unnoticed that Norman "scarcely took part in the conversation and in fact did not appear to be mentally with us," Kilgour subsequently wrote. He also had begun closing his office door which had not been his usual practice, and was sometimes seen scribbling on foolscap sheets of paper or resting on his office couch; in fact, some of the embassy staff thought he looked ill.

On the morning of March 29 he arrived at his office and then asked one of the embassy's Egyptian employees to open the door that led to the roof of the chancery building. Though the ambassador told the employee that he was not needed, he, nevertheless, decided to accompany him. Norman walked around the roof, looking over the sides, and particularly at the highest point which was directly over the garage.

On the same day it was announced in the Egyptian press that Tsuru had been interviewed by the subcommittee. The embassy staff agreed that the news should not be brought to Norman's attention, although he subsequently asked Kilgour if anything further had developed. He answered in the negative to save his chief additional anguish. Although Kilgour never found out whether Norman had ever learned that the subcommittee had again commenced inquiries about him, it would be safe to assume that in a cosmopolitan city such as Cairo, especially in the circle in which Norman moved, it was only a matter of time before the subcommittee's activities would have become known to him. Mrs. Norman later admitted to Kilgour that Herbert had told her that the subcommittee "probably would eventually interview" Tsuru, since he was temporarily teaching at Harvard University. The fact that he was aware of Tsuru's presence at Harvard prompted an RCMP officer to scribble in the margin of Kilgour's report that Norman "must have still been in touch with him."

For the next three days Kilgour saw virtually nothing of his chief. It appears that he had driven out of Cairo to get away from it all. On at least one occasion he was accompanied by a friend who said Norman had slept in the car a great deal of the time and that he had declared he could sleep for an entire year.

On April 1 and 2 Norman was up and about holding talks with senior Egyptian officials. He still appeared "preoccupied though no more than previously."[5] By this point, Tsuru's public testimony to the subcommittee had been released. Norman admitted to the Canadian journalist King Gordon that he had never been as depressed as he had been during the last weeks. He was convinced that the old communist charge would be revived, and that Judge Morris' boast that nothing would obstruct the subcommittee's investigatory work was a sure sign that a new inquiry was about to be initiated. He dwelt on what he euphemistically called his 1950 investigation, admitting that it had not been inquisitorial, only terribly thorough. Convinced that the RCMP had passed on his file to the FBI, he now feared that the FBI, in cahoots with the subcommittee, might extract information out of context and distort whatever was in his file. These comments to Gordon were, of course, deceptive in the extreme, for Norman well knew from his January 1952 interrogation by Messrs. Guernsey, McClellan, and Glazebrook that the most damaging information about him had been supplied to the RCMP by MI5, and not by the FBI. Denigrating the English cousin, however, was less productive than denigrating the American neighbor.

According to Gordon, Norman had no fear that new information might emerge in any renewed investigation. He was very satisfied with the "thoroughness" of the previous one, although he claimed that it had been an ordeal both physically and psychically. He thought that others might become unjustly enmeshed because of the distortions. He also observed that these congressional investigations had no limits when they were intent on destroying someone's name. As an example, he cited the Senate Subcommittee's use of a letter written in September 1940 by William Holland of the Institute of Pacific Relations, stating that any "secret message" to Institute member Philip Lilienthal in Tokyo might be sent in care of Herbert Norman at the Canadian Legation. What Holland seemingly had wanted to say was that any communications not meant for the attention of the Japanese branch of the Institute of Pacific Relations—Lilienthal's mailing address in Tokyo—were to be sent to Norman, in view of growing Japanese criticism of the Institute's excessively pro-Chinese attitude. Norman claimed that he had not known about Holland's letter until it was mentioned in the subcommittee's hearings, and that he naturally would never have agreed to his proposal.

He also thought that External Affairs might be embarrassed if he were once more involved in the subcommittee's questionable activities, despite Pearson's and the Department's complete support. Yet, he felt that neither Ottawa nor Washington could deflect its intentions, if it decided to press for a renewed investigation; as an afterthought, he mentioned that he had awakened the previous night thinking that to be innocent was not sufficient, adding that he had been both conscientious and very discreet in executing his ambassadorial mission. If the question again were to surface he would chuck it all and retire to the country. He characterized the congressional investigations and those who conducted them as "evil." His use of the word evil, according to Gordon, was interesting for he spoke it as if it were an "incarnate" object, something able to destroy life and the world.[6]

At 8:30 the following morning, April 2, Norman visited his Egyptian physician, Dr. Halim Doss. He stayed with him until 10:30, and again visited him that same afternoon between 3:00 and 5:30 p.m. He told the doctor the whole story of his relationship with the subcommittee, and "how he was *worried* about its further investigations."[7] Mentioning that he had discussed the matter with Arthur Kilgour who had minimized the subcommittee's current activities, he felt that the FBI "contained some vicious elements who might not hesitate to frame him if they were able to do so." He spoke of Alger Hiss who had probably been "framed," and that his only mistake had been to deny that he knew Whittaker Chambers—a statement he could not retract.

It is true that the FBI, like any other security organization should be kept on a tight leash, yet the thought that it would attempt to "frame" Norman is preposterous, just as his comments about Alger Hiss border on the absurd, even if they were, no doubt, shared at the time by many from the "Liberal Left." Hiss had been found guilty by twenty of the twenty-four jurors who had sat at both his trials. Despite the fact that he had been defended by America's best legal talent, and had invoked every appeal process the American federal system of law had to offer, all his appeals were rejected. Predictably, if Alger Hiss had been charged in Canada he would have been convicted under the draconian strictures of the Official Secrets Act, after facing a judiciary which was and still is, generally, far more conservative than its American counterpart.

Although Dr. Doss insisted that Norman was exaggerating the subcommittee's actions, noting that it had made no further comments, Norman pointed out that it was working behind closed doors. He then showed him about twelve pages of notes he had written. Some were on the embassy's blue air mail stationery and, according to Dr. Doss' disclosure, they resembled the text of a note found after Norman's suicide. The doctor understood, he later told Kilgour, that Norman had subsequently burned them.

Dr. Doss felt that his patient suffered from a "tremendous sense of guilt." He had, in fact, brought this to his attention. He correctly concluded that "he must have had a very strong religious upbringing." Norman had also maintained that "he had *never* been a communist but during his student days he had become very interested in communism because of its international aspects,"[8] casually observing, in this connection, that Soviet Russia had stood up to Nazi Germany. Kilgour later admitted to Ottawa that he had had a similar conversation with Norman, and that both he and Dr. Doss had assured him that there was no reason to take these prewar experiences so seriously, because many intelligent people had walked the same road. According to the doctor, Norman felt that he had "let the Canadian Government down because it previously had said that he had never been a communist but now he was afraid that a [sub]committee in Washington might show that he had *almost* been a communist."[9] The fear that obviously stalked him was that of public exposure.

The following day, April 3, Norman did not appear at the office, but he telephoned Kilgour to invite him to lunch and a chat, since they had not had an opportunity to talk to each other for several days. Since Kilgour had a prior engagement, he visited with him before lunch for approximately an hour. Kilgour thought he looked "quite weary," and Norman observed that the Washington investigation "had got him down." It was Kilgour's impression that he was unaware that Tsuru had testified, as he talked of the previous RCMP investigation and how tiring it had been. He repeated the assertion that the RCMP had been fed information by the FBI—no mention of MI5—recalling that during the Ottawa investigations he had been asked if he knew a certain Cambridge University economist. When he had said he did, it had taken several hours of questioning to satisfy the RCMP. Available documentary evidence shows that no questioning took place on the subject. Norman also claimed that John Foster Dulles had told him in Tokyo that the only thing Alger Hiss had done was not to cooperate with the FBI. Kilgour surmised that he might have "actually expected another prolonged inquiry." Indeed, "he mentioned the possibility of being recalled to Ottawa for investigation—the result of which might be that he was not properly cleared." Ultimately, the discussion led to the mutual decision that Norman should take an immediate holiday in Spain.

Since the Normans and Arthur Kilgour were planning to attend a Japanese movie that evening, Kilgour was invited for dinner. The proposed holiday was discussed before dinner, and an appropriate draft message to External Affairs on the subject was prepared. Kilgour was to review it the following morning, amend it if necessary and, after Norman's approval, dispatch it to Ottawa. After dinner they picked up two of the Normans' friends, and during the showing of the movie, the ambassador supplied some explanations about its contents. Entitled "Mask of Destiny," it dealt with the self-destruction of the leading character; although his fate had been decided, he was, nevertheless, unable to control the flow of events. During the movie and over drinks afterwards, Norman appeared to feel better, taking an active part in the conversation,[10] and even making arrangements to play croquet the following afternoon.[11]

It was not to be, for on the morning of April 4 he ended his life by jumping off the roof of an eight-storey apartment building. How much seeing the Japanese film the night before may have contributed toward the chemistry of his suicide is an imponderable, as his inspection of the chancery's roof had occurred several days before. . . .

Mrs. Norman strongly denied that Herbert had ever discussed suicide either with her or with Dr. Doss. Indeed, in conversations with others he may have appeared depressed or uneasy, but had never spoken of taking his life. Mrs. Norman wanted this fact conveyed to Lester Pearson—which it was—and also to Prime Minister Louis St. Laurent. What Herbert had discussed with Dr. Doss, according to Mrs. Norman, were his vexations and disquiet over what had developed. She feared that anything said by Herbert's physician might be twisted and overstated.[12] Interestingly, Pearson never publicly discussed the information relayed to him by Mrs. Norman. To have spoken of it would have undercut the notion that Norman had been driven to his death, solely by the activities of the Senate Subcommittee. Politically, it was wiser, even more advantageous, to ignore it and perpetuate the myth. America—specifically the Senate Subcommittee—would be the convenient whipping boy.

But what did Norman supposedly say before his death? According to the Senate Subcommittee report for 1957, the CIA had in its file an April dispatch from a highly reliable source in Cairo stating that on the night before he took his life, he had dined with a physician. He had informed him that he feared Prime Minister St. Laurent was not supporting him and that a Royal Commission of Inquiry would be established. If called to testify "he would have to implicate 60 to 70 Americans and Canadians and that he couldn't face up to it and that he was going to destroy himself."[13]

Before making a textual exegesis of this purported CIA dispatch it should be pointed out that the CIA never denied the existence of a dispatch resembling the text cited by the Senate Subcommittee. Moreover, no agency, no department of the American government, nor the White House have ever denied it. The Diefenbaker government subsequently refuted the existence of any record indicating that prior to Norman's suicide, the St. Laurent government had intended to establish a Royal Commission of Inquiry. The possibility that there may have been unofficial discussions within the government about such a commission was unfortunately never investigated.[14] Nevertheless, there was silence on the American side, especially by the CIA which usually is quick to deny even the most far-fetched story that tangentially might concern it.

However, like any information conveyed through several sources, this CIA dispatch, assuming it exists and had not got its Egyptian events muddled, has obviously undergone some distortion. There is no evidence that Norman dined with any physician on the evening of April 3. He saw Kilgour before lunch and that evening he and his wife dined with him. Then, accompanied by friends they went to see the Japanese movie. Apart from Norman's alleged observation that Prime Minister St. Laurent was not supporting him, the other comment credited to him in the purported conversation with a physician, was about his fear that a "Royal Commission of Inquiry" would be struck and, if called as a witness, his testimony would implicate sixty to seventy Americans and Canadians. Supposing the intelligence and knowledge of the alleged physician with whom he was said to have dined were above average, that individual would have had to be very sophisticated to conjure up the phrase "Royal Commission of Inquiry." Without fear of contradiction, it therefore can be asserted that the nature of such a specialized government body would have been unknown to almost every American and, undoubtedly, to almost every Egyptian. In this instance, the words could only have been voiced by a Canadian or someone familiar with analogous British royal commissions. Only Norman himself could have made such a comment. In line with his remarks about St. Laurent, one can only conclude that the purported conversation had, at least some basis in fact, and that some sort of conversation therefore may have taken place. Only a Royal Commission of Inquiry, with its draconian powers, could have posed questions and would have insisted on the kind of replies that no Senate Subcommittee would have been able to emulate because of lack of jurisdiction and in view of Norman's diplomatic immunity.

The reported conversation, undoubtedly, took place in Cairo between Norman and another individual. Whether he was a physician or someone else is unclear. We know that similar comments were made by him to Kilgour who then reported them to External Affairs: "he mentioned the possibility of being recalled to Ottawa for investigation—the result of which might be that he was not properly cleared."[15]

Ten years later a chronology of the events leading up to Norman's suicide was drafted. It seemingly included all the relevant telegrams sent to and received from Cairo. Nowhere is there a message, either from Louis St. Laurent or Lester Pearson discussing such possibilities.[16]

The only message that we know came from Ottawa was Pearson's handwritten note, sent about a week before Norman's suicide.[17] He might have commented on St. Laurent's uneasiness or he may have made some remarks which, though innocent, may have sufficed to unnerve Norman.

Norman's scribbled suicide notes are so enigmatic that they offer no clear picture of why he actually took his own life. The prudent and reasonable person is placed in the unenviable position of having to weigh and judge jottings made only minutes before his self-destruction, in light of what we now know of his past record. These notes, therefore, must be dissected with the greatest of care.

In the longest, intended for External Affairs, he speaks about being "overwhelmed" by his "consciousness of sin." He asks for God's forgiveness and goes on to say that time and access to the record would show to anyone "impartial" that he was "innocent" of the main allegation, namely, of having conspired or acted against the security of Canada or that of any other state. Claiming never to have violated the secrecy oath as a member of External Affairs, he states that he felt the issue would be obfuscated and twisted. He was exhausted by all of it and, though innocent, was faced by formidable forces. He thought it was better to end it all now than to face further calumny. He then begs for his family's forgiveness.

External Affairs would naturally be upset by the implications of his suicide, the scribbled note continues, but he trusts that an impartial and thorough study would support his "innocence." At this very moment, and because he liked his work in External Affairs, he would, with alacrity, confess to any security breach he may have made. He observes that his weakness has been "illusion," and his chief flaw "naivete." It had been naive of him to think that it was sufficient to be innocent of any act that contravened security. External Affairs, he contends, was aware of his "error," but he had committed no crime. He concludes the note by stating that he was unworthy of his wife whose loyalty had sustained him throughout trials and disappointments.[18]

Then there is the note to his brother Howard, a man who had never lost his belief in Christianity and who, over the years, had been at odds with Herbert about his sequential views of life.[19] Although Norman never specifically mentions the Senate Subcommittee by name, he says that he had been "overwhelmed by circumstances and had lived under illusions too long." Stating that Christianity was the only true road, he asks for Howard's forgiveness because things were not as black as they appeared, though, God knows, they were bad enough.

For what should Howard have forgiven him? Was it for straying from the true Christian path or for planning to take his own life? The answer is unclear. Herbert again claims that he had never betrayed his oath of secrecy, observing that guilt by association had begun to crush him. He was praying to God for forgiveness if it was not too late . . . Yet, why should guilt by association have necessitated God's forgiveness?

In a second note to his brother and sister-in-law, he again pleads innocence, and once more dwells on his own weak Christianity and how it had, nevertheless, helped to sustain him during the previous days.[20]

The fourth note is addressed to his wife. In it he contends that he could no longer live with himself and was unfit to live at all. The short note concludes that he lacked hope of meriting any sympathy.

That Herbert Norman was a sensitive and civilized human being who cared for his fellowmen is attested to in the fifth note addressed to the Swedish minister; it is the shortest and most macabre. He begs forgiveness for choosing his apartment building as the place from which to take the fatal plunge, explaining that it was the only one which would allow him to avoid endangering someone below.[21]

At this point it might be appropriate to examine the qualities potential candidates had to have in the 1930s after having been talent spotted for recruitment by the Communist Party and the Russian intelligence services. The types of persons in whom they were interested were the well-meaning and those who were moved by idealism. The 1946 Royal Commission described them as people who had "a burning desire to reform and improve Canadian society according to their lights." If properly groomed and cultivated through "study groups" and the appropriate literature, such as the periodical *New Masses* to which Norman had subscribed, they would gradually develop what the Royal Commission called "a sense of divided loyalties" or, in extreme cases, "a transferred loyalty." This process was assisted by whatever "sense of internationalism" would have motivated the potential recruit. He was encouraged to develop feelings of loyalty toward an "international ideal," rather than to any particular foreign state. "This subjective internationalism" was then linked through courses of indoctrination and by appropriate Russian propaganda "with the current conception of the national interests" of Soviet Russia and "the current doctrines and policies of Communist Parties throughout the world."[22]

As we have seen, Norman possessed all the right qualities, as even at the bitter end he made sure that no one else suffered. He also had succumbed, for various reasons—some peculiarly Canadian—to the ideological siren of secular optimism and human perfectibility. This probably was the "sin" to which he alluded in his suicide note to External Affairs. Unlike his brother Howard, he had believed in a false god for so long that that sin was partly redeemed by discovering—at the very end—the staying power of his weak Christianity.

This may also, at least partially, explain why the Senate Subcommittee was not specifically mentioned in the notes, and was perhaps only hinted at in the remark that he faced formidable forces, although he was innocent. Was this omission due to his perception that the subcommittee was less at fault than he himself because of his prior activities?

He claims to have lived under an illusion and that he had shown naiveté, that he could not live with himself, was unfit to live, and lacked any hope of meriting sympathy. He says he is innocent of having violated Canada's security and his oath of secrecy, yet his silence about any association with the Communist Party is deafening. Surely, this would have been the time to categorically deny that he was or had ever been a member. He did not do so. Why? Because that part of the *mea culpa* curtain had to be kept tightly drawn. Knowing as we do that he was or had been a member, what are we to make of his denials of all the allegations made against him? Because, to admit even the remotest association with communist elements quickly would have placed in doubt all his other statements.

Norman believed in the great march of history which is part and parcel of communist scripture. No matter what he did, no matter how illegal it was, it could be justified ideologically and psychologically. The laws of communism's dialectical materialism were higher than those governing Canada, higher than any secrecy oath, and greater than thoughts of national security. Moreover, one should differentiate, as Norman had not done, between conveying to unauthorized individuals "secret information" covered by the secrecy oath and "privy information" not covered by that oath. If secret and/or privy material was conveyed by Norman to Moscow during the war when Canada and Soviet Russia were allied, he could have rationalized that Canada's security was not being compromised. However, even if he had passed nothing that was either secret or privy, his denials would not have covered his actions as an agent of disinformation and/or of influence. As pointed out in Brian Crozier's book *Strategy for Survival*, in the United Kingdom and in some other Western states as well—and that would include Canada—"*it is not a punishable offence to be a Soviet agent of influence, even a conscious and paid one.*"[23] (Italics in the original.)

The question of whether or not Norman was an agent of influence must have bothered the mandarins at External Affairs because, almost two weeks after he had committed suicide, someone in its Middle

East Division sent a report to Glazebrook's Defense Liaison II, stating that a selection of Norman's telegraphic reports on political matters had been examined and that a cursory check had been made of his Cairo dispatches. Their quality was considered "outstanding," and no trace had been found that showed any inclination on Norman's part "to sympathize with Communist ideology or practice." On the contrary, in contact with Egyptians and other Arabs, it appeared that he had gone to some trouble to warn them of the dangers which Russian penetration would, in the end, pose to their governments and the peoples of the Middle East. Norman consciously seemed to have developed wide-ranging sources among Egyptians, Arabs, and the diplomatic corps in Cairo, and he had close and friendly relations with the Indian ambassador. This, the report maintains, illustrated that he had not hesitated to pursue any "useful channel," even though he "must have realized that evidence of contact with and dependence on 'neutralist' sources increased his personal vulnerability to irresponsible charges." Of the materials examined only three telegrams had been dispatched after March 14, when the Senate Subcommittee released Emmerson's executive session testimony.[24]

The Middle East Division's analysis is somewhat naive. No agent of influence would have been foolish enough to reveal anything in a telegram or dispatch. Of value to his true masters would have been the type of advice he might have tendered to his government and perhaps to others who could have been influenced by it. What Norman supposedly had said to Egyptians and other Arabs is virtually non-verifiable. Therefore, the Middle East Division's contribution would have been far more significant if his advice to Ottawa on how to handle Middle East events had been juxtaposed with Russian objectives in the region, particularly in Egypt.

Thus, Norman's deep commitment to the cause may help explain his inability to acknowledge the enormity of the evil that had stalked the Russian landscape, expecially during the Stalin era and, subsequently, other regions of the world.

One writer sympathetic to Herbert Norman said about him in 1977 that his "outright naiveté" was "linked to his lack of any strong sense of evil."[25] Three years earlier, almost the same comments were made many miles south of the 49th parallel by a stepson about his stepfather who he considered to have been a "severely repressed and morally rigid person." The stepson recalled that he was "a man capable of inflicting great suffering on himself in order to protect others at all costs." Moreover, until his stepfather's conviction and imprisonment, the stepson asserted he " 'had no sense of evil.' " That man was Alger Hiss.[26] The same characteristics were also noted in the longtime Canadian KGB agent Hugh Hambleton who was convicted in Great Britain under the Official Secrets Act. He, too, never seemed to have been "interested, and never would be, in making any moral judgement of the Soviet regime."[27]

This is not the time to examine the traits which appear to run like threads through the psyches of many who have served the Russian behemoth; let others who follow delve into the matter. If they wish to do so, they might consider the words of the Israeli novelist Amos Oz who said, " 'Whoever ignores varying degrees of evil is bound to become a servant of evil.' "[28]

What exactly were the "overwhelming circumstances" that had decided Herbert Norman to take his own life? Unexpectedly, after a long silence, the Senate Subcommittee on Internal Security again became interested in him, especially after Emmerson's testimony. Some days later, Patrick Walsh attempted to contact Pearson to present a brief dealing with Norman's communist background.[29] Is it possible that Walsh's overtures were mentioned in Pearson's handwritten note to him? Then Tsuru testified before the subcommittee, although Norman apparently was not aware of it. This is possible but not probable, considering the circles in which he moved in Cairo. Even if we discount his purported comments about the establishment of a Royal Commission of Inquiry, he had after all, mentioned to Kilgour "the possibility of being recalled to Ottawa for investigation."

Although Arnold Heeney had been made Canadian Ambassador to Washington by this time, Pearson was still in harness directing External Affairs, and there were others in positions of influence who, in the past, had been sympathetic to Norman's plight. The relative immunity he had enjoyed in the past would probably continue into the future, as long as the Senate Subcommittee desisted from delving into his background and activities. Was it lining up a new surprise witness? Testimony by Jaffe would be damaging in the extreme. Norman undoubtedly knew that he had broken with the American Communist Party and the extreme Left in the late 1940s. Was someone else being groomed to testify against him? Who else was there, and what new evidence might surface, even without the subcommittee's initiatives? Other information it might uncover could again lead to interrogations by Messrs. Guernsey, McClellan, and Glaze-brook. That had to be avoided at all costs.

As in Edgar Allan Poe's classic, *The Pit and the Pendulum*, Norman had escaped several brushes with the pit of destruction. But like on the narrator of Poe's tale of horror, the "walls" were closing in and forcing him inexorably toward the pit. The walls, in this case, were the mounting testimony against him and the fear of possible further revelations concerning his past activities, some of them suspicious. In line with information supplied by the RCMP, the FBI, and MI5, they might have led to a fuller and more vigorous interrogation than the one he had experienced in 1952. Buttressed by a full RCMP field investigation, the façade he had so carefully and cleverly constructed over the years would collapse. Aware of this distinct possibility and dreading, no doubt, that his unmasking would expose others, including perhaps influential friends, Norman decided to commit suicide. Of all the bleak options he may have had, taking his own life must have appeared the least objectionable. No doubt, he was well aware of E. M. Forster's 1930s credo, mouthed by Anthony Blunt and dear to the heart of the Left, "that betraying one's friend was worse than betraying one's country."[30]

Chapter 10

Norman—Pearson

The fact that Egerton Herbert Norman had a charmed career in External Affairs becomes more understandable if juxtaposed with what we may moderately call Lester B. Pearson's inordinate protection of him. Its earliest manifestation was his refusal to attach any significance to the presence of Norman's name in Halperin's notebook. He considered it a case of innocent people being listed in a harmless book of addresses and social engagements. In effect, the matter should have been brought to the attention of the RCMP which Pearson did not do.[1] Indeed, his patronage persisted, despite the suspicions in the minds of the RCMP and the FBI, especially after the RCMP had received information from MI5 about Norman's dubious friends and associates during the period he was at Cambridge.

True enough, the significance of Cambridge University during the 1930s as a KGB and GRU recruiting ground (thanks to the active assistance provided by the British Communist Party), did not begin to crystallize until Burgess and Maclean defected to Moscow in late May 1951. That was several months after Norman had first been questioned by Robertson and Heeney, following his recall to Ottawa from Tokyo. However, by the time Wittfogel appeared before the Senate Subcommittee in August 1951, one would have hoped that his testimony would have moved the Canadian authorities, and Pearson in particular, to question the eminent German academic. In fact, Norman should have been interrogated again, in view of his admission to Glazebrook that he had met Wittfogel[2] who did remember him from New York, although Norman's initial recollections were less specific.

Instead of clearing up the matter, External Affairs, led by Pearson, huffed and puffed and then released the less than truthful statement that Norman had undergone the normal security clearance, according to all the rules applicable to officials of External Affairs. Moreover, because of his prior alleged association with the Communist Party, he had been "very carefully and fully investigated" and given "a clean bill of health," and continued to be a "trusted and valuable official" of External Affairs.[3] Naturally, in a society whose political culture was and still is marked by an inordinate respect for authority Pearson's statement went unquestioned.

According to information received by Terence MacDermot, then High Commissioner in South Africa, there were within External Affairs, senior and especially junior officials who were dissatisfied with what they considered to be an inadequate defense of Norman by Pearson.[4] Yet, MacDermot appears to have kept mum about the 1935 discussions he had with Alexander George Heakes concerning Norman's communist affiliations.

Pearson, wishing, no doubt, to assuage the disgruntled in his department, and operating perhaps on the theory that a good defense is a strong offense, filed a protest note through Donald Matthews, the Canadian chargé d'affaires in Washington, contending that the Senate Subcommittee, by its public reference to Norman, had prejudiced the position of the External Affairs official, not only in the eyes of the Canadian public but also vis-à-vis other countries. Indeed, the reference had been based on "unimpressive and unsubstantiated statements by a former Communist." The note went on to say that Ottawa had "complete confidence" in Norman and hoped that the Senate Subcommittee would be informed of this fact, and of Canada's "regret and annoyance" that its counsel, Judge Robert Morris, had gone out of his way to bring up Norman's name during Wittfogel's testimony. Ottawa desired no publicity about its protest note, because too much had already been said about Norman. (Yet, several days later, Pearson did discuss the note publicly.) Ottawa hoped, the note continued, that the subcommittee would instruct Judge Morris to henceforth "act differently" in matters concerning Canadian officials. Regarding evidence likely to surface before congressional committees about Canadian officials, Ottawa naturally expected their names to be conveyed, in confidence, to Canadian authorities. Any allegations would then be investigated in Canada, and the results referred back to Washington. The note concluded that it was hoped the State Department would agree to this course of action and give Ottawa some assurance that it would become future procedure.[5]

Unbeknown to Ottawa, however, Elizabeth Bentley gave her testimony to the Senate Subcommittee on the same day—August 14—and almost at the same hour as Chargé d'Affaires Matthews handed the protest note to the State Department. When she had been initially questioned by the FBI, after breaking with the Communist Party, she had not mentioned Pearson's name. This may well have been due to the FBI interrogations which focused on Russian intelligence activities in the United States, in which the Bureau was more interested than in any Canadian connection. However, her memory was triggered when she saw Pearson's comments defending Norman in the press. Some days later, after Wittfogel had testified, Bentley approached Judge Morris. They were acquainted with each other, as he had questioned her in the past about her experiences in the communist apparatus. She saw, Bentley remarked ironically, that her friend "Mike Pearson" was making things difficult for him. The judge inquired what she meant by calling him "her friend." She explained, and then was asked by Morris whether she would appear before the subcommittee in executive session. She agreed.[6] Even if she had not done so, he would have had her subpoenaed, a power enjoyed by congressional committees, as well as by the law courts.

After Bentley testified (see Part A in the Appendices), the Canadian Embassy in Washington ascertained through a Canadian news correspondent that Morris had informed him that the subcommittee knew of another Canadian official whose name had been raised by Bentley. It regarded this matter as "very confidential" and would not publicize it. Morris, according to the correspondent, had "mumbled something about 'diplomatic channels.' "[7]

Pearson's note of protest was received by the subcommittee only *after* Bentley had testified. One can imagine its views of Pearson and of his protest note in light of Bentley's testimony. On August 23, Chargé d'Affaires Matthews was called to the State Department, and informed that the Senate Subcommittee would attempt to "proceed with dignity and fairness," and that executive session testimony would be controlled as deemed proper, depending on the particular case. In conjunction with or working through the State Department, it was not averse to cooperating with the Canadian authorities. He also was told that the State Department would explore the matter with the subcommittee to see what it had in mind, and would again approach the Canadian Embassy.

Matthews' reaction was negative, as he believed the subcommittee's "bargaining proposal would 'blow the lid' off Ottawa," and cause it to "view with great suspicion" the request for information transmitted to him on that day. He emphasized that its reply to the State Department did not contain the name of the second Canadian mentioned in the testimony, nor any information relating to what had been said about him.

When it was finally pointed out to Matthews that the subcommittee had not rejected the Canadian note of protest and was willing to exchange information, he appeared to agree to the proposal. He was, however, "suspicious" of what might have been in the subcommittee's letter to the State Department which had not been shown to him.[8]

In line with Morris' mumbled comment to the Canadian correspondent that the matter of the Canadian official identified by Bentley would be handled through diplomatic channels, the State Department was pressed to convey the contents of her testimony to the Canadian Prime Minister Louis St. Laurent. It was explained to Pearson that one of his "friends" would pass on the information to St. Laurent so that Pearson would know it had been done in the proper fashion. Whether the Prime Minister received a verbatim copy of the testimony or a synopsis of it is unclear. Whether he discussed it with Pearson is also unclear, although Pearson tells us that he had promised the State Department that he would discuss it with the Prime Minister. In fairness it must be said that Pearson died before he could deal with this episode in his memoirs. Therefore, his editors were forced to depend "on a few pages of original manuscript, transcript material," plus personal documentation Pearson had made available to others. This is far from desirable, but what emerges from the account we do have is unacceptable.

Pearson tells us that Bentley had supplied the "names of some Canadians who had worked with a communist study group in Washington during the war." This is both erroneous and deceptive. Bentley's testimony, at the minimum, dealt with criminal conspiracy, breaches of the Official Secrets Act and, at worst, possible breaches of the Treason Act. She supplied one name, he tells us, that he

personally suppressed from being made public. That name, well
known in Québec, was that of a person of "unimpeachable loyalty
and considerable achievement." He was, of course, referring to Hazen Sise, the respected architect from Montreal. "During the war,"
according to Pearson, "he was a rather radical young man and went
to some of these study discussions. But he probably did not know
much about what was going on and he certainly was not an agent
of any kind." He may have talked about him, Pearson notes, recounting any unimportant comments he may have made. Through
Bentley's insinuations he therefore had been placed in association
with that particular Canadian to whom he supposedly had conveyed
information, and through him to others "some of whom were or
became Soviet intelligence people."[9]

By no stretch of the imagination was Hazen Sise a person of
"unimpeachable loyalty."As John Sawatsky points out, following
his analysis of Sise's FBI file, he refused to journey to the United
States in 1948 to "appear voluntarily" before a federal Grand Jury
in New York. Since he apparently never crossed into the United
States, following his return to Canada in 1944, he was never questioned by the FBI or any other American police authority. By examining FBI materials on Sise it, however, becomes obvious that he
was questioned by the RCMP. As years later, FBI interest in Sise was
rekindled, it required investigations in cities as far apart as Philadel-
phia and San Francisco.[10] Indeed, in June 1949 following Bentley's
public identification of Sise, the American Consulate General in Montreal informed Washington that it had learned through a "confidential
but thoroughly reliable source"—a euphemism for the RCMP—that
Sise had been "identified with the Secret Section of the Communist
Party in 1935, 1936 and 1937." He had been investigated by Canadian
authorities following Gouzenko's defection, "but his name was not
made public and no evidence was forthcoming at that time linking
him with espionage in Canada."[11] No, Hazen Sise was no babe in
the woods and his "unimpeachable loyalty" to Canada is more than
suspect, even without Bentley's testimony.

That Sise was a "radical" during the war is incorrect since the
more precise description would be a communist. His commitment
to the cause goes back to the 1930s, certainly to the Spanish Civil
War, when he served with the Loyalist forces in Dr. Norman Be-
thune's blood transfusion unit. At the earliest, Pearson appears to
have met Sise in London just before the Second World War.[12] During

that period he would not have disguised his ideological outlook and Pearson would not have been unaware of his political orientation. Despite what Pearson tells us, Sise was not just a "radical."

Not only did the State Department convey Bentley's testimony to Ottawa, but the FBI also passed it on to the RCMP, certainly as early as August 27, 1951, followed by additional information on September 8 and October 3 of the same year.[13]

The file containing the testimony must have reached Pearson, at the very latest by April 3, 1954 via Jack W. Pickersgill, the Secretary of the Cabinet. Stored among the papers of Norman Robertson, his immediate predecessor, who had asked that they be disposed of, Pickersgill transmitted the file to Pearson, informing him in an accompanying letter that he felt he and nobody else should have it, unless he wanted a summary placed elsewhere in order to protect himself.[14]

Since neither Pickersgill's letter nor Bentley's testimony are in the Public Archives in Ottawa among Pearson's papers, it can be assumed that they either were removed or have since been destroyed; by whom or when cannot be established. Canadians need not be chagrined by what appears to have been destruction or removal of documentary evidence, as the Americans appear to have acted in a similar fashion. Elizabeth Bentley's executive session testimony of August 14, 1951 also seems to have disappeared from among the State Department papers. Although listed in the indices, the transcript is missing from the pertinent file in the National Archives in Washington, D.C.[15] When or by whom it was destroyed or removed is also unknown. No doubt, the actions carried out on both sides of the border could be justified by what the French delicately call *les raisons d'état*.

As Louis St. Laurent's papers contain little about the Norman case, one has to speculate what his reaction might have been once he had received the State Department's information about Bentley's testimony. As a small "l" liberal and former corporate lawyer, he likely was not impressed by something which in a court of law and by the canons of scholarship was mere hearsay. On the other hand, as a devout Roman Catholic, opposed to communism and the human repression it fostered, he also might have been uneasy that Bentley had testified under oath. As a former practising attorney he must have known that once people swear to tell the truth, most of them do. Obviously, some do not, which explains why there is a Perjury

Act. But what motive would Bentley have had to lie? She had never actually met Pearson and certainly had not moved in his social circle. In addition, though St. Laurent probably did not know it, it was Bentley who had approached Judge Morris, not the other way round. Based on her prior appearance before the Senate Subcommittee, she knew that she would have to testify under oath, and if she were to bear false witness, the Perjury Act would be enforced. Is it reasonable to suppose she would go out of her way to perjure herself? Not likely.

If St. Laurent did dismiss her testimony about Pearson, as he obviously did, not only would its hearsay aspect have bothered him, but also the possibility that a scandal might develop, should it become public knowledge. In addition, he had just grappled with opposition charges which he had successfully fended off, that his government had failed to adequately protect Canada from communist infiltration. It, therefore, would only be natural for him to be skeptical of further charges along these lines, especially coming from across the border, at a time when Senator McCarthy's anti-communist rhetoric was reaching fever pitch.[16]

What should one make of Elizabeth Bentley's testimony before the Senate Subcommittee? The point must be made that this was not the first time she had raised Hazen Sise's name. Soon after "defecting" in late summer of 1945, she had mentioned him to the FBI as being a member of the communist apparatus,[17] and she publicly identified him as such in early June of 1949; that was naturally denied by Sise.[18] She also dealt with him in her memoirs, written prior to her appearance before the subcommittee, and published several weeks later, in September 1951. No doubt, to avoid a libel charge she had introduced Hazen Sise under the thin disguise of *Harold Sloan*, "a young Canadian" who had been her sub-agent during the war when he had worked for the Canadian government in Washington. She wrote that he had been "recommended for his trustworthiness" to the New York communist apparatus by some of the leading lights in the Canadian Communist Party. He had "had a long and excellent record as a Party member in Canada, including a period of service in the Spanish Civil War."[19]

If the bench mark in evaluating the credibility of any witness is verifiable testimony, then Bentley stood at the head of the class. In fact, some of her testimony to the Senate Subcommittee, as well as the information she subsequently gave to the FBI, were already in the pages of her unpublished memoirs.[20] Mentioned were Sise's marital difficulties and his psychiatric problems.[21] She also refers in her testimony to an aborted attempt in autumn of 1937 to recruit him in Paris into the Russian intelligence services; Sise himself had alluded to the incident in a letter to a London friend.[22] Therefore, based on his own papers, we now know that her comments were no figments of her imagination.[23]

Although the body of her remarks rings true, she, like anyone else, was capable of making minor errors, such as misspelling Sise's name or mixing up the dates on which she had first established contact with him in Washington. Even if her statements about him cannot be corroborated, she was probably telling the truth. Although there may have been much hue and cry about her testimony before congressional committees, no one ever tripped her up on questions of substance.[24]

This brings us to Bentley's important comments about Lester B. Pearson. Based on the fact that she only repeated what Sise had allegedly told her, it must be considered mere hearsay. Why would Sise have given her the "source" of his information which obviously was of considerable importance, and would have been immensely useful to Russian intelligence? It is still a cardinal principle of such operations never to divulge one's source. That applies to intelligence officers and staff personnel, but not to agents such as Hazen Sise. These agents were routinely expected to disclose to their control officer—in that case Elizabeth Bentley—where and how they had acquired information, so that its reliability, especially if it was verbal, could be properly assessed. The procedure is still meticulously followed in the Russian intelligence services, sensitized as they are to possible deception by their perceived opponents. It is most unlikely that they would have trusted an agent such as Sise who in his debriefings would not have disclosed to Bentley the identity of his source. Indeed, if he had been reluctant to do so, Moscow Center would have pressed her to discover it.

It, therefore, would be fair to say that Sise was quite inexperienced in the deadly game of espionage. It is, however, conceivable that he was getting information from someone in the embassy, not necessarily a person of Pearson's functional importance, but someone who would have had access to it, for example, a secretary or a code clerk. Perhaps, not wanting to tell Bentley the truth and in order to throw her off the scent, Sise might have blurted out Pearson's name. Since his office as the liaison for the Canadian National Film Board was down the hall from Pearson's he must have seen him on an everyday basis.[25] But Sise was not one of God's hail-fellow-well-met type persons. According to the FBI, he had a "conceited" manner and spoke an Oxford-accented English,[26] no doubt acquired during his residence in London. In view of his upper middle-class upbringing in one of the wealthier sections of prewar Montreal, and in a society far more deferential to class than the American one, it is difficult to conjure up the picture of a Hazen Sise rubbing shoulders with the embassy's support staff, in an effort to acquire secret and privy information. Marxist-Leninism notwithstanding, it is a stance not unknown to those who, in the abstract and at the expense of other stratas of society want to improve the plight of their fellowmen through the levelling process of the class struggle.

The important point is that what Bentley told the subcommittee and the FBI was something she *believed* to be true, something she had heard from Sise. Whether or not he was telling the truth, misleading her or perhaps even fantasizing is another matter. Her testimony under oath, as well as her comments to the FBI, of and by themselves would be viewed and dismissed as an aberration or conundrum.

There is, however, other evidence, more objective than hers, that increases the uneasiness. Fortunately for Lester Pearson, the Senate Subcommittee never became aware of it. In late October 1944, when Sise had returned to Canada, Pearson contacted External Affairs' Under-Secretary Norman Robertson. He explained to him that he had lunched with Anatoly Gromov, the first secretary of the Russian Embassy in Washington. The Russian had informed him that he had served seven years at the embassy in London. Since he would be seeing Gromov from time to time, Pearson asked Robertson to furnish information about him. In line with his request, the Canadian High Commission in London was asked about Gromov, but no data was available on his "personality."[27]

In the thousands of volumes stored in the archival depositories of External Affairs, the Foreign Office, and the State Department one would be hard pressed to discover a missive sent in wartime from a Deputy Chief of Mission that solicits information about a middle-ranking officer of a Russian Embassy. Even in the worst days of the Cold War, interest in first secretaries of Russian diplomatic missions was the concern, not of the ambassador, but of embassy personnel detailed to answer or expedite such inquiries.

Pearson's request, therefore, was odd, but acquires greater significance when related to the fact that Gromov was Bentley's control officer.[28] His real name was Anatoly Gorski, also known as "Henry." As one of the KGB's most consummate operatives, he had run Blunt, Burgess, Maclean, and Philby, as well as others from the Cambridge circle during the period he served in London. When Maclean was transferred to the British Embassy in Washington, Gromov was detailed to run him. Indeed, in May 1951 he apparently was involved in devising the escape route for Burgess and Maclean to Moscow. Under the disguise of Professor Nikitin, Gromov, subsequently was also involved in the homosexual entrapment of John Watkins, the Canadian Ambassador to Moscow.[29]

In the fall of 1944, about the same time as Pearson wrote to Robertson, Gromov asked Bentley for the whereabouts of Hazen Sise. When she explained that she had dropped him as an agent because of his marital and psychiatric problems, Gromov indicated to her that she should never have done it.[30] Since he was not a person who would allow grass to grow under his feet, it is safe to assume that contact with Sise was re-established through Gromov's associates in Canada. However, Sise's real value to Moscow was not to report the chit-chat he could pick up in the Canadian Embassy, but information he allegedly had received from Pearson, something which Bentley had divulged to the Senate Subcommittee. Can it be that Gromov's luncheon with Pearson was an attempt to reopen the channel of communication disrupted when Bentley dropped Sise as an agent? If so, Pearson's query to Robertson may have been a cautious attempt to ascertain as much about Gromov, as Gromov already knew about him.

The significance of this luncheon could be enhanced if the exact date of the purported dinner prepared by Emma Woikin could be established. It apparently took place some time between early summer, 1944 and late summer, 1945, perhaps at the home of Major Sokolov with Norman and Pearson present.[31] If it occurred after Pearson lunched with Gromov, and keeping in mind the improbability that it was a social occasion, it can be inferred that it was, at the minimum, an attempt to size up Pearson, so to speak, and to reopen the disrupted channel of information. Beyond that it was perhaps the first step to formally recruit Pearson into the Russian intelligence services. They usually are in no rush and sometimes spend considerable time sizing up and reconnoitering someone before an initial approach is even attempted. Bearing in mind that Major Sokolov, the conceivable host, was GRU, a service with which Norman was most likely associated at that time, the probable target may have been Pearson, even if the purported dinner preceded his luncheon with Gromov.

Pearson's handling of the Norman case begins to assume ominous proportions when juxtaposed with Bentley's testimony and comments, his summary dismissal of Norman's name in Halperin's notebook, his lunch with and query about Gromov, and his presence at the purported dinner.

By no stretch of the imagination had Pearson been candid with the Canadian people. He had lied to them in his 1951 statement about Norman, and had deceived the House of Commons during the March-April debates before and following Norman's suicide. Indeed, from 1951 to 1957, as he admitted when pressed by John Diefenbaker and Solon Low, he had been fully aware of Norman's political associations at Cambridge University. These associations, followed by the defections of Burgess and Maclean, Wittfogel's testimony, Norman's interrogations by Messrs. Guernsey, McClellan, and Glazebrook, and the contradictions and inconsistencies that had flowed from these interrogations, should have alerted even the most somnambulent. At that point Norman ought to have been subjected to another security interrogation, buttressed by a full RCMP field investigation of the case, including an interview with Wittfogel. Pearson, one can cogently argue, did not want to act. Was it because he saw in Norman a kindred soul? This might explain why he was probably opposed to any attempts to scrutinize his loyalty to Canada. Whether this attitude was due merely to the personal devotion a superior might have for one of his juniors or because a close friendship had developed, is unanswerable. However, in any equation that attempts to describe a relationship, Bentley's testimony and comments cannot be dismissed by any wave of the hand. In view of the information unearthed about Norman, the evidence about the goals and techniques of the Russian intelligence services (well known to the RCMP, and accumulating during that period), as well as Pearson's reluctance to relate the one to the others, it can be suggested that, at the minimum, Pearson had forfeited his privilege to be a minister of the Crown. Fortunately for him, documentation that could have made this assertation possible was not available for scrutiny at that time. Beyond that, one could suggest that he was negligent in the extreme.

Keeping Bentley's testimony and comments in the forefront, one might even dare to think the unthinkable—that Pearson was Moscow's ultimate mole.

More likely, and seen from a more magnanimous point of view, he was perhaps an unconscious ideological sympathizer. Less generously it might be contended that he could have been a conscious ideological sympathizer who was not under "control." Either stance might have been made easier for him by the "social gospel" which, no doubt, had prevailed in the Methodist household in which he was raised. He gives us a tantalizing, if fleeting glimpse of it when he speaks of "midnight discussion with [Oxford] College friends over the follies of politics that led to war but neglected the evils of poverty and injustice."[32] He tells us no more in his memoirs. If he was an unconscious recruit—not to mention a conscious one—and ideologically sympathetic, both self-restraint and his positions, first as a government official and then as a political leader, had made him more circumspect. His Oxford discussions may be suggestive of interest espoused by someone not dissimilar to Norman who also perceived the inadequacies and evils of his own society but failed to see that behind Moscow's ideological façade far greater evils were being perpetrated, during the interwar and postwar periods, in the name of an ideological social gospel.

These clearly must have been the thoughts that percolated through the minds of the senators and the subcommittee's staff. Certainly they gnawed at Judge Morris' who during the questioning of Emmerson in March 1957 thought it "appropriate . . . to mention . . . [that Wittfogel had] said that to this day no official of the Canadian Government [had] ever called him up or asked him whether or not any of his testimony was, in fact, accurate." Arthur V. Watkins, Utah's Republican Senator, thought that this "very interesting" admission might "have some significance."[33] Pearson was not mentioned by name but the elliptical allusion was there. The fact that Wittfogel had not been invited to Canada for an RCMP interrogation obviously signified that something was amiss. American senators, despite Hollywood's depiction of them as bombastic politicoes, are, by and large, no one's fools, and although some are clearly no giants of intellect, most are savvy when it comes to the real world of politics. Pearson's non-reaction to the idea of having Wittfogel interrogated would have raised suspicions even in the mind of the least perceptive of the breed.

The senators' doubts and those of the subcommittee staff were also heightened by the encounter with Pearson over the subcommittee's desire to question Igor Gouzenko. In an October 1953 interview with the *Chicago Daily Tribune* Gouzenko stated that he felt worthwhile results could be achieved if he could talk to the Senate Subcommittee. Judge Morris expressed a desire to interview him in Canada, and the State Department approached External Affairs to arrange the matter. Pearson, however, rejected the overture on the ground that Gouzenko had been "questioned concerning his alleged statement" to the *Chicago Daily Tribune*. If he had additional information to offer, he should convey it to the Canadian authorities. Gouzenko, Pearson asserted, had denied that he had information beyond what he had given to the 1946 Royal Commission, and he had supposedly claimed that he had been misquoted by the newspaper. Everything of value to Washington and connected with Gouzenko's defection, he contended, had been made available to the American authorities years ago.

Undeterred by Pearson's curt reply, the State Department sent a second note on November 19, in which it raised the stakes. This time the request to make Gouzenko available for questioning was made by Senator William E. Jenner, the chairman of the subcommittee. At that point the proverbial rug was pulled from under Pearson by Gouzenko himself when, in a properly witnessed and signed statement he attested that he had *not* been misquoted by the *Chicago Daily Tribune*. He reiterated his willingness to offer advice to the subcommittee that might prove fruitful in quickly exposing the communist apparatus in the United States. Possibly reacting to the "veiled threat" made by Senator Jenner that he might further raise the stakes by "leaking" Bentley's testimony, Pearson beat a hasty retreat. Provided Gouzenko agreed, he sanctioned a confidential meeting under Canadian auspices between Gouzenko and anyone designated by Washington. It was to be understood that no evidence would be made public without Canadian approval. Pearson's hints that Gouzenko's RCMP protection might be undermined by his actions, certainly must have worried the former Russian code clerk.[34]

The meeting occurred early in January 1954. It was chaired by Mr. Chief Justice J. C. McRuer of the Ontario Supreme Court. Pearson had placed a number of restrictions on the questions Gouzenko could be asked, including the important stricture that no information would be elicited about espionage activities of Canadians or persons resident in Canada.[35] Certainly, as a sovereign state, Canada was well within its rights to handle the matter of espionage on its own, without the assistance or interference of any American body.

Yet, how can one explain Pearson's haste to contradict Gouzenko? Perhaps a case of bad staff work? No, despite his *pro forma* public appreciation of what Gouzenko had done for Canada, he was not particularly fond of the man. For example, it was not until John Diefenbaker had come to power that he was given a monthly government stipend. One might, therefore, suggest that the exercise Pearson had gone through to thwart his meeting with the subcommittee had other reasons. Gouzenko was, without question, a difficult defector and an endless source of concern and bother to the RCMP. More importantly, from Pearson's point of view, he had a mercurial quality. The thought of an unfettered Gouzenko blurting out the story of Colonel Zabotin being asked in 1944 if he knew "Norman," must have crossed his mind. Even though the 1946 Royal Commission's report had dealt with this episode, the impact of any such rendition, in line with the subcommittee's suspicions about Norman, was potentially dangerous. Its reaction might have generated political shock waves that could have shaken many an Ottawa edifice. The espionage activities of Canadians or persons resident in Canada had to be excluded from Gouzenko's testimony. They were.

Pearson wrote to Norman in late December 1953, just days before Gouzenko was questioned by the subcommittee. He noted that Norman no doubt had been following the whole affair with particular interest. He would know better than most how he, Pearson, felt about the business and how annoying and unnecessary it all had been.[36]

Understandably, Pearson's opposition to Gouzenko's appearance was grist for the subcommittee's mill. In line with Bentley's testimony and based on the fact that Wittfogel had not been interrogated by the RCMP, it believed it had the answer. "You will remember, Senator Jenner," Judge Morris observed on March 12, 1957 when Emmerson was being questioned, "when you tried to have Gouzenko testify, that the Canadian authorities would not let you ask any questions whatever about anyone who was a Canadian personality."[37] Again, the name Pearson went unmentioned, but deep suspicions must have been there.

Following the subcommittee's release of Emmerson's testimony on March 14, 1957, the tempo of events began to speed up. On March 20 (see Part C in the Appendices), senior State Department members caucused with Judge Morris and the subcommittee's associate counsel William Rusher. Initially, their discussions dealt with the release of congressional testimony, in this case Emmerson's, in view of the 1951 Canadian objection that material involving Canadians not be released until it was first relayed through the State Department to Ottawa. Judge Morris then read Bentley's testimony of August 14, 1951 to the assembled State Department officials. There is no evidence that either they or Secretary of State John Foster Dulles had been aware of it before that time, although Dulles' predecessor Dean Acheson had known about it. After it had been read, William Rusher remembers that Deputy Assistant Secretary of State Roderick O'Connor "commented dryly" that it would "overload any wires" the State Department possessed.[38]

Therefore, Dulles must have been made aware of its contents, days before Norman committed suicide. It also would be safe to assume that he had been briefed about Pearson's seemingly questionable and excessive protection of him. In view of Dulles' vision of the communist world being a great satanic force, it can well be imagined what all this must have conjured up in his mind. That, as well as the CIA's dispatch about Norman's alleged comments in Cairo just prior to his suicide, might partially explain his three-weeks delay in responding to Pearson's initial protest note of March 18, 1957. The fact that the reply was not signed by Dulles himself (he had departed the previous day for Duck Island on the Canadian side of Lake Ontario), may have been his way of showing disdain for Pearson—possibly a symbolic gesture that went unrecognized at the time. Dulles was not amused by his Canadian counterpart; this was reflected in the State Department's attitude which, unlike that of Ottawa, took Bentley's testimony seriously.[39] Indeed, we are told that at one point, Dulles "had harangued [Pearson] about Canadian policies—in language that was almost violent and certainly abusive."[40] If that incident occurred after March 20, 1957 when he had heard about Bentley's testimony, his treatment of Pearson becomes less of a mystery.

Heeney tells us that in an interview on April 10, President Eisenhower "extended his personal sympathy" on Norman's death. Yet, he would not openly criticize the senators because he felt they would fall like Senator McCarthy.[41] It is, however, safe to assume that following the interview, Eisenhower would have been briefed about Bentley's testimony and Norman, in particular. This may account for his cool remarks at the press conference on April 11, when he was queried regarding the propriety of the Senate Subcommittee's release of publicity about Norman's communist links after he had been cleared by his own government. Eisenhower talked of having "no way of knowing that anybody in Congress deliberately did anything that he thought would damage our relations abroad." In this particular case he thought it a great sorrow to everyone concerned that a misunderstanding should have occurred. Anything that tended to disrupt the close nature of American-Canadian relations was unfortunate. He sincerely hoped that Canada's leadership knew how deeply his government wanted to retain its respect and friendship. Eisenhower was sure that what had occurred could be traced to "inadvertence." He wanted to avoid criticizing anyone, indeed, he hoped that the question could now be "dropped," though he knew that it was of greater importance in Canada than in the United States. He thought that everyone should strive "to restore . . . the fine, firm character of our relationship with Canada just as rapidly as we can."[42] Interestingly, Eisenhower, just as St. Laurent in the House of Commons debates of the preceding days, never spoke the name Egerton Herbert Norman. He may not have been a tower of intellect, but Eisenhower was, by all accounts, a decent and compassionate person. Consequently, his cool reply, keeping in mind that it touched on the suicide of a fellow human being, was out of character. It was as though Norman's name was anathema to him.

Conceivably, to offset Eisenhower's silence Pearson approached St. Laurent four days later, on April 15. If he were asked about Norman at a press conference that evening, Pearson wrote, the Prime Minister might wish to observe that any further statement on the matter would be made by Pearson. However, if St. Laurent felt he should say something himself, Pearson wanted to offer some suggestions. Ottawa's purpose in the Norman matter had been to protect an External Affairs official from "slanderous implications against his loyalty as a Canadian." Moreover, Ottawa had attempted to block disclosures concerning Canadians by the legislative body of another government. "Even if the so-called evidence is fair and valid in any case, and it was not in this case," Pearson claimed, decency dictated that it first be sent to the Canadian government for investigation and for any action to be taken.

The accusation was that the matter had not been cleared up in 1951, when Ottawa had "affirmed and re-affirmed" its confidence in Norman's loyalty and patriotism. Years had passed and there had been no further reference to Norman in the United States. Pearson did "not agree that we should have made all the evidence available at that time." On the contrary, he continued, any such move would have been counter to Ottawa's way of dealing with matters of this nature—a way that had been effective in protecting Canada's interests, and had also been just to the person involved. In the Norman case, he argued, disclosure would have focused greater attention than necessary on the matter. In the atmosphere of 1951 this "would have been unjust and unfair" to Norman and might have forced him out of External Affairs.

When it again erupted in the previous month, immediate and what was thought effective action was taken. In view of the information leaked by Washington, it appeared to Pearson that more had to be done than merely to affirm Ottawa's confidence in Norman's loyalty. Accordingly, as St. Laurent knew, he had stated that the purported evidence in the charges against Norman was based only on the communist associations during his student days. External Affairs had known about them, had examined them "exhaustively," and had decided, at that time, that there was nothing in them that contradicted External Affairs' view that he was a "loyal and trustworthy" government official. There was "no evidence," Pearson held, that Norman had "had any Communist associations while he was with the Department." This seemed to him "to be the crux of the matter;" Norman "should not be condemned and persecuted because of any Communist illusions as a student, which he may have once had, but which he had long since abandoned." Pearson had a very selective memory, indeed. Conveniently, he had forgotten the information and the string of associations and contacts during Norman's years in External Affairs.

In the House of Commons debate Diefenbaker had demanded that the question be answered whether the Senate Subcommittee statements were untrue. According to Pearson, a response of yes or no was impossible, without examining all the testimony, since many statements were untrue and some were true, "though implications drawn from them were false and malicious." If he had given a categorical response, Pearson contended, without releasing all the evidence, a "wrong impression" would have been created that would have been very unfair to Norman who could not now defend himself. If the evidence were released now, "we would merely be raking up a lot of old insinuations and charges dealing with situations and activities" which pre-dated Norman's entrance into External Affairs and, "did not affect his loyal service to the Department subsequently." All the evidence against Norman, "even by implication dealt with his student activities and to drag all that up now and make it all public would seem to me to be unfair and unjust." On the contrary, all the evidence, even by implication, did not deal *solely* with Norman's activities as a student. Pearson's comment was deceptive.

He then waxed hot and heavy on the charge that he had been lax in his duties and weak in Norman's defense, because he had not made public all the charges nor replied to them in 1951. He wanted to add, though this could not, of course, be said publicly that Norman himself had been grateful that this stance had not been taken, and that the matter had been allowed to die. It was not Canada's fault that it had been resurrected.[43] Based on what we now know, the memorandum was filled with distortions and half–truths, and was a self-serving document.

Though St. Laurent was getting on in age and perhaps was not in the very best of health, he was an astute and experienced politician. He obviously bought none of what Pearson had written. When asked at the press conference whether the Norman question would be an election issue, he replied in the negative, observing it would be unfortunate if that occurred. He thought that the Norman case was an "unfortunate tragedy," and although he had not had close contacts with the man, he had had a "really affectionate" regard for the External Affairs official.[44] With that, St. Laurent had deftly sidestepped Pearson's approach.

Between Eisenhower's statement of April 11 and that of St. Laurent on April 15, a debate took place in the United States Senate. Pressed by Senator Richard L. Neuberger (Democrat of Oregon), the Chairman of the Senate's Judiciary Committee, Senator James O. Eastland (Democrat of Mississippi), defended his subcommittee's action of having released the information to the press. Neatly and discreetly, Eastland summed it up: "The distinguished Senator asks me why this information was not submitted through channels to Canada. There are certain facts on the record which I could go into, but it is not my intention to do so at this time. There are also facts off the record which I would not divulge on this floor. But there was a sound reason for the action which was taken." Moreover, like Judge Morris and others, Eastland noted that Wittfogel had never been questioned by the RCMP.[45]

Months after this debate it was proposed to Judge Morris by a member of the subcommittee staff that Eastland ask Dulles about Norman's purported comments in Cairo, reported by the CIA, regarding the establishment of a Royal Commission of Inquiry.[46] At present, documentation is not available to establish whether or not this was done, however, Norman's purported comments were noted in the Judiciary Committee's 1957 report. We do know that, over a year later, on May 22, 1958, Eastland wrote to Dulles. He did so, he explained, following Dulles' receipt of a report detailing an Executive branch investigation of Norman's death, conducted in Cairo. The report, he claimed, was circulated among interested government departments, and approximately thirty persons had had access to it. Eastland contended that because it contained interviews with people in Cairo who had been aware of Norman's activities just prior to his suicide, it would be of interest to the Senate Subcommittee. It wished to see it because it contained "an explanation of his motive for taking his own life." Supposedly, this explanation had been ascertained in an interview with his physician in Cairo, in which "Norman is said to have told the doctor of his desperate state of mind and his fears of a forthcoming investigation regarding his Communist associations." He feared not only for his own safety, but was apprehensive that if the investigation were held, he would have to involve others aside from himself. Eastland presumed that this included both Americans and Canadians. He pointed out that the report was in no way related to nor should it be confused with the CIA dispatch mentioned after Norman's suicide.

Eastland felt that this report had received considerable circulation within the government, and that it was "entirely proper to request that a copy of the document be turned over to the Subcommittee." Dulles would recall, he continued, that when Gouzenko defected, Prime Minister Mackenzie King had stated that Canada had been used as a base for espionage against the United States. Moreover, in its 1946 report the Royal Commission had observed that only a small fraction of Russia's espionage activities in Canada had been uncovered by Gouzenko's revelations.[47] Due to lack of documentation, Dulles' reply to Eastland's missive is unknown; it is, however, possible that any response to so sensitive a matter might have been oral.

Aside from the small group of Americans who knew about Bentley's testimony and had suspicions about Pearson because of it, there was one Canadian who was aware of it. That was Pearson's political opponent John Diefenbaker who apparently had received a copy of it after he became Prime Minister, but from whom is unknown. Reading it could only have strengthened his suspicions about Pearson. They were reflected in his desire to see Norman's entire RCMP file, selected portions of which had been supplied to him, one month after he became Prime Minister.[48] Like St. Laurent, Diefenbaker was an experienced lawyer, and though he, no doubt, realized that what Bentley had said was mere hearsay, he was well aware of the fact that people usually do not perjure themselves once they have sworn to tell the truth. He believed Bentley, and this belief manifested itself in December 1964 when Pearson, now Prime Minister, approached him about Gerda Munsinger, a suspected East German communist agent who had bedded at least one Diefenbaker cabinet minister. Faced with what he considered to be Pearson's attempt to blackmail him, he referred to Bentley's testimony "which had implicated Pearson himself," he tells us. According to Diefenbaker, the Prime Minister tried to assuage him.[49]

Pearson's version of this exchange, as one would expect, is different. Diefenbaker, he alleged, waved his fist at him and threatened him with scandal, contending that he knew all about Pearson when he was a communist. In response, Pearson laughed at him, observing that he was no doubt alluding to Bentley's testimony before the Senate Subcommittee. He characterized Bentley as that "deranged woman," stating there was nothing to what she had said. When Dean Acheson had sent someone to Ottawa to inform him of it, Pearson claimed, he had proposed that the testimony be published.[50] As J. L. Granatstein points out, the interview was "extraordinary," as blackmail had been attempted by both sides.[51]

Whether Pearson ever told Acheson's emissary that the testimony ought to be published, cannot be verified. What is of note, however, is his description of Bentley as someone who was "deranged." She points out in her memoirs that after she had "defected," the American Communist Party, in an attempt to destroy her credibility, had circulated the rumor that she had been an inmate in a mental institution.[52] Surely, Pearson could have chosen more appropriate language to dismiss Bentley's hearsay evidence than to repeat the communist canard that she was demented.

Subsequent events would appear to support the possibility that Diefenbaker's blackmail had only partially succeeded. The Munsinger Affair arose in the House of Commons inadvertantly, only fifteen months later, in March of 1966. A judicial inquiry was instituted, and a report handed down six months later in September of that year. Why Diefenbaker did not then divulge Bentley's testimony is open to speculation, but Pearson's prevailing popularity and the hearsay nature of her comments were undoubtedly factors that made him decide against it.

Over the years, much has been said about the Norman case that has little basis in fact. One can argue that some of it was a calculated attempt to blur what had occurred, to disinform, and to cast aspersions in other directions. The RCMP for one has come in for its share of the blame, with the FBI close behind, and J. Edgar Hoover playing the role of the avenging angel. The CIA, it was murmured, had also been involved but the lead roles were reversed for the senators and the staff of the Senate Subcommittee on Internal Security. It was claimed that the demonic forces let loose during that period had inevitably consumed Egerton Herbert Norman. History and politics are much more complicated than any such sophomoric view of a world which only rarely is composed of black and white, but more often of shades of grey.[53]

Congressional committees, though not stipulated by the American Constitution, are a fact of life, sanctioned by custom and convention and justified, on more than one occasion, by the law courts. Indeed, according to the courts the purview of these committees is virtually unlimited, since it is their legitimate right to investigate all manner of things for possible legislative enactments. Like any organized body it can be misused and corrupted in the hands of politicians. It would, however, be fair to contend that, by and large, committees of Congress have, over the decades, performed their tasks with integrity and dispatch. The problem that doggedly follows anyone who tries to examine the Norman episode is the unending charge that it was a manifestation of "McCarthyism." More than a host of KGB agents, the notorious senator from Wisconsin probably did more to hurt and disrupt legitimate congressional investigations of activities harmful to the security of the United States and its allies.[54] He certainly deserves the Lenin Prize for his methods and actions. But McCarthy was not a member of that particular Senate Subcommittee, which had the perfect right to investigate Norman at least during the period he was a resident of the United States, studying at two of its best known institutions of higher learning (Harvard and Columbia universities). He had received funds from an American foundation (Rockefeller), and had been associated with an American body (the Institute of Pacific Relations) that subsequently attracted the attention of the subcommittee as a communist-front organization.

Norman's work with American counterintelligence in Tokyo after the war also was a legitimate matter of concern as well as his associations with American diplomats.

One can cogently argue that, after a certain point, perhaps the wiser political move would have been to convey to the Canadian authorities any feelings of uneasiness about Norman and his activities. But what confidence could the subcommittee have had in these authorities? It distrusted Pearson and that mistrust was shared by the Eisenhower administration, especially Secretary of State John Foster Dulles and, no doubt, others. Pearson's complaint that an American congressional body had no right to delve into the activities of a serving Canadian diplomat was convenient. He well knew that political collisions of that nature are rarely resolved in public forums.

In any examination of the Norman case, one cannot ignore the direct or tangential presence and activities of Lester B. Pearson. His involvement in External Affairs' slipshod handling of Norman's scrutiny after he had been recalled from Tokyo, would have been unacceptable in anyone else's case. It is unlikely that others would have been treated in the same generous manner. Norman was part of the establishment, despite his impecunious position in 1935, in the sense that he was the child of missionary parents. For complex, sociopolitical and historical reasons, missionary children on both sides of the border have always led particularly charmed lives. They are members of a special status group, and usually treated in a manner not likely to be enjoyed by others. That attitude toward them, especially in government service, certainly was prevalent through the 1950s. Nor must we forget that mandarins, Canadian ones in particular, have a tendency to treat their own as a privileged class, supposedly exempt from the scrutiny applied to others. This background and the existing links between Norman and Pearson might explain most of what happened.

However, there remains an enormous web of coincidences which is difficult to unravel and often fractures the laws of probability. Aside from Pearson's "disinformation" about Bentley's testimony, there is Wittfogel's non-interrogation, the Gouzenko imbroglio of 1953, Pearson's disregard of the significance of the Halperin notebook, the purported Emma Woikin dinner, and Pearson's inordinate interest in Anatoly Gromov.

Then there is his continuing contact with Hazen Sise during the time he was Prime Minister. Sise had written to him seeking his support on a non-sensitive civic matter. This is a prerogative that any taxpayer might enjoy. His desire to communicate with someone he had known in the past and who now held the highest office in the country is understandable. He was also entitled to a reply and, in view of the information the RCMP and the FBI had in their files about him, any correspondence could have been handled by an assistant to the Prime Minister.[55] Loyalty to a friend (which Pearson conveniently forgot in Ambassador Kirkwood's case), surely has its limitations.

On the American side, doubts about Pearson would not have lain fallow. Aside from Eastland, Dulles, and perhaps Eisenhower, other American political leaders must have questioned his actions. Moreover, at times, his general orientation in world affairs was perceived in Washington as anti-American. Dean Acheson must have had his suspicions aroused, certainly by the autumn of 1952. How he saw Pearson's interventions in the Korean ceasefire negotiations at the United Nations, is spelled out in his memoirs, published when Pearson was still alive. They are, therefore, circumspect, but his disillusionment, one might even argue, his hostility toward him are clearly there.[56] Acid tongued, he summed it up for Anthony Eden by calling Pearson " 'an empty glass of water.' "[57]

Keeping in mind that Secretary of State John Foster Dulles' brother Allen was Director of the CIA, it goes without saying that the information John Foster had about Pearson would have been conveyed to Allen and vice versa. How Bentley's testimony was perceived and used by the astute Allen is open to speculation. Believing Pearson to be garrulous and indiscreet, it is unlikely that he would have buried anything about him in the files. That he would have conveyed what he knew to President John F. Kennedy is more than likely. That the information was, in turn, passed on by Allen Dulles' successors in the CIA to presidents Johnson and Nixon is possible and probable. We know that Johnson and Pearson mutually disliked each other,[58] and the former, it appears, expressed that to him in the very clearest terms imaginable.[59]

If Ottawa, at times, complained about not being consulted on certain matters of high political importance, one may ask whether Washington did so because it did not have the same confidence in Lester Pearson[60] that it had had in Mackenzie King or St. Laurent. However, its suspicions might have gone far to explain its attitude toward Pearson and its reaction to the policies he pursued while he was Secretary of State for External Affairs, as well as when he was Prime Minister.

It can be suggested that certain of Washington's less altruistic political denizens may have perceived him as an ideological sympathizer and even a conscious agent of the communist apparatus, but not under its "control." Because of his high political office, he may, therefore, have been seen as an agent of influence. Nor would it be unreasonable to speculate that by the spring of 1957, at the latest, misleading information might have been passed on to him by the Americans. This would have been done deliberately, in the hope that he would convey it to Moscow. The ploy would have been to disinform the Russians about American plans and policies. Regrettably, this theory cannot be tested at present, as documentation for the period in question cannot be examined at this time.

One perceptive writer has noted that the "curious dichotomy between the public Pearson and the private man will likely never be resolved." Arnold Heeney is credited with observing that despite "his attractive public qualities, Pearson kept a large part of himself in reserve." His informality and easy manner sometimes led others to believe that "he sympathized with them more than was really the case." Though groomed for Canada's highest office he "never achieved the reputation of being a master of the political arts." It can be argued that in the "sphere of political drama, Pearson was a failure."[61] The preceding pages dealing with the Norman case would lend support to these comments about Pearson.

To follow a "cold trail" is always difficult. In a society such as Canada's whose political culture craves secrecy, it is even harder to delve into the immediate past. Tradition and custom are often a greater impediment in this respect than any Official Secrets Act which, in the Canadian setting, is more often invoked to camouflage the peccadilloes of politicians and mandarins than to protect legitimate state secrets.

This mania for secrecy is reflected in the limited documentation that was released under the Canadian Access to Information Act. Although it has made it possible to write this work, what was withheld, possibly to hide additional warts in the Norman case, is difficult to assess. That information was withheld is not open to question. Fortunately, there is the House of Commons, the functioning Canadian public forum, which could make it possible to net much of what happened.

Let us hope that among Her Majesty's 282 loyal stalwarts one can be found who will stand up in the House to ask pertinent questions. Candidly answered in a manner befitting the central role this legislative body plays in Canada's political life, the responses might help draw back a curtain that has too long remained closed. The initial three questions are simple enough:

1. Did the Government of Canada, following Egerton Herbert Norman's suicide, acquire information that showed that he had connections with the Communist Party before or during his employment by the Department of External Affairs?

2. Did the Government of Canada, following Egerton Herbert Norman's suicide, acquire information that showed that he had contributed funds to the Canadian Communist Party before or during his employment by the Department of External Affairs?

3. Did the Government of Canada acquire information that showed that Egerton Herbert Norman had been identified and discussed by Anthony Blunt as someone who, like himself, was associated with the Russian intelligence services?

In view of the accumulative information supplied by the RCMP, MI5, and the FBI, answers to these three questions should lead to additional ones, especially those regarding the manner in which Norman was security cleared. Only then will it be possible to remove forever the obfuscation surrounding the case of Egerton Herbert Norman. Only then will it be possible to examine it, as it should have been done by the House of Commons, almost thirty years ago.

Appendices

Appendix A

Internal Security Subcommittee

STENOGRAPHIC TRANSCRIPT OF HEARINGS

Subcommittee to Investigate the Administration
of the Internal Security Act and Other Internal Security Laws

OF THE

COMMITTEE ON THE JUDICIARY UNITED STATES SENATE

Washington D. C.
AUGUST 14, 1951

Volume 96
EXECUTIVE SESSION[1]—CONFIDENTIAL
ELIZABETH T. BENTLEY[2] (Clinton, Connecticut)
TUESDAY, AUGUST 14, 1951

United States Senate,

Subcommittee to Investigate the Administration of the Internal Security Act and Other Internal Security Laws of the Committee on the Judiciary,

Washington, D.C.

The subcommittee met at 4:30 p.m., pursuant to call, in room 424, Senate Office Building, Honorable Pat McCarran [Democratic Senator from Nevada] (chairman) presiding.

Present: Senators McCarran, [James O.] Eastland [Democratic Senator from Mississippi], and [Willis] Smith [Democratic Senator from North Carolina].

Also present: Senators [Joseph R.] McCarthy [Republican from Wisconsin] and [Herman] Welker [Republican from Idaho];[3] [Judge] Robert Morris, Subcommittee Counsel; and Benjamin Mandel, Director of Research.

THE CHAIRMAN: The committee will come to order.

You may proceed, Mr. Morris.

MR. MORRIS: Mr. Chairman, Miss Bentley having been sworn [in] this morning I do not believe it will be necessary to swear her in again.[4]

THE CHAIRMAN: Yes.

MR. MORRIS: Miss Bentley, while you were operating in Washington did you, Mr. Golos, or any member associated with you at that time have any particular connection with the Canadian Legation?

MISS BENTLEY: Yes, we did. Mr. Golos had always had connections with the Canadians[5] [and] with Fred Rose,[6] who is now in jail for espionage up there.

MR. MORRIS: Who was that?

MISS BENTLEY: Fred Rose.

MR. MORRIS: You had dealings with him?

MISS BENTLEY: From Sam Carr,[7] with Tim Buck, who is head of the Canadian [Communist] Party. As a result, any Canadians who came to the United States and were in a position to help us were turned over to us. As a result of this, in 1942 Mr. Hazen Size, S—i—z—e,[8] came down and was promptly turned over to us. He brought a letter signed, I think, by Fred Rose.[9]

MR. MORRIS: He was a conscious, direct agent, is that right?

MISS BENTLEY: Yes, he had quite a background of Communist activity and had fought in Spain besides.

MR. MORRIS: Would you say his Communist background was open and notorious?

MISS BENTLEY: According to him he was fairly open. I don't know how open that would be.

MR. MORRIS: But you say he fought in the Spanish War?

MISS BENTLEY: He didn't fight, but he drove a truck with the Loyalists and was almost picked up for service with the Russian Intelligence. He was to report to a contact in Paris, but due, I believe, to the Stavisky affair his Soviet contact didn't show up and therefore he returned to Canada.[10]

MR. MORRIS: It is your testimony that he was a direct agent and conscious agent and worked directly with you?

MISS BENTLEY: That is right.

MR. MORRIS: What were some of the sources of his information?

MISS BENTLEY: I would say part of his information came from the material he was getting. He was part of the Canadian [National] Film Board.[11]

MR. MORRIS: Will you tell us about that?

MISS BENTLEY: I think we had an American Film Board which made pictures for the General Staff. Therefore he had that type of material. But his most valuable material came from Mike Pearson.

MR. MORRIS: Who is Mike Pearson?

MISS BENTLEY: That is really his nickname, it's really Lester Pearson, and he was second in charge of the Canadian Legation during that period,[12] which would be from 1942 to 1943 when I lost Hazen Size.

MR. MORRIS: Was he a coun[sellor] to the Canadian Legation?

MISS BENTLEY: I don't know the precise title, but Hazen said he was the top man in the Legation. I understand from Hazen that Pearson knew Hazen was a Communist[13] and was willing to help. Pearson by virtue of his position used to sit in on American functions, particularly British ones re British policies, all of which was super hush-hush.[14]

MR. MORRIS: Then he used to give the information he obtained to Hazen Size?

MISS BENTLEY: That is correct, and he passed it on to me.

MR. MORRIS: Do you have any question now that Hazen Size was a Communist?

MISS BENTLEY: Hazen Size said [Pearson] knew that he was a Communist? (sic) Hazen Size said he knew.

MR. MORRIS: Nevertheless he was giving this information to Hazen Size?

MISS BENTLEY: That is correct.

MR. MORRIS: Hazen Size turned it over to you?

MISS BENTLEY: That is correct.

MR. MORRIS: What did you do with it?

MISS BENTLEY: That was turned over to Golos during his lifetime, and later on to his succeeding agent.

MR. MORRIS: And it went on to the Soviets?

MISS BENTLEY: That is right.

THE CHAIRMAN: I would like to ask a question. What was the nature, the manner, in which the information was conveyed to you? Was it by documents or by microfilm or how was it?

MISS BENTLEY: No, Mr. Hazen Size made notes and turned the notes over to me. Once in a while he would forget to make notes and would remember it and I would write it down, but he generally wrote notes.

MR. MORRIS: Your relations with Size were over a long duration?

MISS BENTLEY: Roughly two years. As a matter of fact, [w]e only dropped [him] because he was starting to go to a psychiatrist.[15] In espionage you don't trust a person who goes to a psychiatrist and your orders are to drop him. I immediately dropped him when he started going to a psychiatrist.

MR. MORRIS: Do you have any further questions, Mr. Chairman?

THE CHAIRMAN: No. Do any of the other Senators have questions?

MR. MORRIS: We have the testimony of Edward C. Carter taken in executive session. The date of this is June 15, 1951. Mr. Carter, in discussing the Washington chapter of the I[nstitute of] P[acific] R[elations],[16] testified as follows:

> MR. CARTER: I would guess, and this is just a guess, during the war, fairly early in the war, a great many businessmen and experts of all kinds, engineers and lawyers, were coming to Washington in connection with the war effort. A good many of them were members of the I[nstitute of] P[acific] R[elations] from Boston, San Francisco, Seattle, and so on. Also there was a very large number of Chinese, Filipinos, Canadian[s], British, and so on, in Washington, many of whom were members of the I[nstitute of] P[acific] R[elations] in their own countries. For example, Mike Pearson, present External Affairs Minister of Canada, was at the Legation here and was very active in the Canadian Institute.

That is the Canadian Institute of Pacific Relations.

> So it was a natural extension in order to serve our members from all over the world and profit by their recent contacts with China, the Philippines, and other countries.

That is page 81 of the executive session of that day, Volume 49. I would like that incorporated into this record to show, Mr. Chairman, the connection between the I[nstitute of] P[acific] R[elations] and Mike Pearson, who has been identified as Lester B. Pearson.

I think, Mr. Mandel, if you would tell us the present position of Mr. Pearson it would be helpful.

MR. MANDEL: In Who's Who for 1950-51, page 2132, Mr. Pearson is listed as Under Secretary of State for External Affairs in Canada since 1946 and as Chairman of the First Political Committee of the United Nations in April-May, 1947.

MR. MORRIS: Now, Mr. Chairman, I made the suggestion that in view of the very high position that Mr. Pearson has [as Secretary of State for External Affairs] in the Canadian Government that this be an executive session.

THE CHAIRMAN: This is an executive session, and all who are in attendance here are bound by that obligation.

MR. MORRIS: You know, Senator, we had testimony that [Egerton] Herbert Norman, who was the acting Canadian U[nited] N[ations] delegate and now acting delegate to the United Nations, was identified by Dr. Karl August Wittfogel[17] on last Tuesday as then a member of a Communist cell; it was a study group.

Now this study group met in the home of Moses Finkelstein in New York City during late 1937, and early 1938, and that was the basis of Wittfogel's knowledge. I would like to put into the record, Mr. Chairman, further activities on the part of Norman in the Institute of Pacific Relations showing that he was tied in with the Institute.

We introduced some exhibits the other day, but I think Mr. Mandel should insert the official positions at the biennial conferences.

MR. MANDEL: I read from the publication called War and Peace in the Pacific, which is headed A Preliminary Report of the Eighth Conference of the Institute of Pacific Relations on wartime and postwar cooperation of the United Nations in the Pacific and Far East, Mont Tremblant, Quebec, December 4 to 14, 1942. Page 155 of this report lists the conference membership by countries.

Under Canada is the following: Under Canadian Secretariat, E[gerton] H[erbert] Norman, Department of External Affairs, Ottawa, Canadian Legation, Tokyo, 1940 to 1942. Then I read now from Security in the Pacific, a preliminary report of the Ninth Conference of the Institute of Pacific Relations at Hot Springs, Virginia, January 6 to 17, 1945. On page 150 we find Norman, E[gerton] H[erbert], 1942 in parenthesis, which means the previous conferences attended.

Far Eastern Division, Department of External Affairs, Ottawa, Canadian Legation. Tokyo, 1940 to 1942. Author of Japan's Emergence as a Modern State and Soldier and Peasant in Japan.

Finally I read from the volume entitled Problems of Economic Reconstruction in the Far East, a report of the Tenth Conference of the Institute of Pacific Relations held at Stratford-on-Avon, England, September 5 to 20, 1947. I read from page 114 listing members of the conference.

> Canadian Legation, including E[gerton] Herbert Norman (1942-45)—
> being the previous conferences he had attended. Chief Canadian liaison
> mission in Japan. Formerly Canadian member of the Far Eastern Com-
> mission, Washington.

MR. MORRIS: The purpose of those three entries, Mr. Chairman, is to show that [Egerton] Herbert Norman had been active in the Institute of Pacific Relations acting as a conference member of three triennial conferences, the last three conferences that they had held.

THE CHAIRMAN: I would like to ask the witness, what was the nature of the information or data that you received when you made the notes?

MISS BENTLEY: Well, it was what we classified as political material, Senator, not military. It consisted of arrangements between Britain and Canada, it consisted of all the inner confidential data that the Dominion had.

THE CHAIRMAN: Did it have to do with top confidential secrets?

MISS BENTLEY: Yes, definitely.

THE CHAIRMAN: Did it have to do with her activity during the war, that is, Canada's activity during the war?

MISS BENTLEY: Some of it, yes. Some of it was plans for developments after the war, I mean as to what groups you should deal with, and so on.

THE CHAIRMAN: Did it have to do with anything pertaining to the action of Canada or Great Britain with reference to her relationship to Russia?

MISS BENTLEY: Yes, definitely.

MR. MORRIS: Could you remember, Miss Bentley, with any degree of particularity some of the reports?

MISS BENTLEY: Not offhand. I would have to sit down and try to think it out. It is rather hard suddenly to try and give what they were.

MR. MORRIS: Mr. Chairman, this is a development we encountered last night when Miss Bentley came into town and we had a short session.

THE CHAIRMAN: My questions go just to the nature of the information she received.

MR. MORRIS: Yes.

THE CHAIRMAN: It could have been some information of no importance whatever. From her answers it is indicated that it was information of [a] very highly important nature.

MR. MORRIS: And it was something that occurred many times, not once or twice?

MISS BENTLEY: Yes, it occurred many times.

THE CHAIRMAN: Now you passed information on to someone else?

MISS BENTLEY: Yes, I passed it on to whoever was my Soviet superior at that moment.

THE CHAIRMAN: From there do you know where it went?

MISS BENTLEY: Yes, I know it went to Moscow.

MR. MORRIS: Did you know a man named [John] Grierson, Miss Bentley?

MISS BENTLEY: Grierson I understand was with the [Canadian National] Film Board. He was Hazen Size's superior.

MR. MORRIS: You do not know his first name?

MISS BENTLEY: No.

THE CHAIRMAN: You were asked did you know him.

MISS BENTLEY: I can't remember offhand. Grierson was very, very close to the Party. I am not entirely sure that he wasn't a Party member, but he was extremely close.[18]

THE CHAIRMAN: The question was did you know him [?]

MISS BENTLEY: Personally?

THE CHAIRMAN: Yes, that is the question.

MISS BENTLEY: No, I knew him through Mr. Size, who told me

that Grierson's policy was to get, in quotes, "as many persons into the Party as he could."

MR. MORRIS: Was his first name John?

MISS BENTLEY: I think so.

MR. MORRIS: You say he is Size's superior?

MISS BENTLEY: I think so.

MR. MORRIS: But he was in Canada?

MISS BENTLEY: I think he was down here also. I think he came down on trips. I have to sit down and think on that because I am not sure.

THE CHAIRMAN: Is there anything further?

MR. MORRIS: I think that is all, Senator.

THE CHAIRMAN: Any questions, Senators?

MR. MORRIS: Senator, I wonder if you deem it advisable or not, that one of the people active in the Secretariat of the I[nstitute of] P[acific] R[elations] was Fred[erick] Poland, who was involved in the Canadian espionage case. Now we have the record of Fred[erick] Poland. I do not know whether it is particularly appropriate for this time. He is a Canadian. The only thing in connection with this particular thing today is that he is a Canadian, and he was involved in the Canadian espionage ring.[19]

THE CHAIRMAN: He is not known to this witness?

MR. MORRIS: No.

THE CHAIRMAN: I think we will defer that.

MR. MORRIS: That is all, Senator.

THE CHAIRMAN: When is the next meeting?

MR. MORRIS: Thursday morning at 10 a.m., Senator.

THE CHAIRMAN: Thank you, Miss Bentley. We appreciate your coming here, and we appreciate your manner of testifying, which has been clear, helpful, and we appreciate it.

MISS BENTLEY: Thank you very much.

THE CHAIRMAN: That will be all.

(Whereupon, at 5 p.m., the executive session was closed.)

Appendix B

Office Memorandum * UNITED STATES GOVERNMENT

To: Director, FBI (100-364301[-7]) Date: September 28, 1951

From: S[pecial] A[gent in] C[harge], New York

Subject: HAZEN EDWARD SISE, w[ithout] a[lias].
         ESP[IONAGE].—R[USSIAN]

Re bu[reau] let[ter], 9/20/51.

[Within these brackets material was deleted by the FBI as allowed under the United States Freedom of Information Act. The deleted material might be a reference to Bentley's testimony in executive session before the Subcommittee on Internal Security on August 14, 1951, six weeks previously.]

It should be pointed out that while they are set out in question and answer form no stenographer was present and that the answers are not a stenographic transcript [, the document reads].

1. Q—Was HAZEN SISE conscious that the info[rmation] he was supplying source (BENTLEY) was actually being delivered to the Russians?

   A—Miss BENTLEY stated that this question was not discussed between them. However, she said she cannot see how SISE could have failed to know this. Prior to the first meeting she and GOLOS had with SISE there was already in existence a Communist system wherein members of the Com[munist] Pa[rty][1] organization who were coming to the U[nited] S[tates] would bring messages from Canadian Communist leaders to GOLOS. These messages dealt with C[ommunist] P[arty] members and matters and espionage matters. The individuals bringing these messages would upon their return to Canada carry with them messages which were given to them by GOLOS. On one of these occasions a R[oyal] C[anadian] A[ir] F[orce] Officer brought a letter of introduction for HAZEN SISE to GOLOS. BENTLEY said she did not see this letter, but it was her impression that it was from FRED ROSE, who was the most frequent forwarder of letters to GOLOS. Subsequent to this delivery of the letter, the R[oyal] C[anadian] A[ir] F[orce] Officer took GOLOS and BENTLEY to the "Flat Iron" Building (at the junction of 5th Ave., Broadway and 23rd St., N[ew] Y[ork] C[ity]), where he introduced SISE to them.

BENTLEY said she had only seen this R[oyal] C[anadian] A[ir] F[orce] Officer on the one occasion and does not recall his name.[2]

Another reason BENTLEY believes SISE was aware he was working for the Russians is based upon her recollection of statements made by SISE that he had almost made contact with the Russians once before. He told her he drove a truck in Spain during the Spanish Civil War. While in Spain he was contacted by the GPU.[3] To the best of her recollection SISE was either on his way home and was told to go via Paris or was simply told to go to Paris and was given a password or recognition signal and told to meet a man at a designated place and time. SISE told her he followed these instructions and no contact was made with him at the time designated. He returned to the meeting place on the following two days and remained in Paris for about a week but was not contacted. Following his return to Canada, SISE learned from someone in Canada that the individual whom he was expected to contact in Paris had been involved in some way in the "Stavisky Affair," and it was necessary for him to flee France before the contact with SISE could be consummated.[4]

2. Q – If not what was the cover story source used at the time?

   A – There was no cover story used.

3. Q – If SISE was conscious:
   - (a) How was he recruited
   - (b) When
   - (c) By whom
   - (d) Where

   A – BENTLEY believed SISE had been a member of the C[ommunist] P[arty] in Canada and that he had been a Communist before going to Spain. She stated she based this belief on statements made by SISE to that effect.[5] It was her further belief that SISE'S contact with GOLOS and herself was the first instance in which he had been in contact with the Russians with the exception of the abortive attempt at Paris mentioned above. She again stated it was her belief that FRED ROSE had sent SISE to them, and in further explaining her reason for this belief, she said that while ROSE, SAM CARR and TIM BUCK all corresponded with GOLOS, ROSE was the most frequent correspondent and on one occasion visited GOLOS in N[ew] Y[ork]. As stated above, she actually did not see the note received by GOLOS on the occasion on which SISE was introduced to GOLOS.

4. Q – Under what circumstances was the initial contact made with source:
   - (a) Method of recognition
   - (b) Where
   - (c) When
   - (d) Upon whose instructions
   - (e) Frequency of meetings
   - (f) Methods used to arrange meetings (routine and emergent)
   - (g) Cover story for meetings (story to give if found together)
   - (h) Safety and danger signals, if any.

   A – Most of the points of this question have been covered in other questions, however, they are being specifically reiterated here.
   - (a) SISE was introduced by the unknown R[oyal] C[anadian]

A[ir] F[orce] Officer following delivery of a letter of introduction to GOLOS.

(b) This introduction took place at an entrance of the Flat Iron Building, N[ew] Y[ork] C[ity].

(c) The initial meeting with SISE, according to BENTLEY'S statements in this interview, took place in the Spring or Summer of 1942. (It will be noted that she had previously stated that she contacted SISE in Washington in the late Spring of 1943.)

(d) Probably upon FRED ROSE'S instructions.

(e) After SISE went to Washington, D.C., she met him every two weeks at first, and later met him once a month. She said she travelled to Washington about every two weeks, but as time went on and she acquired other contacts, she did not see SISE on every occasion.

(f) As to the methods used to arrange meetings with SISE, Miss BENTLEY stated she would simply call him on the telephone at his office and tell him where to meet her. She said they would frequently meet at the Mayflower Hotel in Washington and frequently dined at a French Restaurant, The L'Escargo[t], which was at that time located across the street from the Mayflower Hotel. Emergency meetings were arranged in the same manner as regular meetings. On one occasion she said she called SISE at his residence.

(g) She advised that so far as she can recall they planned no cover story.

(h) She also[6] was unable to recall any arrangements for safety and danger signals made between SISE and herself. In this regard she stated the use of such signals did not occur with any[7] great frequency in the period in which she was contacting SISE.

5. Q – What other intelligence did SISE supply source?
   (a) Types, detailed.
   (b) His sources and whether they were conscious or unconscious.
   (c) Dates.

   A – She stated SISE was a member of the Canadian [National]

Film Board and furnished her with info[rmation] obtained as a result of this employment, including info[rmation] he received from the American equivalent of the Canadian [National] Film Board. She stated that none of this info[rmation] was of any great importance to the Russians but she accepted it any way in order to make SISE feel he was accomplishing something. In addition, he supplied her with info[rmation] which he obtained from LESTER PEARSON[8] having to do with diplomatic conferences and affairs which PEARSON was party to. Miss BENTLEY states that she cannot recall details of this info[rmation].

(b) BENTLEY stated that so far as she knew the Canadian [National] Film Board and "MIKE" PEARSON[9] were the only sources which SISE had available to him on a regular basis. In addition, he sometimes picked up stray bits of gossip at the Canadian Legation. BENTLEY'S comments on whether or not PEARSON was conscious of SISE'S role in Soviet Espionage are set out below.

(c) She is unable to recall dates when she obtained info[rmation] from SISE other than meetings occurring with him between the period of Spring and Summer of 1942 (sic) and continuing until sometime in 1944.

6. Q –Had SISE been operated by anyone else? Names.

   A – BENTLEY has no knowledge of this. Reference is made to the answer of Question #3 above.

7. Q –Length of time he was operated?

   A – She stated she was in contact with SISE from the Spring of 1942 to sometime in 1944. She stated SISE during the latter part of this period was having some kind of marital difficulty[10] and mentioned to her that he planned to consult with a psychiatrist.[11] She told her Soviet Superior "BILL" (who has not been identified) about this and he told her to discontinue meeting with SISE. Later she was asked by JACK (who has been identified as JOSEPH KATZ[12] and was the successor to "BILL" as her Soviet Superior) if she knew where SISE was. Upon her reply that she did not know of his whereabouts, he told her SISE should not have been dropped but no further effort was made through her to pick SISE up again.

8. Q– Was source informed that intelligence could be expected from PEARSON through SISE?

A – SISE told BENTLEY that he could get info[rmation] from PEARSON. It is her belief based upon statements made by SISE that PEARSON had known SISE quite well in Canada. It was her further belief also based on statements by SISE, that he, SISE was well known as a Communist to his friends in Canada, and it was because of this fact that he had been able to obtain his position on the Canadian [National] Film Board through the assistance of one [John] GRIERSON, who headed this board and who, according to BENTLEY, based upon further statements by SISE, was a member of the C[ommunist] P[arty].

9. Q – If so, who informed source and how was it said?

A – She was informed of this by HAZEN SISE.

10. Q – Was SISE operated in a net or individually?

A – SISE was operated as an individual although he was contacted on the occasion of BENTLEY'S visits to Washington to contact her other sources, some of which were networks and some of which were individuals.

11. Q – If a net, identification of personalities.

A – See answer above.

12. Q – Did SISE have a cover name?

A – Not so far as BENTLEY knew.

13. Q – Did he use it?

A – No.

14. Q – Who gave him this name?

   A – See above.

15. Q – To whom did source pass the intelligence received from SISE?

   A – The info[rmation] was passed on to JACOB GOLOS during the early part of her contact with SISE. GOLOS in turn would pass it on to his Soviet Superiors. Following GOLOS' death she passed the material on to "CATHERINE" and "BILL", both of whom are unknown to date.

16. Q – Under what circumstances?

   A – Miss BENTLEY was closely associated with GOLOS and contacted him almost daily at her home and office and at his office. It was, therefore, a simple matter to turn over the material to him. After his death she turned it over to "BILL" or "CATHERINE", whom she met approximately every two weeks by pre-arrangement subsequent to her trips to Washington, D.C.

17. Q – Was it written or oral?

   A – She received info[rmation] from SISE in both oral and written form. She stated the written material was notes which he made of info[rmation] which came to his attention. She does not remember that he ever passed her info[rmation] in the form of documents obtained in the course of his business. She is unable at present to furnish any details as to the exact content of this material.

18. Q – Can source detail it?

   A – No, other than it had to do with internal policies of the British Empire and joint policies of the U[nited] S[tates] and Canada.

19. Q – Was the source aware of PEARSON's political ideology?

   A – From info[rmation] BENTLEY received from SISE she got the

impression that PEARSON was a "left-winger."[13] It is her recollection that SISE told her PEARSON was in sympathy with
the Loyalist cause in the Spanish Civil War. She is also of the
belief that the fact that PEARSON moved in the same circles
as SISE socially gave an indication that he, PEARSON, was a
"left-winger." It was also her recollection that SISE told her
that PEARSON was a friend of [John] GRIERSON, who, as is
stated above, was head of the Canadian [National] Film Board
and, according to SISE, was a Communist who was planting[14]
other Communists in the Canadian [National] Film Board.[15]

20. Q –If so, from whom did source hear it?

A – From SISE only.

21. Q –Can source recall any remarks regarding PEARSON by SISE or
others?

[A–] None, other than those mentioned in answer to question #19.

22. Q –Can source name any other Canadians who were known as
sources of intelligence. (Identification & detailed circumstances).

A – She stated that about October, 1943, FRED ROSE came to
N[ew] Y[ork] to contact GOLOS. The purpose of this visit
was to establish contact with the Russians through GOLOS
for a group of about 10 individuals who were in the Canadian
Government and one individual who was in the International
Labour Organization. It was ROSE'S desire to set this group
up as an espionage ring to siphon material through GOLOS.
GOLOS' death occurred before anything could be done about
this matter; subsequently a number of Canadian Communists
came to N[ew] Y[ork] bearing notes from ROSE to her. These
continued until about June, 1944. BENTLEY spoke to her principal, "BILL," about this matter and suggested going to Canada to contact ROSE. He advised against it because at that
time BENTLEY was handling a large group of people already.
It is her belief that some of the people who were involved
with ROSE in this matter were revealed as a result of the
disclosures of IGOR GOUZENKO.

BENTLEY, in speaking of the individuals who brought notes from Canada, stated that in most instances she did not know the names of these people and in the few instances in which she learned the names she has since forgotten them. Besides the above mentioned R[oyal] C[anadian] A[ir] F[orce] Officer whom she described as young, blond and "Jewish", these contacts were:

a Canadian "WAC",[16] small, thin build;

FRED ROSE'S "current girlfriend";

a young married couple who were visiting N[ew] Y[ork] on vacation;

a Canadian newspaperman who accompanied ROSE to N[ew] Y[ork] in October, 1943, whom she described as rather good-looking with dark complexion. It is her belief that this news-paperman travelled to Finland or Sweden subsequent to this visit to N[ew] Y[ork]. With regard to the visit of ROSE and this newspaperman, she recalled that they were taken by GO-LOS and herself to the Russian Skazka Restaurant, which was operated by an American Communist. She recalled further that they were treated with considerable deference by the restaurant owner because of the fact that ROSE was a member of the Canadian Parliament.

23. Q – Did source ever hear of Egerton Herbert Norman? If so, details.

A – No.

24. Q – Does the name [deleted], one time lawyer and officer in the Canadian Wartime Information Board, and associated with HAZEN SISE, mean anything to source?

A – No.

25. Q – Did source know of any espionage operations in Canada which have not in part or in full been publicized?

A – Not unless there were names appearing on the list which FRED ROSE had, which had not been publicized. She stated that she does not presently recall these names other than that she believes the individual who was a member of the I[nternational] L[abour] O[rganization] was [name deleted], and she believes this individual may have been publicized as a result of the revelations of GOUZENKO.

26. Q—Did it ever come to source's attention that the Russians operated from a base in the U[nited] S[tates] against Canada and vice versa?

   If so, can source offer info[rmation] on:
   (a) Methods employed
   (b) Border crossings
   (c) Agent running
   (d) Lines of communications (routine and emergency)
   (e) Courier lines (intelligence & bodies)
   (f) Cover
   (g) Documentation
   (i) Live and dead letter boxes[17]
   (j) Other personalities
   (k) Dates

   A—She has no knowledge of this other than info[rmation] she obtained with regard to the proposed setup made by FRED ROSE.

It would appear that BENTLEY'S answers to the above questions are an interpretation and an enlargement of the statements furnished by her with regard to SISE in 1945. She has stated that the info[rmation] with regard to PEARSON was overlooked by her at that time.

Appendix C

March 20, 1957

3:05 P.M.

Meeting with State Department Officers

Present: Robert Morris [Counsel of the Senate Subcommittee on Internal Security]
William Rusher [Associate Counsel of the Senate Subcommittee on Internal Security]
Rod[erick] O'Connor [Deputy Assistant Secretary of State for Congressional Relations, State Department]
Robert Cartwright [Deputy Administrator, Bureau of Security and Counselor Affairs, State Department]
Ernest Lister [Deputy Director, British, Commonwealth, and North European Affairs, State Department]

O'CONNOR: Canada has taken the view for the last six years or so that our State Department should pass on their views to the Canadian Government. Our interest here is to work out a plan for [the] State [Department] and the Subcommittee to cooperate in this. [The] State [Department] should get the first crack at this kind of testimony which is derogatory information against foreign officials of a friendly government.

MORRIS: Canada knew about our testimony concerning Norman and there has been an exchange of information.[1]

(Morris then read the secret memorandum to the group.)[2]

O'CONNOR: Our concern is not so much with the substance of this [information] but in the method in which it is handled. I feel it should be submitted to [the] State [Department] first.

MORRIS: Because a foreign national crosses the trail must we stop our investigation? What about [the Japanese national, Shigeto] Tsuru[?] We will have to ask him about it.

O'CONNOR: Let us go over the executive [session testimony] with you and then we can determine [the matter].

MORRIS: We operate on such a close margin, we can't wait for [the transcript of the subcommittee's testimony] to be presented to the Canadian Parliament and then wait for their decision. We would be out of business economically [because of the expense of bringing witnesses back or holding them over].

O'CONNOR: We do present a lot of executive session testimony from other committees.

(Morris then read Elizabeth Bentley's testimony of August 14, 1951 concerning [Lester] Pearson to the group. Bentley's testimony was executive [session testimony].)

MORRIS: What would you do with this? Release it?

O'CONNOR: I am sure that would blow us out of the water on our northern border.[3] The release of that kind of testimony would get us into a terrific jam with our Canadian friends. Before you do anything with it, give our top people a chance to talk it over with the Chairman [of the Senate Judiciary Committee which governed the Subcommittee on Internal Security].

MORRIS: The second thing. Could you check with the FBI on the truth and the accuracy of our evidence on Norman[?]

O'CONNOR: The information furnished us recently from the FBI is nothing more than you have.

MORRIS: The third thing. What do you suggest about how to protect the United States security against Norman [?] The FBI knew about [Alger] Hiss and [Klaus] Fuchs but nothing happened until it was brought out. In this case Norman and [John K.] Emmerson had what looked to us like an emergency meeting [in Beirut] and they got together. We still do not know what happened. Emmerson wants to change his testimony.[4] What do we do about it? You tell us.

O'CONNOR: Not about our guy (Norman).

MORRIS: About Norman too.

MORRIS: What will the State Department do to protest Pearson's attack on the Senate [?]

O'CONNOR: Why do you say that[?]

(Morris describes Pearson's attack.)[5]

O'CONNOR: I haven't seen his attack.

O'CONNOR: I don't know what liaison we have with security organizations of [the] Canadian Government. I don't know if there are any channels with the Canadian Government, such as FBI through the Royal [Canadian] Mounted [Police].

MORRIS: We are not interested in Canadian security. Our concern is American security.

CARTWRIGHT: We have unusually close relations over many years with Canadian officials. There is no question about that. But we do not know about this case.

(Morris points out that no Canadian official approached [Professor Karl A.] Wittfogel who gave [the] Subcommittee original information concerning Norman.)[6]

[?]: Maybe the Canadian Government doesn't tell Pearson everything.

O'CONNOR: Maybe they weigh their evidence against ours.

(Morris asked [the] staff to check [the] files for [a] letter of transmittal to [the] State Department, transmitting [the] Bentley August 14, 1951 testimony to [the] State Department.)

MORRIS: What about [Guy] Burgess and [Donald] Maclean [?] Should we clear through the British Government——? What is the standard?

MORRIS: What about [Ludwig] Racjhmann (sic)?[7]

O'CONNOR: I think what we are talking about are friendly allied governments. This is probably a test case for allied governments.

O'CONNOR: As far as the Communist countries are concerned, unload your guns and fire away. This case obviously has to go way up stairs.

O'CONNOR: Suppose we got a couple of guys in [a] foreign forei[g]n service and we made advances to their governments and said that we had evidence that they smell. Should we let them know that our officials will not deal with them?

LISTER: We cannot tell a foreign government what they should do about their representatives.

LISTER: If there is any more public reference to Norman we are at [sic] trouble with Canada.

O'CONNOR: The only answer is to have the questioning so limited [a]s just to allow [Emmerson] to make the correction about his letter [to Norman]. Is it not possible to have him correct this in some sort of staff hearing [?] Just handled by the staff and not bring in the Senators.

MORRIS: Why don't you consult the [State] Department on that [?] We will go ahead with our executive session and there won't be anything in open [session] until we discuss this with you.

CARTWRIGHT: Is there any element in the Canadian Government which would be more sympathetic?

LISTER: Pearson is a hero. Right now he is cooperating to the fullest extent with our government in defense contracts.

MORRIS: This is just what I mean. Look at the situation. There are many Americans frightened about Pearson. There are a good many Canadians in the U.N. who are pro-Communist.[8] Why, Pearson has even objected to Americans employed in the U.N. when they were called before the Subcommittee during our U.N. hearings.

O'CONNOR: Why can't we delete some of the materials from the executive session if it is published?

Adjourned: 4:10 P.M.

Abbreviations

The Amerasia Papers: A Clue to the Catastrophe of China

United States Senate, Committee on the Judiciary, *The Amerasia Papers: A Clue to the Catastrophe of China*, Prepared by the Subcommittee to Investigate the Administration of the Internal Security Act and Other Internal Security Laws, 91st Congress, 1st Session (Washington, D.C.: Government Printing Office, 1970), 2 Vols.

CIA Papers

Archives of the Central Intelligence Agency, Langley, Virginia

Committee on the Judiciary, *Internal Security Annual Report for 1957*

United States Senate, Committee on the Judiciary, *Internal Security Annual Report for 1957*, Report of the Committee of the Judiciary, made by its Subcommittee to Investigate the Administration of the Internal Security Laws, 85th Congress, 2nd Session (Washington, D.C.: Government Printing Office, 1958)

External Affairs Papers

Archives of the Department of External Affairs, Ottawa

FBI Papers

Archives of the Federal Bureau of Investigation, Washington, D.C.

Hearings, *Institute of Pacific Relations*, Part . . .

United States Senate, Committee on the Judiciary, *The Institute of Pacific Relations,* Hearings before the Subcommittee to Investigate the Administration of the Internal Security Act and Other Internal Security Laws, . . . Congress, . . . Session, Part . . . (Washington, D.C.: Government Printing Office)

Hearings, *Scope of Soviet Activity in the United States,* Part . . .

United States Senate, Committee on the Judiciary, *Scope of Soviet Activity in the United States,* Hearings before the Subcommittee to Investigate the Adminstration of the Internal Security Act and Other Internal Security Laws, . . . Congress, . . . Session, Part . . . (Washington, D.C.: Government Printing Office)

Hearings, *State Department Loyalty Investigations,* Part . . .

United States Senate, Committee on Foreign Relations, *State Department Employee Loyalty Investigations,* Hearings before a Subcommitee of the Committee on Foreign Relations . . . to Investigate whether there are Employees in the State Department Disloyal to the United States, 81st Congress, 2nd Session (Washington, D.C.: Government Printing Office, 1950)

NA

National Archives, Washington, D.C.

PAC	Public Archives of Canada, Ottawa
PRO	Public Record Office, London, England
RCMP (CSIS) Papers	Archives of the Royal Canadian Mounted Police, now in the possession of the Canadian Security Intelligence Service, Ottawa
Records of the Senate Subcommittee on Internal Security (1951-1975), RG 46, NA	Records of the United States Senate Subcommittee on Internal Security of the Senate Judiciary Committee (1951-1975), RG 46, NA
Report of the 1946 Royal Commission on Espionage in Canada	*Royal Commission to Investigate the Circumstances Surrounding the Communication, by Public Officials and Other Persons in Positions of Trust, of Secret and Confidential Information to Agents of a Foreign Power* (Ottawa: King's Printer, 1946)
Report on the Institute of Pacific Relations	United States Senate, Committee on the Judiciary, *Report of the Institute of Pacific Relations*, Report No. 2050, 82nd Congress, 2nd Session (Washington, D.C.: Government Printing Office, 1952)
Testimony of Former Russian Code Clerk Relating to the Internal Security of the United States	United States Senate, Committee on the Judiciary, *Testimony of Former Russian Code Clerk Relating to the Internal Security*

of the United States. Questioning on January 4, 1954, in Ottawa, Canada, of Igor Gouzenko, former Code Clerk in the Soviet Embassy at Ottawa, by Representatives of the Internal Security Subcommittee of the Committee on the Judiciary . . . , Document No. 5, 84th Congress, 1st Session (Washington, D.C.: Government Printing Office, 1955)

US Army Intelligence and Security Command

United States Army Intelligence and Security Command, Fort Meade, Maryland

Notes

PREFACE

[1]Henry L. Stimson and McGeorge Bundy, *On Active Service in Peace and War* (New York: Harper, 1948), p. 226.

[2]See, for example, Roberta Wohlstetter, *Pearl Harbor: Warning and Decision* (Stanford: Stanford University Press, 1962) and Gordon Prange, *At Dawn We Slept* (New York: McGraw-Hill, 1981).

CHAPTER 1

[1]Sidney Katz, "What Kind of Man *Was* Herbert Norman?", *Maclean's Magazine*, September 28, 1957, p. 92; Charles Taylor, *Six Journeys: A Canadian Pattern* (Toronto: Anansi, 1977), p. 148.

[2]Norman's scholarship, however, has not gone uncriticized. See, for example, John Whitney Hall, "E. H. Norman on Tokugawa Japan," *The Journal of Japanese Studies,* Vol. 3, No. 2 (Summer 1977), pp. 365-374, and the exegesis of Norman's seminal study *Japan's Emergence as a Modern State. Political and Economic Problems of the Meiji Period* (New York: Institute of Pacific Relations, 1940), by George Akita, "An Examination of E. H. Norman's Scholarship," *The Journal of Japanese Studies*, Vol. 3, No. 2 (Summer 1977), pp. 375-419. For the rejoinder, see Herbert P. Bix, "The Pitfalls of Scholastic Criticism: A Reply to Norman's Critics," *ibid.*, Vol. 4, No. 2 (Summer 1978), pp. 391-411. An approbatory appraisal of the corpus of Norman's scholarly work is to be found in John W. Dower's "E. H. Norman, Japan and the Uses of History," in E. Herbert Norman, *Origins of the Modern Japanese State. Selected Writings of E. H. Norman*, ed. by John W. Dower (New York: Pantheon, 1975), pp. 3-101.

[3]Roger W. Bowen (ed.), *E. H. Norman: His Life and Scholarship* (Toronto: University of Toronto Press, 1984).

[4]Taylor, p. 110.

[5]*Ibid.*, pp. 109-113.

[6]Norman's transcript records, University Archives, Thomas Fisher Rare Book Library, University of Toronto.

[7]Norman's letter quoted in Taylor, p. 113.

[8] Norman's letter quoted in Roger W. Bowen, "Cold War, McCarthyism, and Murder by Slander: E. H. Norman's Death in Perspective," in Bowen, p. 51.

[9]Taylor, p. 114.

[10]An unsigned memorandum entitled, Draft: Egerton Herbert Norman, January 29, 1968, p. 1, Norman File, RCMP (CSIS) Papers. See also Bowen, "Cold War, McCarthyism, and Murder by Slander," p. 62.

[11]Halperin's transcript records, University Archives, Thomas Fisher Rare Book Library, University of Toronto.

[12]*The Soap-Box* (Toronto), No. 1 (February 1932).

[13]*The Varsity* (University of Toronto), January 9, 1933, pp. 1, 4.

[14]Norman's letter quoted in Taylor, pp. 110, 114-115. On the Canadian government's prosecution of the leadership of the Canadian Communist Party see *The Globe and Mail* (Toronto), November 13, 1931, pp. 1, 2, and November 14, 1931, pp. 1, 3.

[15]Norman's letter quoted in Bowen, p. 25.

[16]Norman's letter quoted in Taylor, p. 115 and also Bowen, p. 25.

[17]Norman's letter quoted in Bowen, p. 25.

[18]Norman's letter quoted in Bowen, "Cold War, McCarthyism, and Murder by Slander," p. 51.

[19]Taylor, p. 115.

[20]Gary D. Kelly (compiler), *Historical Club of the University of Toronto. List of Members and Subjects for the Years 1905-1960* (Toronto: Sidney Hermant, 1964), item 216.

[21]Bowen, p. 25.

[22]Norman's letter quoted in Taylor, p. 119.

[23]E. H. Norman, "The Monk and the Devil," *Acta Victoriana*, Vol. 55, No. 7 (May-June 1931), pp. 10-14 and E. H. Norman, "All Our Yesterdays," *ibid.*, Vol. 57, No. 2 (Second Fall Term 1932), pp. 10-17. Unlike his brother Howard, Herbert remarked years later, "he had left religion behind." Henry S. Ferns, *Reading from Left to Right* (Toronto: University of Toronto Press, 1983), p. 200.

CHAPTER 2

[1]Charles Taylor, *Six Journeys: A Canadian Pattern* (Toronto: Anansi, 1977), pp. 115-116.

[2]Thomas E. B. Howarth, *Cambridge Between Two Wars* (London: Collins, 1978), p. 213; Michael Straight, *After Long Silence* (London: Collins, 1983), p. 60.

[3]Norman's letter quoted in Roger W. Bowen, "Cold War, McCarthyism, and Murder by Slander: E. H. Norman's Death In Perspective," in Roger W. Bowen (ed.), *E. H. Norman: His Life and Scholarship* (Toronto: University of Toronto Press, 1984), p. 51.

[4]Andrew Boyle, *The Fourth Man* (New York: Dial Press/James Wade, 1979), pp. 103, 108. See also Hugh Thomas, *John Strachey* (London: Eyre Methuen, 1973).

[5]Victor Kiernan to the writer, February 4, 1985.

[6]Bowen, "Cold War, McCarthyism, and Murder by Slander," p. 50.

[7]Henry S. Ferns, *Reading from Left to Right* (Toronto: University of Toronto

Press, 1983), p. 203. On Guest at Cambridge, see Bruce Page, David Leitch, and Phillip Knightley, *The Philby Conspiracy* (Garden City, New York: Doubleday, 1968), pp. 41-50, Boyle, pp. 63-64, 66, 69, 95, 154, Howarth, pp. 158, 209, 212 and Carmel Haden Guest (ed.), *David Guest. A Scientist Fights for Freedom (1911-1938)* (London: Lawrence and Wishart, 1939), *passim*. On Guest's death in Spain see, Hugh Thomas, *The Spanish Civil War* (New York: Harper and Row, 1961), pp. 547-548.

[8]Michael Straight to the writer, April 17, 1985.

[9]Norman's letter quoted in Bowen, "Cold War, McCarthyism, and Murder by Slander," p. 52 and Taylor, pp. 116-118. See also Peter Stansky and William Abrahams, *Journey to the Frontier: Two Roads to the Spanish Civil War* (Boston: Little, Brown, 1966), pp. 131-413.

[10]John Cornford, *John Cornford. A Memoir*, ed. by Pat Sloan (London: Jonathan Cape, 1938), p. 124; Stansky and Abrahams, p. 246; Howarth, p. 213. See also Cornford's comment about how to handle the bourgeoisie. Straight, p. 67.

[11]Stansky and Abrahams, pp. 387-390. See also Thomas, *The Spanish Civil War*, pp. 346-348.

[12]Norman's letter quoted in Bowen, "Cold War, McCarthyism, and Murder by Slander," p. 52 and Taylor, pp. 118-119.

[13]Chapman Pincher, *Their Trade is Treachery* (London: Sidgwick & Jackson, 1981), pp. 127, 131.

[14]Boyle, pp. 100-101; Neal Wood, *Communism and British Intellectuals* (London: Gollancz, 1959), pp. 221-223.

[15]James Klugmann, *History of the Communist Party of Great Britain* (London: Lawrence and Wishart, 1968-1969), 2 Vols.

[16]Tom Driberg, *Guy Burgess: A Portrait with Background* (London: Weidenfeld and Nicolson, 1956), p. 18; Pincher, *Their Trade is Treachery*, pp. 127, 130-131, 136.

[17]Straight, pp. 59-61.

[18]Victor Kiernan to the writer, October 20, 1984.

[19]Chapman Pincher, *Too Secret Too Long* (London: Sidgwick & Jackson, 1984), p. 614 fn. 20.

[20]See Richard Allen (ed.), *The Social Gospel in Canada: Papers of the Interdisciplinary Conference on the Social Gospel in Canada, March 21-24 1973, at the University of Regina* (Ottawa: National Museums of Canada, 1975).

[21]Cyril Powles, "E. H. Norman and Japan," in Bowen, p. 22.

[22] Taylor, pp. 109-111.

[23]Powles, "E. H. Norman and Japan," p. 21.

[24]Taylor, p. 110.

[25][Philip J. Jaffe], A typescript about E. Herbert Norman, p. 3, Jaffe material, Mark Gayn Papers, Thomas Fisher Rare Book Library, University of Toronto. See also Abbott to Hoover, May 15, 1957, Referrals File 100-346993-163, FBI Papers and Morris to the File, April 30, 1957, Norman File, Records of the Senate Subcommittee on Internal Security (1951-1975), RG 46, NA.

[26]See the epic Byzantine poem *Digenes Akrites*, edited with an introduction,

translation and commentary by John Mavrogordato (Oxford: The Clarendon Press, 1956).

[27]Powles, "E. H. Norman's Japan," p. 20. See also Ferns, p. 205.

[28]An unsigned and untitled memorandum, April 24, 1957, Norman File, Records of the Senate Subcommittee on Internal Security (1951-1975), RG 46, NA. See also Chapman Pincher, *Too Secret Too Long*, pp. 387, 417.

[29]An unsigned memorandum entitled Draft: Egerton Herbert Norman, p. 8, January 1, 1968, Norman File, RCMP (CSIS) Papers.

[30]Edwin Eagle to the writer, September 3, 1985.

[31]Norman's letter quoted in Bowen, p. 26.

[32]*Ibid.*, p. 26.

[33]Taylor, p. 117.

[34]Victor Kiernan, "Herbert Norman's Cambridge," in Bowen, p. 41; Victor Kiernan to the writer, February 4, 1985.

[35]Victor Kiernan, "Herbert Norman's Cambridge," pp. 40-41.

[36]Taylor, p. 116.

[37]Kiernan, "Herbert Norman's Cambridge," p. 41.

[38]Victor Kiernan to the writer, November 9, 1984.

[39]Kiernan, "Herbert Norman's Cambridge," p. 44 fn. 9; Victor Kiernan to the writer, October 20, 1984.

[40]Christopher Andrew, "F. H. Hinsley and the Cambridge moles," in Richard Langhorne (ed.), *Diplomacy and Intelligence during the Second World War; Essays in Honour of F. H. Hinsley* (Cambridge: Cambridge University Press, 1985), p. 27.

[41]Ferns, p. 203. On the incident at the Cambridge War Memorial see Page, Leitch, and Knightley, p. 48, Boyle, pp. 107-108, Howarth, p. 214, and Cornford, pp. 102-104.

[42]Howarth, *passim*; Thomas Howarth to the writer, November 21, 1984; Boyle, *passim*.

[43]Kiernan, "Herbert Norman's Cambridge," pp. 44-45 fn. 9 and Ferns, p. 206. On Kitson Clark's conservative orientation see Howarth, pp. 199, 224, and Ferns, pp. 73-74.

[44]Norman's letter quoted in Taylor, pp. 112, 114.

[45]Kiernan, "Herbert Norman's Cambridge," pp. 44-45 fn. 8.

CHAPTER 3

[1]Guernsey to Glazebrook, January 4, 1952, Glazebrook to Heeney, February 28, 1952, and [Heakes] to Martin, March 30, 1957, Norman File, External Affairs Papers; an unsigned, undated memorandum entitled E. H. Norman: Security Clearance, p. 18, and an unsigned, undated memorandum entitled Egerton Herbert Norman, Brief of Information and Investigation, p. 2, Norman File, RCMP (CSIS) Papers; Lord Tweedsmuir to the writer, October 26, 1985.

[2]Henry S. Ferns, *Reading from Left to Right* (Toronto: University of Toronto Press, 1983), p. 207; two letters from Geoffrey Andrew to the writer,

March 11, 1985 and from Elizabeth MacDermot to the writer, March 16, 1985.

³Abbott to Hoover, May 15, 1957, Referrals File 100-346993-163, FBI Papers.

⁴Morris to the File, April 30, 1957, Norman File, Records of the Senate Subcommittee on Internal Security (1951-1975), RG 46, NA.

⁵Philip J. Jaffe, *The Amerasia Case from 1945 to the Present* (New York, 1979), pp. 1-13.

⁶Abbott to Hoover, May 15, 1957, Referrals File 100-346993-163, FBI Papers and Morris to the File, April 30, 1957, Norman File, Records of the Senate Subcommittee on Internal Security (1951-1975), RG 46, NA.

⁷Jaffe, *The Amerasia Case*, pp. 1-13. See also Howard L. Boorman and Richard C. Howard (eds.), *Biographical Dictionary of Republican China* (New York: Columbia University Press, 1967), I, pp. 293-296; Donald W. Klein and Anne B. Clark (eds.), *Biographic Dictionary of Chinese Communism 1921-1965* (Cambridge: Harvard University Press, 1971), I, pp. 160-163, Philip J. Jaffe, *The Rise and Fall of American Communism* (New York: Horizon Press, 1975), pp. 12, 56, and Arthur N. Young, *China and the Helping Hand 1937-1945* (Cambridge: Harvard University Press, 1963), pp. 187-188.

⁸Abbott to Hoover, May 15, 1957, Referrals File 100-346993-163, FBI Papers and Morris to the File, April 30, 1957, Norman File, Records of the Senate Subcommittee on Internal Security (1951-1975), RG 46, NA.

⁹*Ibid.*

¹⁰[Philip J. Jaffe], A typescript about E. Herbert Norman, p. 2, Jaffe material, Mark Gayn Papers, Thomas Fisher Rare Book Library, University of Toronto and an unsigned, untitled memorandum, April 24, 1957, Norman File, Records of the Senate Subcommittee on Internal Security (1951-1975), RG 46, NA.

¹¹Abbott to Hoover, May 15, 1957, Referrals File 100-346993-163, FBI Papers and Morris to the File, April 30, 1957, Norman File, Records of the Senate Subcommittee on Internal Security (1951-1975), RG 46, NA.

¹²Holmes to Heeney, July 3, 1950, Folder 10 (Correspondence July-December 1950), Box 1, George Ignatieff Papers, Archives, Trinity College, University of Toronto.

¹³Hearings, *Institute of Pacific Relations*, Part 10 (March 4, 5, 6, 7, 10, 14, and 21, 1952), pp. 3470-3472.

¹⁴Ivan Avakumovic, *The Communist Party in Canada* (Toronto: McClelland and Stewart, 1975), p. 128. MacLeod was high up in the Communist Party, editor of its mouthpiece the *Canadian Tribune* and close to the party's guiding light Tim Buck. See Tim Buck, *Yours in the Struggle: The Reminiscences of Tim Buck* (Toronto: NC Press, 1977), pp. 277-278, 302-307, 310, 322-323.

¹⁵Hearings, *Institute of Pacific Relations*, Part 10 (March 4, 5, 6, 7, 10, 14, and 21, 1952), pp. 3470-3472. See also Jaffe, *The Amerasia Case*, p. 4 and Boorman and Howard, p. 294.

¹⁶*The Washington Post and Times Herald*, April 19, 1957, p. All.

¹⁷Patrick Walsh to the writer, November 5, 1984. See also William Rusher,

Special Counsel (New Rochelle, New York: Arlington House, 1968), p. 230. The account of Walsh's subsequent activities for the RCMP as a paid informant must be approached with care. See John Baker White, *Pattern for Conquest* (London: Hale, 1956), pp. 126-130. On Leopold, see Alan Phillips, *The Living Legend* (London: Cassell, 1957), pp. 63-67, 75-76.

18[Philip J. Jaffe], A typescript about E. Herbert Norman, p. 9, Jaffe material, Mark Gayn Papers, Thomas Fisher Rare Book Library, University of Toronto.

19John Sawatsky, *For Services Rendered: Leslie James Bennett and the RCMP Security Services* (Toronto: Doubleday, 1982), p. 256.

20Charles Taylor, *Six Journeys: A Canadian Pattern* (Toronto: Anansi, 1977), p. 119.

21*Ibid.*, pp. 118-119. On Norman's stipend, see Rockefeller Archive Center, Pocantico Hills, North Tarrytown, New York. On Stalin's machinations in Spain during the civil war, see the consummate study by Burnett Bolleten, *The Spanish Revolution. The Left and the Struggle for Power during the Civil War* (Chapel Hill: University of North Carolina Press, 1979), *passim.*

22Ferns, p. 214.

23Interview with Robert Bryce, *The Toronto Star*, April 5, 1981, p. B12.

24Hearings, *Scope of Soviet Activity in the United States*, Part 57 (March 26, 27, and April 4, 1957), pp. 3739-3744.

25See for example S[pecial] A[gent in] C[harge] (Boston) to the Director, FBI, January 4, 1951, File 100-346993-25, FBI Papers.

26On Norman's courses at Columbia University, see Rockefeller Archives Center, Pocantico Hills, North Tarrytown, New York.

27Hearings, *Institute of Pacific Relations*, Part 1 (July 25, 26, 31, August 2, and 7, 1951), pp. 312, 318-320.

28*Ibid.*, Part 2 (August 9, 14, 16, 20, 22, and 23, 1951), pp. 482-484.

29*Ibid.*, Part 12 (March 28, 29, 31, and April 1, 1952), pp. 4152-4153.

30*Ibid.*, Part 11 (March 10, 12, 13, 19, 21, 25, and 27, 1952), pp. 3962-3963.

31*Ibid.*, Part 12 (March 28, 29, 31 and April 1, 1952), p. 4154; Moses Finley [Finkelstein] to the writer, March 5, 1985.

32Moses Finley [Finkelstein] to the writer, March 31, 1985.

33Hearings, *Institute of Pacific Relations*, Part 1 (July 25, 26, 31, August 2, and 7, 1951), pp. 318-319.

34Committee on the Judiciary, *Internal Security Annual Report for 1957*, p. 106 fn.

35Italics added. Norman to Glazebrook, August 13, 1951, Vol. 10, Pearson Papers, MG 26, N1, PAC.

36G. L. Ulmen, *The Science of Society: Toward an Understanding of the Life and Work of Karl August Wittfogel* (The Hague: Mouton, 1978), pp. 172, 175.

37Andrew Boyle, *The Fourth Man* (New York: Dial Press/James Wade, 1979), pp. 37, 63.

38Ulmen, pp. 176, 209, 218, 221.

39Ulmen, pp. 327-328 and Wittfogel to Mandel, August 22, 1951, Norman

File, Records of the Senate Subcommittee on Internal Security (1951-1975), RG 46, NA. See also Committee on the Judiciary, *Internal Security Annual Report for 1957*, p. 106 fn.

[40]Boorman and Howard, pp. 294-295; Ulmen, pp. 105, 176-179, 203-205, 218, 224, 286, 372. See also Chi Ch'ao-ting's comments about Wittfogel in his Columbia University doctoral dissertation, *Key Economic Areas in Chinese History* (London: Allen & Unwin, 1936), pp. xvi, 11, fn. 18, 28.

[41]Committee on the Judiciary, *Internal Security Annual Report for 1957*, p. 106 fn.

[42]*The Globe and Mail* (Toronto), August 17, 1951, p. 2.

[43]Ulmen, p. 329.

[44]*The Gazette* (Montreal), April 15, 1957, p. 8.

[45]A minute by Sir Robert Scott, entitled United States Congressional Accusations, August 16, 1951, FO/371/91165, PRO.

[46]*The Globe and Mail* (Toronto), August 10, 1951, pp. 1-2.

[47]Committee on the Judiciary, *Internal Security Annual Report for 1957*, p. 102; Hearings, *Scope of Soviet Activity in the United States*, Part 56 (March 12 and 21, 1957), p. 3675.

[48]Memorandum for Mr. Pearson, August 11, 1951, Vol. 10, Pearson Papers, MG 26, N1, PAC.

[49] Committee on the Judiciary, *Internal Security Annual Report for 1957*, p. 106 fn.

[50]Roger W. Bowen, "Cold War, McCarthyism, and Murder by Slander: E. H. Norman's Death in Perspective," in Roger W. Bowen, *E. H. Norman: His Life and Scholarship* (Toronto: University of Toronto Press, 1984), p. 62.

[51]Taylor, p. 120.

[52]Holmes to Heeney, July 3, 1950, Folder 10 (Correspondence July-December 1950), Box 1, George Ignatieff Papers, Archives, Trinity College, University of Toronto.

[53]C. B. F[ahs], Reception celebrating Indonesian Independence Day, August 17, 1951, Norman File, Records of the Senate Subcommittee on Internal Security (1951-1975), RG 46, NA.

[54]*Report on the Institute of Pacific Relations*, pp. 224-225. On the Russian officers see the testimony of Alexander Barmine, Igor Bogolepov, and Ismail Akhmedoff. Hearings, *Institute of Pacific Relations*, Part 1 (July 25, 26, 31, August 2, and 7, 1951), Part 13·(April 2-June 20, 1952), and United States Senate, Committee on the Judiciary, *Interlocking Subversion in Government Departments*, Hearing before the Subcommittee to Investigate the Administration of the Internal Security Act and Other Internal Security Laws, 83rd Congress, 1st Session, Part 15 (October 28-December 2, 1953) (Washington, D.C.: Government Printing Office, 1953).

[55]Italics in the original. Watson (Washington) to Garvey, January 14, 1953, FO/371/103562, PRO. See also John N. Thomas, *The Institute of Pacific Relations: Asian Scholars and American Politics* (Seattle: University of Washington Press, 1974).

[56]Jaffe, *The Amerasia Case*, pp. 1-13; Frederick Vanderbilt Field, *From*

Right to Left: An Autobiography (Westport: Lawrence Hill, 1983), pp. 127-129, 168-169; Thomas, *The Institute of Pacific Relations*, pp. 23-24, 28; Boorman and Howard, p. 295.

⁵⁷*Report on the Institute of Pacific Relations*, p. 224. On the Russian officers see the sworn testimony of Alexander Barmine and Igor Bogolepov, Hearings, *Institute of Pacific Relations*, Part 1 (July 25, 26, 31, August 2, and 7, 1951), and Part 13 (April 2-June 20, 1952).

⁵⁸Watson (Washington) to Garvey, January 14, 1953, FO/371/103562, PRO. See also Holmes to Heeney, July 3, 1950, Folder 10 (Correspondence July-December 1950), Box 1, George Ignatieff Papers, Archives, Trinity College, University of Toronto. On Lattimore's editorship of *Pacific Affairs*, see Thomas, *The Institute of Pacific Relations*, pp. 15-22, and on Norman's contributions to *Pacific Affairs*, see Bowen, "Cold War, McCarthyism, and Murder by Slander," p. 62.

⁵⁹Jaffe, *The Amerasia Case*, pp. 14-38, 47-52; Thomas, *The Institute of Pacific Relations*, pp. 49-51. See also *The Amerasia Papers: A Clue to the Catastrophe of China*, 2 Vols.

⁶⁰[Philip J. Jaffe], A typescript about E. Herbert Norman, p. 9, Jaffe material, Mark Gayn Papers, Thomas Fisher Rare Book Library, University of Toronto; Bowen, "Cold War, McCarthyism, and Murder by Slander," p. 52.

⁶¹Abbott to Hoover, May 15, 1957, Referrals File 100-346993-163, FBI Papers and Morris to the File, April 30, 1957, Norman File, Records of the Senate Subcommittee on Internal Security (1951-1975), RG 46, NA.

⁶²Ian M. Drummond, *Political Economy at the University of Toronto: A History of the Department, 1888-1982* (Toronto: Faculty of Arts and Sciences, University of Toronto, 1983), p. 168.

⁶³Klein and Clark, p. 161.

⁶⁴On Coe's activities, see United States Senate, Committee on the Judiciary, *Morgenthau Diary (China)*, Prepared by the Subcommittee to Investigate the Administration of the Internal Security Act and Other Internal Security Laws, 89th Congress, 1st Session (Washington, D.C.: Government Printing Office, 1965), 2 Vols.; John Morton Blum, *From the Morgenthau Diaries 1941-1945* (Boston: Houghton Mifflin, 1967), *passim*; John Keith Horsefield (ed.), *The International Monetary Fund, 1945-65* (Washington, D.C.: The International Monetary Fund, 1969), I, p. 339; Rusher, pp. 83, 91, 93-99, 103; Young, pp. 233, 326, 329, 353; *New York Times,* December 4, 1952, pp. 1, 20, May 16, 1956, p. 17, and February 21, 1959, p. 4. On White's activities, see Whittaker Chambers, *Witness* (New York: Random House, 1952), *passim*; Elizabeth Bentley, *Out of Bondage* (New York: Devin-Adair, 1951), pp. 135-136, 142-143, 198 and James Barros, "Alger Hiss and Harry Dexter White: The Canadian Connection," *Orbis*, Vol. 21, No. 3 (Fall 1977), pp. 593-605.

⁶⁵"The Reminiscences of K'ung Hsiang-hsi," (typescript), p. 132, Oral History Collection, Columbia University, New York.

⁶⁶Rockefeller Archive Center, Pocantico Hills, North Tarrytown, New York.

⁶⁷Norman to Skelton, August 10, 1935, Skelton to Norman, October 11, 1935, Norman to Skelton, October 1, 1936, Norman to Keenleyside, October 8, 1936, Keenleyside to Norman, October 13, 1936, Skelton to Norman, March 12, 1938, Norman to Skelton, March 17, 1938, Norman to Skelton, [mid-June 1938], Skelton to Bruce, June 18, 1938, Norman to Skelton, October 8, 1938, Norman to Skelton, June 27, 1938, Skelton to Blair, July 11, 1939, and Blair to Skelton, July 20, 1939, File 80-L, Volume 1562, RG 25, G1, PAC.

⁶⁸Taylor, p. 123.

⁶⁹[Philip J. Jaffe], A typescript about E. Herbert Norman, p. 9. Jaffe material, Mark Gayn Papers, Thomas Fisher Rare Book Library, University of Toronto.

⁷⁰George Ignatieff, *The Making of a Peacemonger: The Memoirs of George Ignatieff* (Toronto: University of Toronto Press, 1985), p. 119.

⁷¹Ferns, p. 207.

⁷²Summary of Information on Edgerton [sic] Herbert Norman, April 11, 1951, CIA Papers. See also Hearings, *Scope of Soviet Activity in the United States*, Part 56 (March 12 and 21, 1957), p. 3660 and Rusher, p. 196.

⁷³General Headquarters, Far East Command, Military Intelligence Section, General Staff, to the Assistant Chief of Staff, Washington, November 30, 1950, US Army Intelligence and Security Command.

⁷⁴Ferns, p. 207.

⁷⁵Taylor, p. 123.

⁷⁶*Commission of Inquiry Concerning Certain Activities of the Royal Canadian Mounted Police* (Ottawa: Minister of Supply and Services, 1981), Vol. 1 (Second Report—Freedom and Security under the Law), p. 61, and John Sawatsky, *Gouzenko: The Untold Story* (Toronto: Macmillan, 1984), p. 283. See also Reginald Whitaker, "Origins of the Canadian Government's Internal Security System, 1946-1952," *Canadian Historical Review*, Vol. 65, No. 2 (June 1984), pp. 154-183.

⁷⁷Robert Cecil, "The Cambridge Comintern," in Christopher M. Andrew and David Dilks (eds.), *The Missing Dimension: Governments and Intelligence Communities in the Twentieth Century* (London: Macmillan, 1984), pp. 181-182. See also Boyle, pp. 114, 167-168, 188-189, 220.

⁷⁸Ferns, p. 176. On Skelton see Norman Hillmer, "The Anglo-Canadian Neurosis: The Case of O. D. Skelton," in Peter Lyon (ed.), *Britain and Canada: Survey of a Changing Relationship* (London: Cass, 1976), pp. 61-84.

⁷⁹Buck, p. 337.

⁸⁰Civil Service Examination Papers in 1936 for Third Secretary, Department of External Affairs, File 1 (Correspondence 1935-1945), Box 1, George Ignatieff Papers, Archives, Trinity College, University of Toronto.

⁸¹Sawatsky, *For Services Rendered*, pp. 254-255.

CHAPTER 4

¹Henry S. Ferns, *Reading From Left to Right* (Toronto: University of Toronto Press, 1983), pp. 218-219. See also Charles Taylor, *Six Journeys: A Canadian Pattern* (Toronto: Anansi, 1977), p. 124.

²That it was an "intrusion," see Roger W. Bowen, "Cold War, McCarthyism, and Murder by Slander: E. H. Norman's Death in Perspective," in Roger W. Bowen, *E. H. Norman: His Life and Scholarship* (Toronto: University of Toronto Press, 1984), p. 54.

³New York report on an interview with Norman, September 5, 1942, File 100-346993-X, FBI Papers.

⁴Lester B. Pearson, *Mike: The Memoirs of the Right Honourable Lester B. Pearson* (Toronto: University of Toronto Press, 1972), I, p. 195.

⁵Ferns, p. 219. See also Taylor, p. 125.

⁶Hearings, *Scope of Soviet Activity in the United States*, Part 57 (March 26, 27, and April 4, 1957), p. 3744.

⁷A report by FBI Boston, October 16, 1946, File 100-346993-2, FBI Papers.

⁸Ferns, pp. 219-220. For the itinerary, see Stevie Cameron, "Forming Canada's Intelligence Service Wasn't Easy," *The Citizen* (Ottawa), March 15, 1986, p. B5.

⁹Bowen, "Cold War, McCarthyism, and Murder by Slander," p. 55.

¹⁰A report by FBI Boston, October 16, 1946, File 100-346993-2, FBI Papers. See also an untitled and undated memorandum about Norman, p. 3, File 100-346993-29, and Ladd to the Director, October 19, 1950, p. 2, File 100-346993-9, FBI Papers. Apparently among Tsuru's books was a "complete record of the Nye munitions investigations largely prepared by Alger Hiss." Hearing, *Scope of Soviet Activity in the United States*, Part 56 (March 12 and 21, 1957), p. 3660.

¹¹Hearings, *Scope of Soviet Activity in the United States*, Part 57 (March 26, 27, and April 4, 1957), p. 3744.

¹²Remer to Langer, July 21 and October 9, 1942, Langer to Donovan, October 12, 1942, Pearson to Donovan, November 4, 1942, and a memorandum by Donovan, November 5, 1942, CIA Papers. On Remer's relationship with the Institute of Pacific Relations, see Hearings, *The Institute of Pacific Relations*, Part 1 (July 25, 26, 31, August 2 and 7, 1951), pp. 147, 161; Part 2 (August 9, 14, 16, 20, 22, and 23, 1951), pp. 393, 443, 445, 476; Part 6 (January 24, 25, 26, and 30, 1952), p. 1802; Part 8 (January 29, February 6, 8, 11, 12, 14, 15, 18, 19, 20, and 21, 1952), pp. 2809, 2810, 2832; Part 10 (March 4, 5, 6, 7, 10, 14, and 21, 1952), pp. 3280-3281, 3310-3311 and Part 14 (May 2, June 20, 1952), pp. 5226, 5254, 5259.

¹³Peter St. John, "Canada's Accession to the Allied Intelligence Community 1940-45," *Conflict Quarterly*, Vol. 4, No. 4 (Fall 1984), pp. 13-14. See also Bowen, "Cold War, McCarthyism, and Murder by Slander," p. 30 fn. 27, and Ferns, p. 204.

¹⁴[Philip J. Jaffe], A typescript about E. Herbert Norman, p. 9, Jaffe material, Mark Gayn Papers, Thomas Fisher Rare Book Library, University of Toronto.

¹⁵Abbott to Hoover, May 15, 1957, Referrals File 100-346993-163, FBI Papers and Morris to the File, April 30, 1957, Norman File, Records of the Senate Subcommittee on Internal Security (1951-1975), RG 46, NA.

¹⁶[Philip J. Jaffe], A typescript about E. Herbert Norman, p. 10, Jaffe material, Mark Gayn Papers, Thomas Fisher Rare Book Library, University of Toronto.

[17]An unsigned, untitled memorandum, April 24, 1957, Norman File, Records of the Senate Subcommittee on Internal Security (1951-1975), RG 46, NA.

[18]Abbott to Hoover, May 15, 1957, Referrals File 100-346993-163, FBI Papers and Morris to the File, April 30, 1957, Norman File, Records of the Senate Subcommittee on Internal Security (1951-1975), RG 46, NA. See also Elizabeth Bentley, *Out of Bondage* (New York: Devin-Adair, 1951), p. 203.

[19][Philip J. Jaffe], A typescript about E. Herbert Norman, p. 9, Jaffe material, Mark Gayn Papers, Thomas Fisher Rare Book Library, University of Toronto.

[20]*Ibid.*, pp. 10-11.

[21]Ferns, pp. 165-172, 213.

[22]Victor Kiernan to the writer, November 9, 1984.

[23]*The Gazette* (Montreal), April 18, 1957, p. 8. See also Taylor, p. 138.

[24][Philip J. Jaffe], A typescript about E. Herbert Norman, p. 11, Jaffe material, Mark Gayn Papers, Thomas Fisher Rare Book Library, University of Toronto.

[25]Pearson, I, pp. 132-134.

[26]*Ibid.*, III, p. 168.

[27]Ferns, pp. 165-172, 178, 197-212. On the Japanese academic Kei Shibata, see *Kodansha's Dictionary of Economics* [in Japanese] (Tokyo: Kodansha, 1980), p. 524.

[28]Bowen, "Cold War, McCarthyism, and Murder by Slander," p. 55. See also Taylor, p. 126.

[29]Bowen, "Cold War, McCarthyism, and Murder by Slander," p. 55, and Taylor, p. 126. On Norman's date of recruitment, see Roundtree to Willoughby (G-2 GHQ Inter-Office Memorandum), November 30, 1950, US Army Intelligence and Security Command.

[30]Taylor, p. 126. See also Bowen, "Cold War, McCarthyism, and Murder by Slander," pp. 55-56.

[31]Bowen, "Cold War, McCarthyism, and Murder by Slander," p. 53.

[32]Thorpe to Mackenzie King, January 31, 1946, Norman File, External Affairs Papers.

[33]Roundtree to Willoughby (G-2 GHQ Inter-Office Memorandum), November 30, 1950, US Army Intelligence and Security Command.

[34]Charles A. Willoughby, *Shanghai Conspiracy. The Sorge Spy Ring* (New York: Dutton, 1952), p. 16. See also Willoughby's interview with Harold Greer which Willoughby never publicly disavowed. *Toronto Daily Star*, May 3, 1957, p. 1.

[35]*Toronto Daily Star*, May 3, 1957, p. 1.

[36]Agent Report by Lee M. Martin, CIC, Re: Egerton Herbert Norman, June 3, 1957, US Army Intelligence and Security Command.

[37]*Ibid.*

[38]On Isaacs' prior communism, see *The Amerasia Papers: A Clue to the Catastrophe of China*, I, p. 38 and II, p. 1760.

[39]John K. Emmerson, *The Japanese Thread* (New York: Holt, Rinehart,

and Winston, 1978), pp. 256-261; Hearings, *Institute of Pacific Relations*, Part 3 (September 14, 18, 19, 20, 25, 1951), pp. 748-750; Hearings, *Scope of Soviet Activity in the United States*, Part 56 (March 12 and 21, 1957), pp. 3670-3672; Glazebrook to the Commissioner of the RCMP, September 21, 1951, Norman File, RCMP (CSIS) Papers.

[40]Agent Report by Lee M. Martin, CIC, Re: Egerton Herbert Norman, June 3, 1957, US Army Intelligence and Security Command.

[41]Sanzo Nosaka to the writer, November 7, 1984. See also Willoughby, p. 16.

[42]General Headquarters, Far East Command, Military Intelligence Section, General Staff, to the Assistant Chief of Staff, G-2, Washington, D. C., November 30, 1950, US Army Intelligence and Security Command, and John Stewart Service to the writer, April 28, 1985. On John Stewart Service's involvement in the Amerasia case, see his *The Amerasia Papers: Some Problems in the History of US-China Relations* (Berkeley: Center for Chinese Studies, University of California, 1971).

[43]Agent report by Lee M. Martin, CIC, Re: Egerton Herbert Norman, June 3, 1957, US Army Intelligence and Security Command.

[44]General Headquarters, Far East Command, Military Intelligence Section, General Staff, to the Assistant Chief of Staff, G-2, Washington, D.C., November 30, 1959, US Army Intelligence and Security Command.

[45]Willoughby, p. 16.

[46]Hearings, *Scope of Soviet Activity in the United States*, Part 57 (March 26, 27, and April 4, 1957), p. 3743.

[47]Hearings, *Institute of Pacific Relations*, Part 10 (March 4, 5, 6, 7, 10, 14, and 21, 1952), pp. 3473, 3547.

[48]Hearings, *Scope of Soviet Activity in the United States*, Part 56 (March 12 and 21, 1957), p. 3658.

[49]Hearings, *Institute of Pacific Relations*, Part 10 (March 4, 5, 6, 7, 10, 14, and 21, 1952), p. 3568.

[50]Laughlin to Ladd, August 23, 1951, Referrals File 100-346993-29, FBI Papers.

[51]Summary of Information on Edgerton [sic] Herbert Norman, April 11, 1951, CIA Papers.

[52]*The Amerasia Papers: A Clue to the Catastrophe of China*, II, p. 1714.

[53]Bowen, "Cold War, McCarthyism, and Murder by Slander," p. 62.

[54]General Headquarters, Far East Command, Military Intelligence Section, General Staff, to the Assistant Chief of Staff, G-2, Washington, D.C., November 30, 1950, US Army Intelligence and Security Command.

[55]Willoughby to Lacey (G-2 Inter-Office Memorandum), December 10, 1950, US Army Intelligence and Security Command.

[56]Summary of Information on Edgerton [sic] Herbert Norman, April 11, 1951, CIA Papers. On Norman's comments at the January 1945 conference, see *The Amerasia Papers: A Clue to the Catastrophe of China*, II, pp. 1272-1302.

[57]Roger W. Bowen, "Irony or Tragedy." in Bowen, p. 196.

[58]Taylor, pp. 129-130, 134.

[59]Pearson, II, pp. 145-147.

[60]Norman to Pearson, February 8, 1950, Vol. 10, Pearson Papers, MG 26, N1, PAC. See also Taylor, pp. 135-136.

[61]Hearings, *Scope of Soviet Activity in the United States*, Part 56 (March 12 and 21, 1957), p. 3660; also a six-page untitled, undated, and unsigned memorandum dealing with Egerton Herbert Norman, US Army Intelligence and Security Command.

[62]Heeney to Norman, February 22, 1950. Vol. 10, Pearson Papers, MG 26, N1, PAC.

[63]R. Barry Farrell, *The Making of Canadian Foreign Policy* (Scarborough: Prentice-Hall, 1969), p. 54.

[64]Glazebrook to Ignatieff, December 4, 1950, Folder 10 (Correspondence July-December 1950), Box 1, George Ignatieff Papers, Archives, Trinity College, University of Toronto.

CHAPTER 5

[1]An unsigned and undated memorandum entitled The Norman Case: Some Factors and Considerations, p. 1, Norman File, RCMP (CSIS) Papers.

[2]Report of the 1946 Royal Commission on Espionage in Canada, pp. 63-64, 71, 85, 124-125, 133, 135, 137-145, 707, 729, 731.

[3]*Ibid.*, p. 707.

[4]*The Gouzenko Transcripts: The Evidence Presented to the Kellock-Taschereau Royal Commission of 1946*, ed. by Robert Bothwell and J. L. Granatstein (Ottawa: Deneau, 1982), pp. 312-321.

[5]*The Globe and Mail* (Toronto), March 5, 1947, p. 8; *The Toronto Star*, March 5, 1947, p. 3.

[6]An unsigned memorandum entitled Egerton Herbert Norman, a[lso] k[nown] a[s] E. Herb Norman, Herb Norman, May 23, 1950, p. 1, Norman File, RCMP (CSIS) Papers.

[7]Director, FBI to the S[pecial] A[gent in] C[harge] (Boston), October 16, 1946, File 100-346993-1; FBI (San Francisco) to the FBI (Washington), February 17, 1947, File 100-346993-3; and FBI (Boston) to the FBI (Washington), March 11, 1947, File 100-346993-4, FBI Papers. See also John Sawatsky, *Men in the Shadows* (Toronto: Doubleday, 1980), p. 145.

[8]An unsigned and undated memorandum entitled The Norman Case: Some Factors and Considerations, p. 1, Norman File, RCMP (CSIS) Papers.

[9]Lester B. Pearson, *Mike: The Memoirs of the Right Honourable Lester B. Pearson* (Toronto: University of Toronto Press, 1975), III, p. 166.

[10]See Viktor Suvorov, *Inside the Aquarium. The Making of a Top Soviet Spy* (New York: Macmillan, 1986), pp. 184-185.

[11]Hearings, *Scope of Soviet Activity in the United States*, Part 57 (March 26, 27, and April 4, 1957), pp. 3744-3745.

[12]*Testimony of Former Russian Code Clerk Relating to the Internal Security of the United States*, p. 45. See also Robert J. Lamphere and Tom Shachtman, *The FBI-KGB War. A Special Agent's Story* (New York: Random House, 1986), pp. 134, 137, 153.

¹³Born in Germany, Fuchs had fled to Great Britain because he was both Jewish and a communist. During the war, he was briefly interned in Canada where he had been sent by the British who considered him a German national and thus an enemy alien. A very talented mathematician and physicist, he worked on the atomic bomb project during the war and acquired British nationality. Fuchs now lives in communist East Germany. See Andrew Boyle, *The Fourth Man* (New York: Dial Press/James Wade, 1979), pp. 248-249, 251, 295-296, 348-349.

¹⁴Hoover to Bolling, November 1, 1950, File 100-346993-6, FBI Papers.

¹⁵General Headquarters, Far East Command, Military Intelligence Section, General Staff, to the Assistant Chief of Staff, G-2, Washington, D.C., November 30, 1950, US Army Intelligence and Security Command.

¹⁶Charles Taylor, *Six Journeys: A Canadian Pattern* (Toronto: Anansi, 1977), p. 136.

¹⁷Hearings, *State Department Loyalty Investigations*, Part 1 (March 8, 9, 13, 14, 20, 21, 27, 28, April 5, 6, 20, 25, 27, 28, May 1, 2, 3, 4, 26, 31, June 5, 6, 7, 8, 9, 12, 21, 22, 23, 26, 28, 1950), p. 565.

¹⁸Canadian Ambassador (Washington) to the Sec. of State for External Affairs, No. 914, April 21, 1950; The Sec. of State for External Affairs to the Head of the Canadian Liaison Mission (Tokyo) No. 87, April 28, 1950; Head of the Canadian Liaison Mission (Tokyo) to the Sec. of State for External Affairs, No. 68, May 2, 1950, Norman File, External Affairs Papers.

¹⁹An unsigned, untitled, and undated memorandum in the files of the subcommittee alleges that Norman's report had been approved by General Thorpe. The report cited who had been interviewed and with whom the question had been discussed. When the report got to Willoughby "he saw that every one of the sources used was communist." He brought the report to MacArthur's attention and Thorpe was returned to the United States. Norman File, Records of the Senate Subcommittee on Internal Security (1951-1975), RG 46, NA.

²⁰A report on Norman, May 23, 1950 sent to an unknown addressee, File 100-346993-6, FBI Papers. In the preface to his book, Norman expressed his debt to Tsuru "whose penetrating criticism has been of the greatest aid especially in matters relating to Japanese economic history." E. Herbert Norman, *Japan's Emergence as a Modern State. Political and Economic Problems of the Meiji Period* (New York: Institute of Pacific Relations, 1940), p. xiii.

²¹ Hearings, *Scope of Soviet Activity in the United States*, Part 57 (March 26, 27, and April 4, 1957), pp. 3744-3745. See also Director, FBI to the Legal Attaché (Ottawa), April 25, 1957, File 100-346993-108, FBI Papers.

²²Laughlin to Ladd, August 23, 1951, Referrals File 100-346993-29, FBI Papers.

²³General Headquarters, Far East Command, Military Intelligence Section, General Staff, to the Assistant Chief of Staff, G-2, Washington, D.C., November 30, 1950, US Army Intelligence and Security Command.

²⁴See the unsigned marginal minute in MacNeil to Glazebrook, September 29, 1951, Norman File, External Affairs Papers.

²⁵ An unsigned and undated memorandum entitled The Norman Case: Some Factors and Considerations, pp. 4-5, Norman File, RCMP (CSIS) Papers.

²⁶An unsigned and undated memorandum entitled E. H. Norman: Security Clearance, p. 1, Norman File, RCMP (CSIS) Papers.

²⁷An unsigned and undated memorandum entitled The Norman Case: Some Factors and Considerations, p. 1, Norman File, RCMP (CSIS) Papers.

²⁸An unsigned and undated minute as well as George Glazebrook, Memorandum for the File, March 21, 1952, Norman File, External Affairs Papers.

²⁹H[enry] S. Tadeson, Edgerton [sic] Herbert Norman and the marginal minutes, [September] 1950, Norman File, RCMP (CSIS) Papers and Summary of Information on Edgerton [sic] Herbert Norman, April 11, 1951, CIA Papers.

³⁰ On Norman's desire to teach and his visits to Hamilton, see Rockefeller Archive Center, Pocantico Hills, North Tarrytown, New York.

³¹See Roger W. Bowen, "Cold War, McCarthyism, and Murder by Slander: E. H. Norman's Death in Perspective," in Roger W. Bowen (ed.), *E. H. Norman: His Life and Scholarship* (Toronto: University of Toronto Press: 1984), p. 50.

³²H[enry] S. Tadeson, Edgerton [sic] Herbert Norman and the marginal minutes, [September] 1950, Norman File, RCMP (CSIS) Papers.

³³MacNeil to Glazebrook and the marginal minutes, September 29, 1950, Norman File, External Affairs Papers.

³⁴Glazebrook to Pearson, September 15, 1950, Norman File, External Affairs Papers.

³⁵MacNeil to Glazebrook, October 11, 1950, Norman File, RCMP (CSIS) Papers. On Norman and Holmes, see Chapter 3, pp. 24-25. On "Norman" and Norman Freed and Norman Veall, see Report of the 1946 Royal Commission on Espionage in Canada, pp. 23, 505. See also *Vestnik* (Toronto), December 16, 1944, p. 4 and December 20, 1944, p. 4.

³⁶Unsigned and undated notes, Norman File, External Affairs Papers.

³⁷Italics added. [Heeney] to Wrong, October 14, 1950, Norman File, External Affairs Papers. On the Fuchs incident see Chapman Pincher, *Too Secret Too Long* (London: Sidgwick & Jackson, 1984), pp. 116-117.

³⁸[Heeney] to Pearson, October 14, 1950, Norman File, External Affairs Papers.

³⁹[Wrong] to Heeney, October 17, 1950, Norman File, External Affairs Papers.

⁴⁰Glazebrook to Pearson, October 18, 1950, Norman File, External Affairs Papers.

⁴¹[Wrong] to Robertson, October 23, 1950, Norman File, External Affairs Papers.

⁴²See the unsigned and undated memorandum entitled The Norman Case: Some Factors and Considerations, Norman File, RCMP (CSIS) Papers.

⁴³On Norman-Bryce see Chapter 3, p. 15, and on Walsh-Leopold, see Chapter 3, p. 14. Apparently "Norman spent a good deal of time with his old friend Robert Bryce" after he was recalled from Tokyo. James Littleton, *Target Nation. Canada and the Western Intelligence Network* (Toronto: Lester

& Orpen Dennys, 1986), p. 34. It is interesting to note that in September 1945 when Igor Gouzenko was seeking assistance in order to defect he was directed to John Leopold who made an appointment to see Gouzenko the following morning. That night personnel from the Russian Embassy forced their way into Gouzenko's apartment, but fortunately, he was hiding with a neighbor (June Callwood, *Emma* (Toronto: Stoddart, 1984), pp. 122-123 and John Sawatsky, *Gouzenko: The Untold Story* (Toronto: Macmillan, 1984), p. 37. Leopold's sluggish and inexplicable reaction to Gouzenko's desperate need for assistance was not forgotten. When Gouzenko subsequently met Leopold he refused to ride in the same automobile with him and maintained that Leopold "was a spy." He requested that the RCMP never bring Leopold into his presence again. His RCMP bodyguard was perplexed. See Sawatsky, *Gouzenko: The Untold Story*, p. 62.

[44] An unsigned and untitled memorandum, October 24, 1950, Norman File, External Affairs Papers.

[45] An unsigned memorandum entitled Draft: Egerton Herbert Norman, January 29, 1968, p. 9, Norman File, RCMP (CSIS) Papers.

[46] Pearson, III, p. 169.

[47] *The Gazette* (Montreal), April 18, 1957, p. 8.

[48] File 100-346993-75, FBI Papers.

[49] Director, FBI to the Attorney General, April 26, 1957, File 100-346993-104 and Hoover to McLeod, April 26, 1957, File 100-46993-111, FBI Papers.

[50] *The Gazette* (Montreal), April 18, 1957, p. 8.

[51] McClellan to Glazebrook, November 22, 1950, and the attached report, Norman File, RCMP (CSIS) Papers. On Norman's view of the Moscow spy trials see Chapter 3, pp. 14-15.

[52] See Chapter 4, p. 35.

[53] Pearson, III, p. 168.

[54] An unsigned, undated, and untitled memorandum, Norman File, External Affairs Papers. As to the marginal RCMP note that it was all an assumption, see the memorandum by T. M. Guernsey, Re: Egerton Herbert Norman, December 1, 1950, which is the note to the FBI, Norman File, RCMP (CSIS) Papers. On Christ and communism see Chapter 1, p. 5. On the Moscow spy trials, see Chapter 3, p. 35. Though according to Norman he saw little of Holmes during the war he certainly saw him in 1951 when Holmes worked for the UN Secretariat and Norman was representing Canada in the UN. See Sidney Katz, "What Kind of Man *Was* Herbert Norman?", *Maclean's Magazine*, September 28, 1957, p. 88.

[55] Donald N. Brown to the writer, December 17, 1985. Since Brown retired from the RCMP as Superintendent having served in the Force for 29 years, 22 in the Crime Detection Laboratories, and having testified in over 600 cases, it is safe to say that he is an "expert."

[56] T. M. Guernsey, Re: Egerton Herbert Norman, December 1, 1950, which is the note to the FBI, Norman file, RCMP (CSIS) Papers.

[57] Heeney to Wood, December 1, 1950, Norman File, RCMP (CSIS) Papers.

[58] Boyle, pp. 357-358, 370.

[59] Two letters Heeney to Wood, December 1, 1950, Norman File, RCMP (CSIS) Papers.

[60]Wood to Heeney, December 6, 1950, Norman File, External Affairs Papers.

[61]M[cClellan] to Glazebrook, January 23, 1951, Norman File, RCMP (CSIS) Papers.

CHAPTER 6

[1]See Chapter 3, p. 12.

[2][Heakes] to Martin, March 30, 1957; see also [Heakes] to Martin, June 8, 1951, Norman File, External Affairs Papers.

[3][Heakes] to Martin, June 8 and 11, 1951, Norman File, External Affairs Papers.

[4]Martin to Pearson, June 13, 1951, Norman File, External Affairs Papers.

[5]See Chapter 3, p. 19.

[6]Cabinet Summary, August 15, 1951, Norman File, RCMP (CSIS) Papers.

[7]See Chapter 3, p. 18.

[8]Charles Taylor, *Six Journeys: A Canadian Pattern* (Toronto: Anansi, 1977), pp. 138-139. See also C. B. F[ahs], Reception celebrating Indonesian Independence Day, August 17, 1951, Norman File, Records of the Senate Subcommittee on Internal Security (1951-1975), RG 46, NA and *The Globe and Mail* (Toronto), August 17, 1951, pp. 1-2.

[9]A[rnold] D. P. H[eeney], Memorandum for Mr. Glazebrook, August 30, 1951, Norman File, RCMP (CSIS) Papers. It would appear that General and Mrs. George Stratemeyer could be included among this group in Tokyo who perceived Norman "as far to the left." Mrs. Stratemeyer claimed that Norman's farewell party "was the only time while [General] MacArthur was in Japan that the Russians ever attended a social function." W[illiam] A. R[usher], Memorandum to the File, May 10, 1957. Norman File, Records of the Senate Subcommittee on Internal Security (1951-1975), RG 46, NA.

[10]Glazebrook, Memorandum for [the] File, September 13, 1951, Norman File, External Affairs Papers.

[11] Taylor, p. 140.

[12]Henry S. Ferns, *Reading from Left to Right* (Toronto: University of Toronto Press, 1983), pp. 211-212; Memorandum of Conversation (Bessie Touzel and James Barros), April 17, 1985.

[13]Transcripts of the Hearings of the [Kellock-Taschereau] Royal Commission to Investigate the Facts Relating to and the Circumstances Surrounding the Communication, by Public Officials and Other Persons in Positions of Trust of Secret and Confidential Information to Agents of a Foreign Power, Volumes 1-2, Microfilm Reels T-1368 (pp. 769-770), and T-1369 (pp. 3558, 3837), RG 33/62, PAC.

[14]Ferns, pp. 213-214.

[15]Memorandum of Conversation (Bessie Touzel and James Barros), April 17, 1985.

[16]Sigvaldason to Glazebrook, No. 3745, September 8, 1951, Norman File, RCMP (CSIS) Papers.

[17]See Chapter 4, pp. 38-39.

[18]Glazebrook to Commissioner of the RCMP, September 21, 1951, Norman File, RCMP (CSIS) Papers.

[19]An unsigned and undated memorandum entitled E. H. Norman: Security Clearance, pp. 17-18, Norman File, RCMP (CSIS) Papers.

[20]Guernsey to Glazebrook, January 4, 1952, Norman File, External Affairs Papers.

[21]An unsigned and undated memorandum entitled E. H. Norman: Security Clearance, p. 18, Norman File, RCMP (CSIS) Papers.

[22]Untitled memorandum of conversation (McClellan, Guernsey, Norman, and Glazebrook), January 1952, and Glazebrook's marginal note, Norman File, External Affairs Papers.

[23]John Sawatsky, *Men in the Shadows* (Toronto: Doubleday, 1980), pp. 100-103 and fns.; John Sawatsky, *For Services Rendered: Leslie James Bennett and the RCMP Security Service* (Toronto: Doubleday, 1982), p. 31; Chapman Pincher, *Too Secret Too Long* (London: Sidgwick & Jackson, 1984), pp. 409-410.

[24]Untitled memorandum of conversation (McClellan, Guernsey, Norman, and Glazebrook), January 1952, Norman File, External Affairs Papers.

[25]See Chapter 2, p. 10.

[26]Italics added.

[27]The official archives of the University of Toronto do not show that Norman was doing postgraduate work in 1935-1936.

[28]See Chapter 3, pp. 13, 14.

[29]See Chapter 3, p. 12.

[30]See Chapter 2, p. 7.

[31]See Chapter 3, p. 12.

[32]See Chapter 2, pp. 10-11.

[33]Italics added.

[34]See Chapter 3, pp. 17-18.

[35]Sawatsky, *Men in the Shadows*, pp. 96-98.

[36]Italics added.

[37]See Chapter 3, p. 13.

[38]See Chapter 1, pp. 3-5.

[39]On The Apostles see Andrew Boyle, *The Fourth Man* (New York: Dial Press/James Wade, 1979), pp. 70-71, 75; Michael Straight, *After Long Silence* (London: Collins, 1983), pp. 92-94 and Richard Deacon, *The Cambridge Apostles: A History of Cambridge University's Elite Intellectual Secret Society* (New York: Farrar, Straus & Giroux, 1986).

[40]See Chapter 5, p. 51.

[41]Roger W. Bowen, "Cold War, McCarthyism, and Murder by Slander: E. H. Norman's Death in Perspective," in Roger W. Bowen (ed.), *E. H. Norman: His Life and Scholarship* (Toronto: University of Toronto Press, 1984), p. 63. See also Taylor, p. 139.

[42]Sawatsky, *For Services Rendered*, pp. 253-254.

[43]An unsigned and undated memorandum entitled Egerton Herbert Norman: Brief of Information and Investigation, p. 10, Norman File, RCMP (CSIS) Papers.

[44]George Glazebrook, Memorandum for Mr. Heeney, January 18, 1952, and Heeney's minute and marginal comments, Norman File, External Affairs Papers. On the suspicions of General George Pearkes, see [Pearkes] to [Diefenbaker], August 10, 1951, Frames 051918-051920, (File Herbert Norman), Reel M-7442, Volume 64, Series 1940-1956, Diefenbaker Papers, PAC.

[45]George Glazebrook, Memorandum for Mr. Heeney, January 22, 1952, and Heeney's minute and marginal comments. On the RCMP minute see the RCMP copy, Norman Files, External Affairs and RCMP (CSIS) Papers. On Norman's note to Glazebrook of August 13, 1951, see Chapter 3, p. 17.

[46]Arnold Heeney, *The Things That Are Caesar's* (Toronto: University of Toronto Press, 1972), pp. 98, 144.

[47]George Glazebrook, Memorandum for Mr. Heeney, February 6, 1952, Norman File, External Affairs and RCMP (CSIS) Papers.

[48]George Glazebrook, Memorandum to Mr. Heeney, January 29, 1952, Norman File, External Affairs Papers.

[49]George Glazebrook, Memorandum for Mr. Heeney, February 28, 1952, Norman File, External Affairs Papers.

[50]E[gerton] H[erbert] N[orman], Memorandum for Mr. Glazebrook (probably some time in March 1952), Norman File, External Affairs Papers.

[51]See Chapter 3, pp. 13-14.

[52]George Glazebrook, Memorandum for Mr. Heeney, March 10, 1952, Norman File, RCMP (CSIS) Papers.

[53]George Glazebrook, Memorandum for the File, March 21, 1952, Norman File, External Affairs Papers.

[54]George Glazebrook, Memorandum for the File, March 31, 1952, Norman File, External Affairs Papers. On Nicholson, see Sawatsky, *Men in the Shadows*, p. 108.

CHAPTER 7

[1]Lester B. Pearson, *Mike: The Memoirs of the Right Honourable Lester B. Pearson* (Toronto: University of Toronto Press, 1975), III, p. 169.

[2]Canada, Parliament, House of Commons, *Debate, Official Report*, 22nd Parliament, 5th Session, Vol. III (April 12, 1957) (Ottawa: Queen's Printer, 1957), p. 3493.

[3]*The Gazette* (Montreal), April 18, 1957, p. 8.

[4]*The Globe and Mail* (Toronto), August 17, 1951, p. 1.

[5]Charles Taylor, *Six Journeys: A Canadian Pattern* (Toronto: Anansi, 1977), p. 140.

[6]*Ibid.*, p. 140.

[7]James Eayrs, *In Defence of Canada: Appeasement and Rearmament* (Toronto: University of Toronto Press, 1965), pp. 16-27. See also Robert Bothwell and John English, " 'Dirty Work at the Crossroads': New Perspectives on the Riddell Incident," *The Canadian Historical Association. Historical Papers 1972*, pp. 263-285.

[8]Taylor, p. 140.

[9]Pearson to Norman, March 3, 1953, Vol. 10, Pearson Papers, MG 26, N1, PAC.

[10]Norman to Pearson, March 9, 1953, Vol. 10, *ibid.*

[11]The pertinent files are 601.4244/2-2453 and 742.521/3-3153, RG 59, NA.

[12][Norman] to Pearson, April 24, 1956, Vol. 10, *ibid.* See also [Norman] to Léger, April 19, 1956, Norman File, External Affairs Papers.

[13]Christine Kirkwood, "The Story of Stadacona 1956-1957" (typescript in the possession of the author); [Norman] to Kirkwood, March 28, 1956, Kirkwood to Burbridge, May 8, 1963, Burbridge to Kirkwood, May 17, 1963, Kirkwood to Burbridge, March 26, 1965, Kirkwood to Pearson, August 7, 1963, Pearson to Kirkwood, December 4, 1963, Mrs. Christine Kirkwood's Private Papers. On the Spencer episode, see Pearson, III, pp. 173-175.

[14]Taylor, pp. 145-146. On the question of Anglo-Swiss and Australian-Canadian diplomatic representation in Egypt, see *New York Times*, November 2, 1946, p. 5 and *The Sydney Morning Herald*, November 9, 1956, p. 1.

[15]Committee on the Judiciary, *Internal Security Annual Report for 1957*, p. 102.

[16]John K. Emmerson, *The Japanese Thread* (New York: Holt, Rinehart & Winston, 1978), p. 333. On General Willoughby's comments, see Hearings, *Institute of Pacific Relations*, Part 2 (August 9, 14, 16, 20, 22, and 23, 1951), p. 374.

[17]Emmerson, pp. 333-336. On Bentley, see the *New York Times*, December 4, 1947, p. 47; Elizabeth Bentley, *Out of Bondage* (New York: Devin-Adair, 1951), *passim.*

[18]McManus to Morris, March 21, 1957, Norman File, Records of the Senate Subcommittee on Internal Security (1951-1975), RG 46, NA.

[19]Hearings, *Scope of Soviet Activity in the United States*, Part 56 (March 12 and 21, 1957), pp. 3645-3685 and Emmerson, pp. 334-337.

[20]Herter to Eastland, March 22, 1957 and Eastland to Herter, March 22, 1957, Norman File, Records of the Senate Subcommittee on Internal Security (1951-1975), RG 46, NA.

[21]Committee on the Judiciary, *Internal Security Annual Report for 1957*, p. 106-107.

[22]*The Amerasia Papers: A Clue to the Catastrophe of China*, II, pp. 1679-1762.

[23]Robert Morris, *No Wonder We are Losing* (Plano: University of Plano Press, 1958), *passim.*

[24]Hoover to Tolson, Boardman, Belmont, and Nichols, April 10, 1957, File 100-346993-52, FBI Papers. See also the comment by Senator Arthur V. Watkins (Republican of Utah) in United States Congress, *Congressional Record*, Vol. 103, Pt. 4 (March 25-April 12, 1957), p. 5613.

[25]Judge Robert Morris to the writer, August 5, [1985].

[26]Hoover to Tolson, Boardman, Belmont, and Nichols, April 12, 1957,

File 100-346993-56 and Director, FBI to Boardman, Nichols, Belmont, and Roach, April 15, 1957, File 100-346993-55, FBI Papers.

²⁷A six-page, untitled, undated, and unsigned memorandum dealing with Egerton Herbert Norman, US Army Intelligence and Security Command.

²⁸Agent Report by Lee M. Martin, CIC, Re: Egerton Herbert Norman, June 3, 1957, *ibid.*

²⁹Judge Robert Morris to the writer, August 5, [1985].

³⁰Canada, Parliament, House of Commons, *Debates, Official Report*, 22nd Parliament, 5th Session, Vol. III (March 15, 1957) (Ottawa: Queen's Printer, 1957), pp. 2349-2350. 2370.

³¹Norman to External [Affairs], No. 227, March 19, 1957, Norman File, External Affairs. See also Canada, Parliament, House of Commons, *Debates, Official Report*, 22nd Parliament, 5th Session, Vol. III (April 4, 1957) (Ottawa: Queen's Printer, 1957), p. 3059.

³²Pearson to Diefenbaker, March 29, 1957, Norman File, External Affairs Papers.

³³Patrick Walsh to the writer, March 27, 1985 and *The Gazette* (Montreal), April 19, 1957, p. 4. For the brief, see Walsh to Pearson, March 25, 1957, Norman File, Records of the Senate Subcommittee on Internal Security (1951-1975), RG 46, NA.

³⁴Peter Stursberg, *Lester Pearson and the American Dilemma* (Toronto: Doubleday, 1980), pp. 160-161.

³⁵Hearings, *Scope of Soviet Activity in the United States*, (March 26, 27, and April 4, 1957).

³⁶[Heakes] to Martin, March 30, 1957, Norman File, RCMP (CSIS) Papers.

³⁷Canada, Parliament, House of Commons, *Debates, Official Report*, 22nd Parliament, 5th Session, Vol. III. (April 10, 1957) (Ottawa: Queen's Printer, 1957), p. 3357.

³⁸[Heakes] to Martin, April 4, 1957, Norman File, External Affairs Papers. He also wrote Martin a letter from Toronto on the same day expressing the same thoughts. [Heakes] to Martin, April 4, 1957, Norman File, *ibid.*

³⁹ [Heakes] to Martin, April 5, 1957, Norman File, External Affairs Papers.

⁴⁰Martin to [Heakes], April 6, 1957, and Glazebrook's marginal minute, Norman File, External Affairs Papers.

⁴¹Canada, Parliament, House of Commons, *Debates, Official Report*, 22nd Parliament, 5th Session, Vol. III (April 4, 1957) (Ottawa: Queen's Printer, 1957), pp. 3058-3059.

⁴²Diefenbaker to McFaul, April 8, 1957, Frame 20702, (File 861 Egypt), Reel M-5560, Vol. 29, First Leader of the Official Opposition, Diefenbaker Papers, PAC.

⁴³Patrick Walsh, *Canada's Watergate: the Story of Treason in Ottawa*, (Flesherton: The Canadian League of Rights, 2nd rev. ed., 1983), pp. 36-37.

⁴⁴Canada, Parliament, House of Commons, *Debates, Official Report*, 22nd Parliament, 5th Session, Vol. III (April 12, 1957) (Ottawa: Queen's Printer, 1957), pp. 3466, 3492-3502. On the suspicion of Norman's supposed "double check" in 1951 see George [Pearkes] to [Diefenbaker], August 10, 1951,

Frames 051918-051920, (File Herbert Norman), Reel M-7442, Vol. 64, Series 1940-1956, Diefenbaker Papers, PAC.

⁴⁵Paul Martin, *A Very Public Life* (Toronto: Deneau, 1985), II, pp. 137, 248-266, 290.

⁴⁶Hoover's marginal minute in Belmont to Boardman, April 18, 1957, File 100-346993-101, FBI Papers.

⁴⁷Pearson to Davis, April 17, 1957, Norman File, External Affairs Papers.

⁴⁸George Glazebrook, Further Statements on the Norman Case, April 26, 1957, Norman File, RCMP (CSIS) Papers.

⁴⁹G[eorge] G[lazebrook], Memorandum for the Minister, May 13, 1957, Norman File, External Affairs Papers.

CHAPTER 8

¹Leo Heaps, *Hugh Hambleton, Spy. Thirty Years with the KGB* (Toronto: Methuen, 1983).

²Michael Straight, *After Long Silence* (London: Collins, 1983).

³See Chapter 3, p. 24.

⁴Chapman Pincher, *Their Trade is Treachery* (London: Sidgwick & Jackson, 1981), pp. 127-128 and Chapman Pincher, *Too Secret Too Long* (London: Sidgwick & Jackson, 1984), p. 396.

⁵See Chapter 2, pp. 10-11.

⁶See Chapter 5, p. 52.

⁷Henry S. Ferns, *Reading from Left to Right* (Toronto: University of Toronto Press, 1983), p. 209.

⁸Pincher, *Their Trade is Treachery*, pp. 127, 139.

⁹Pincher, *Too Secret Too Long*, pp. 387, 417.

¹⁰Nigel West, *A Matter of Trust: MI5, 1945-72* (London: Weidenfeld and Nicolson, 1982), p. 76.

¹¹David C. Martin, *Wilderness of Mirrors* (New York: Harper & Row, 1980), pp. 106-109, 149. See also West, pp. 74-77.

¹²Iain Elliot, "Eastern Approaches," *The Times Literary Supplement*, October 26, 1984, p. 1207.

¹³See Chapter 4, pp. 36-37.

¹⁴See Chapter 3, pp. 24-25.

¹⁵Pincher, *Their Trade is Treachery*, p. 127.

¹⁶See Chapter 4, pp. 32-33.

¹⁷See Chapter 3, p. 12.

¹⁸See Chapter 4, pp. 33, 36.

¹⁹See Chapter 6, p. 73.

²⁰See Chapter 4, pp. 28-31.

²¹*Ibid.*, pp. 38-40.

²²*Ibid.*, p. 42.

²³Ferns, p. 213.

²⁴On Moscow's decision in the early 1950s to discontinue recruitment through the party, see Ladislav Bittman, *The KGB and Soviet Disinformation* (Washington, D.C.: Pergamon-Brassey, 1985), pp. 23-24.

²⁵Andrew Boyle, *The Fourth Man* (New York: Dial Press/James Wade, 1979), pp. 298-299, 362-363, 371; Pincher, *Their Trade is Treachery*, pp. 111, 187-188; Martin, pp. 44-45, 48-50, 61; West, pp. 31, 38.

²⁶Boyle, *passim* and Pincher, *Too Secret Too Long, passim.*

²⁷See the thoughtful study by Richard H. Shultz and Roy Godson, *Dezinformatsia: Active Measures in Soviet Strategy* (Washington, D.C.: Pergamon-Brassey, 1984), pp. 132-133, 193-194.

²⁸Ferns, pp. 208-209.

²⁹Charles Taylor, *Six Journeys: A Canadian Pattern* (Toronto: Anansi, 1977), p. 129.

³⁰*Ibid.*, pp. 128-130, 134-135. See also Roger W. Bowen, "Cold War, McCarthyism, and Murder by Slander: E. H. Norman's Death in Perspective," in Roger W. Bowen (ed.), *E. H. Norman: His Life and Scholarship* (Toronto: University of Toronto Press, 1984), pp. 59-61.

³¹E. W. T. Gill, Note for the File: Mr. Herbert Norman, October 1, 1952, Norman File, External Affairs Papers.

³²John Sawatsky, *For Services Rendered: Leslie James Bennett and the RCMP Security Service* (Toronto: Doubleday, 1982), pp. 171-183.

³³See Ford to James, November 22, 1948; James to Ford, November 23, 1948; Norman's dispatch No. 461, October 15, 1948; Gascoigne to Scarlett, January 20, 1949, and various attached minutes, FO/371/69827, PRO.

³⁴See Chapter 3, p. 13.

³⁵Howard L. Boorman and Richard C. Howard (eds.), *Biographical Dictionary of Republican China* (New York: Columbia University Press, 1967), I, p. 294.

³⁶See Chapter 3, p. 24.

³⁷*Ibid.*, p. 23.

³⁸On Chi Ch'ao-ting's career, see [Philip J. Jaffe], "My Chinese Cousin: Chi Ch'ao-ting" (typescript), Folder 5, Box 5, Philip J. Jaffe Papers, Robert W. Woodruff Library, Emory University, Atlanta; Boorman and Howard, I, pp. 293-297; Donald W. Klein and Anne B. Clark (eds.), *Biographic Dictionary of Chinese Communism 1921-1965* (Cambridge: Harvard University Press, 1971), I, pp. 160-163.

³⁹Straight, pp. 101-104, 120-121, 129-130, 134-135, 143-144, 157, 167-168.

⁴⁰Pincher, *Too Secret Too Long*, p. 160.

⁴¹John Barron, *KGB; the Secret Work of Soviet Secret Agents* (New York: Reader's Digest Press, 1974), pp. 379, 384.

⁴²Report of the 1946 Royal Commission on Espionage in Canada, pp. 39-40.

⁴³*Ibid.*, pp. 14-15.

⁴⁴Memorandum of Conversation (McClellan, Guernsey, Norman, and Glazebrook), January 1952, p. 24, Norman File, External Affairs Papers.

⁴⁵Elizabeth Bentley, *Out of Bondage* (New York: Devin-Adair, 1951), pp. 104-105, 158, and Parts A and B of the Appendices to this work.

⁴⁶Hoover to Berle, February 5, 1943, File 894.00B/62, RG 59, NA. Though the Russian naval staff had nothing to offer the Americans concerning the

Japanese Navy, GRU's Far Eastern experts provided American military intelligence "firsthand information of Japanese troop movements and dispositions in Manchuria, which they obtained by actual contact and by the infiltration of intelligence agents." John R. Deane *The Strange Alliance* (New York: Viking, 1962), pp. 237-239.

[47]On Sorge's activities, see Charles A. Willoughby, *Shanghai Conspiracy. The Sorge Spy Ring* (New York: Dutton, 1952); Chalmers A. Johnson, *An Instance of Treason* (Stanford: Stanford University Press, 1964); and Frederick W. Deakin and G. R. Storry, *The Case of Richard Sorge* (New York: Harper & Row, 1966); Gordon Prange, *Target Tokyo* (New York: McGraw-Hill, 1984). On the special intelligence section, see Peter St. John, "Canada's Accession to the Allied Intelligence Community 1940-45," *Conflict Quarterly*, Vol. 4, No. 4 (Fall 1984), p. 13.

[48]Pincher, *Too Secret Too Long*, p. 551.

[49]Ferns, p. 223.

[50]See Chapter 5, p. 54.

[51]Report of the 1946 Royal Commission on Espionage in Canada, p. 29.

[52]See Chapter 5, pp. 54-55, 65.

[53]Vladimir and Evdokia Petrov, *Empire of Fear* (New York: Praeger, 1956), p. 198; John Barron, KGB *Today: The Hidden Hand* (London: Hodder & Stoughton, 1984), pp. 352, 397; Pincher, *Too Secret Too Long*, pp. 355-356; Robert J. Lamphere and Tom Shachtman, *The FBI-KGB War. A Special Agent's Story* (New York: Random House, 1986), p. 195. See also the executive session testimony by Nicholas Dozenberg on May 21, 1940 in United States House of Representatives, Special Committee on Un-American Activities, *Investigation of Un-American Propaganda Activities*, Hearings before the Special Committee to Investigate Un-American Activities, 76th Congress, 3rd Session, Part 13 (April 11-May 21, 1940), (Washington, D.C.: Government Printing Office, 1941).

[54]Stevie Cameron, "Forming Canada's Intelligence Service Wasn't Easy," *The Citizen* (Ottawa), March 15, 1986, p. B5.

[55]David Beaubier to the writer, September 16, 1985, and also June Callwood, *Emma* (Toronto: Stoddart, 1984), pp. 98-99.

[56]Callwood, p. 95-100.

[57]Report of the 1946 Royal Commission on Espionage in Canada, p. 497.

[58]Oleg Penkovskiy, *The Penkovskiy Papers*, trans. by Peter Deriabin, (Garden City, New York: Doubleday, 1965), p. 273.

[59]Lester B. Pearson, *Mike: The Memoirs of the Right Honourable Lester B. Pearson* (Toronto: University of Toronto Press, 1972), I, p. 229.

[60]David Beaubier to the writer, September 16 and 27, 1985.

[61]Callwood, p. 99.

[62]Pearson, II, p. 147.

[63]Dean Acheson, "Crisis in Asia—An Examination of U.S. Policy." *State Department Bulletin*, Vol. XII (January 23, 1950), pp. 111-118; Dean Acheson, *Present at the Creation* (New York: Norton, 1969), pp. 355-357.

[64]Harry Temple, "Deaf Captains: Intelligence, Policy, and the Origins of the Korean War," *International Studies Notes*, Vol. 8, Issues 3-4 (Fall-Winter 1981-1982), pp. 19-23.

[65]See Chapter 4, p. 43.

[66]Aside from *A Matter of Trust: MI5, 1945-72* (London: Weidenfeld and Nicolson, 1982), already cited, Nigel West is also the author of *MI5: British Security Service Operations, 1909-1945* (London: Bodley Head, 1981), *MI6: British Secret Intelligence Service Operations, 1909-1945* (London: Weidenfeld and Nicolson, 1983), as well as *A Thread of Deceit: Espionage Myths of World War II* (New York: Random House, 1985).

[67]Dodd, Mead & Company to the writer, August 28, 1984.

[68]The writer to Anatoly Golitsyn, September 17, 1984.

[69]Anatoly Golitsyn to the writer, December 1, 1984.

[70]See Chapter 2, p. 7.

[71]Pincher, *Too Secret Too Long*, p. 382.

[72]Barton Whaley, *Soviet Clandestine Communication Nets. Notes for a History of the Structure of the Intelligence Services of the USSR* (Cambridge: Massachusetts Institute of Technology, Center for International Studies, March 1969), p. 87.

[73]Whaley, pp. 97-106. To penetrate Japan, see Nadezhda and Maiia Ulanovskaia, *Istoriia odnoi semi* [*One Family's Story*] (in Russian) (New York: Chalidze, 1982), p. 78. Aino Kuusinen, *Before and After Stalin* (London: Michael Joseph), pp. 103-127; Whittaker Chambers, *Witness* (New York: Random House, 1952), pp. 225, 364-369, 388, 397, 409-410, 437.

[74]Report of the 1946 Royal Commission on Espionage in Canada, pp. 20-21; Igor Gouzenko, *This Was My Choice* (Toronto: Dent, 1948), pp. 242-243.

[75]Whaley, p. 148.

[76]Whaley, p. 86 and John Sawatsky, *Men in the Shadows* (Toronto: Doubleday, 1980), p. 93. See also Penkovskiy, p. 277.

[77]Peter Deriabin and Frank Gibney, *The Secret World* (Garden City, New York: Doubleday, 1959), p. 243. See also Penkovskiy, pp. 277, 285. On the tensions between KGB and GRU, see Peter Deriabin, *Watchdogs of Terror* (New Rochelle, New York: Arlington House, 1972), p. 215; Barron, pp. 15, 343-345; Viktor Suvorov, *Inside Soviet Military Intellegence* (New York: Macmillan, 1984), pp. 46-50; Peter Deriabin with T.H. Bagley, "Fedorchuk, the KGB, and the Soviet Succession," *Orbis*, Vol. 26, No. 3 (Fall 1982), p. 619; Brian Freemantle, *KGB* (London: Michael Joseph/Rainbird, 1983), 60-61.

CHAPTER 9

[1]See Chapter 7, p. 107.

[2]Unless cited otherwise, what follows is based on a report by Norman's deputy Arthur Kilgour, about the events in Cairo before and after Norman's suicide. Kilgour to Léger, April 10, 1957, Norman File, RCMP (CSIS) Papers. Kilgour's subsequent version of these days is slightly inaccurate, based as it was on memory. Arthur Kilgour, "On Remembering Herbert Norman," in Roger W. Bowen (ed.), *E. H. Norman: His Life and Scholarship* (Toronto:

University of Toronto Press, 1984), p. 77. See also Charles Taylor, *Six Journeys: A Canadian Pattern* (Toronto: Anansi, 1977), p. 147. As to the affidavit, see E[gerton] H[erbert] N[orman] to Glazebrook, March 12, 1952, and the attached documents especially the affidavit, Norman File, RCMP (CSIS) Papers.

[3]See Chapter 4, p. 41.

[4]Italics added. Kilgour to Léger, April 10, 1957, Norman File, RCMP (CSIS) Papers.

[5]Kilgour to Léger, April 10, 1957, Norman File, RCMP (CSIS) Papers.

[6]King Gordon to [Pearson], April 7, 1957, Vol. 44, Pearson Papers, MG 26, N1, PAC. On Holland's letter, see Hearings, *Institute of Pacific Relations*, Part 1 (July 25, 26, 31, August 2 and 7, 1951), pp. 320-321, and *ibid.*, Part 14 (May 2, June 20, 1952), pp. 5030-5031.

[7]Italics added.

[8]Italics added.

[9]Italics in the original.

[10]Kilgour to Léger, April 10, 1957, Norman File, RCMP (CSIS) Papers.

[11]Taylor, p. 147.

[12]Holmes to Pearson, July 18, 1957, Vol. 44, Pearson Papers, MG 26, N1, PAC.

[13]Committee on the Judiciary, *Internal Security Annual Report for 1957*, p. 101 fn.

[14]Canada, Parliament, House of Commons, *Debates, Official Report*, 24th Parliament, 1st Session, Vol. I (May 15-16, 1958) (Ottawa: Queen's Printer, 1958), pp. 92, 137-138.

[15]This chapter, p. 149.

[16]Chronology—Part II, February 23, 1967, Norman File, External Affairs Papers.

[17]See Chapter 7, pp. 111-112.

[18]Kilgour to External Affairs, No. 260, April 6, 1957, Norman File, External Affairs Papers.

[19]H[oward] Norman to Pearson, April 13, 1957, Vol. 44, Pearson Papers, MG 26, N1, PAC.

[20]Taylor, p. 149.

[21]Kilgour to External Affairs, No. 259, April 6, 1957, Norman File, RCMP (CSIS) Papers.

[22]Report of the 1946 Royal Commission on Espionage in Canada, pp. 72-73. On the *New Masses*, see Chapter 4, p. 36.

[23]Italics in the original. Brian Crozier, *Strategy of Survival* (New Rochelle, New York: Arlington House, 1978), p. 136.

[24]Middle East Division to D[efense] L[iaison] II, April 17, 1957, Norman File, External Affairs Papers.

[25]Taylor, p. 119.

[26]Allen Weinstein, *Perjury: the Hiss-Chambers Case* (New York: Knopf, 1978), pp. 526-527.

[27]Leo Heaps, *Hugh Hambleton, Spy. Thirty Years with the KGB* (Toronto: Methuen, 1983), p. 53.

[28]*The New York Times*, January 16, 1986, p. 17.

[29]See Chapter 7, p. 111.

[30]Andrew Boyle, *The Fourth Man* (New York: The Dial Press/James Wade, 1979), p. 384.

CHAPTER 10

[1]See Chapter 5, p. 53.

[2]See Chapter 3, p. 17.

[3]*Ibid.*, p. 19.

[4][Holmes] to [MacDermot], Labour Day, [1951], File 54, MacDermot Papers, Special Collections, Bishop's University, Lennoxville, Québec.

[5]Memorandum of Conversation (W. D. Matthews and H. Freeman Matthews) and attachments, August 14, 1951, File 742.001/8-1451, RG 59, NA. On Pearson's public discussion of the note, see *The Globe and Mail* (Toronto), August 17, 1951, pp. 1-2.

[6]Judge Robert Morris to the writer, June 26, 1985.

[7]Satterthwaite to Bonbright, August 16, 1951, File 742.001/8-1651, RG 59, NA.

[8]Memorandum of Conversation (Matthews and Raynor), August 24, 1951 and attachment, File 742.001/8-2451, RG 59, NA.

[9]Lester B. Pearson, *Mike: The Memoirs of the Right Honourable Lester B. Pearson* (Toronto: University of Toronto Press, 1975), III, pp. xi, 168.

[10]John Sawatsky, "Pearson's Friend was a Soviet Spy: FBI Report," *The Gazette* (Montreal), January 8, 1982, pp. 1, 9.

[11]Hinkle (Montreal) to the Sec. of State, June 7, 1949, File 842.00B/6-749, RG 59, NA.

[12][Sise] to [Pearson], September 8, 1939, Vol. 13, Folder 2, Sise Papers, MG 30, D187, PAC.

[13]Memorandum for Inspector [Cecil] Bayfield, January 12, 1954. File 100-364301-11, FBI Papers. See also [Commissioner RCMP] to Bayfield, August 24, 1951 and Bayfield to the Commissioner RCMP, August 28, 1951, Norman File, RCMP (CSIS) Papers.

[14]J. W. Pickersgill to the writer, March 20, 1986.

[15]The missing State Department file is 711.001/6-2052, RG 59, NA.

[16]See J. W. Pickersgill, *My Years with Louis St. Laurent* (Toronto: University of Toronto Press, 1975), pp. 146-149.

[17]Bentley's FBI code name was "Gregory." See Strickland to Ladd, Underground Espionage (NKVD) in Agencies of the United States Government, October 21, 1946, p. 192, File 65-56402-1802, FBI Papers. See also Elizabeth Bentley, *Out of Bondage* (New York: Devin-Adair, 1951), pp. 286-289, 294.

[18]*The Gazette* (Montreal), June 6, 1949, p. 1; *The Globe and Mail* (Toronto), June 6, 1949, p. 1; *New York Times*, June 6, 1949, p. 8.

[19]Bentley, p. 158. Bentley's identification of Harold Sloan as "a young Canadian" had its repercussions years later. Igor Gouzenko believing that "Harold Sloan" was Pierre Trudeau compiled a seventeen-page pamphlet

entitled *Memorandum: Trudeau, a Potential Canadian Castro*. He distributed it during the Liberal Party convention of 1968 to prevent Trudeau's election as party leader upon Pearson's retirement. See also John Sawatsky, *Gouzenko: The Untold Story* (Toronto: Macmillan, 1984), pp. 211-216.

[20]Bentley, pp. 104-105, 158.

[21]*Ibid.*, p. 158.

[22][Sise] to O'Donnell, October 12, 1937, Vol. 6, Folder 7 (Correspondence 1936-1937, Spain), Sise Papers, MG 30, D187, PAC.

[23]See Sise to his father, April 10, 1947, and Dr. J. J. O'Connell to P. F. Sise, December 9, 1947 and P. F. S[ise] to Dr. J. J. O'Connell, December 24, 1947, Vol. 3, Folder 11, Sise Papers, MG 30, D187, PAC.

[24]Robert J. Lamphere and Tom Shachtman, *The FBI-KGB War. A Special Agent's Story* (New York: Random House, 1986), pp. 36-41, 195, 207-208, 219, 253-254, 279-285.

[25]Naturally, once the war had commenced, Sise attempted to acquire a position in External Affairs. Unfortunately, for him, he was 34 years of age and this was held against him. He did not get the job of liaison officer between the Canadian National Film Board and the American authorities in film matters until mid-December 1942. See [Sise] to [Robertson], December 23, 1939, Robertson to [Sise], January 8, 1940, and Robertson to Grierson, December 16, 1942, Vol. 13, Folder 2, and for the Robertson letter to Grierson see Vol. 13, Folder 12, Sise Papers, MG 30, D187, PAC.

[26]Hazen Edward Sise, June 19, 1956, File 100-364301-15, FBI Papers.

[27]Pearson to Robertson, October 25, 1944, Wrong to Ritchie, October 30, 1944, [Ritchie] to Biddulph, November 7, 1944 and [Ritchie] to Wrong, November 15, 1944, File AR 1079/1, Vol. 2120, External Affairs Papers, RG 25, A12, PAC.

[28]Bentley, p. 299 and Lamphere and Shachtman, p. 39.

[29]Chapman Pincher, *Too Secret Too Long* (London: Sidgwick & Jackson, 1984), pp. 48, 76, 121, 171, 342, 379, 396, 416. See also John Barron, *KGB; The Secret Work of Soviet Secret Agents* (New York: The Reader's Digest Press, 1974), p. 167. On the escape route, see Vladimir and Evdokia Petrov, *Empire of Fear* (New York: Praeger, 1956), p. 272. As to Professor Nikitin, see John Sawatsky, *For Services Rendered: Leslie James Bennett and the RCMP Security Services* (Toronto: Doubleday, 1982), p. 180.

[30]Strickland to Ladd, Underground Espionage (NKVD) in Agencies of the United States Government, October 21, 1946, p. 192, File 65-56402-1802, FBI Papers.

[31]See Chapter 8, pp. 136-137.

[32]Pearson, I, pp. 50-51.

[33]Hearings, *Scope of Soviet Activity in the United States*, Part 56 (March 12 and 21, 1957), p. 3675.

[34]Canada, Parliament, House of Commons, *Debates, Official Report*, 22nd Parliament, 1st Session, Vol. I (November 25, 1953) (Ottawa: Queen's Printer, 1953), pp. 325-327, 351-353. See also *Chicago Daily Tribune*, October 26, 1953, pp. 1-2 and November 21, 1953, pp. 1-2. On Jenner's "veiled threat," see Sawatsky, *Gouzenko: The Untold Story*, p. 127.

[35]*Testimony of Former Russian Code Clerk Relating to the Internal Security of the United States*, p. 7.

[36][Pearson] to Norman, December 28, 1953, Vol. 44, Pearson Papers, MG 26, N1, PAC.

[37]Hearings, *Scope of Soviet Activity in the United States*, Part 56 (March 12 and 21, 1957), p. 3660.

[38]William A. Rusher to the writer, June 25, 1985.

[39]Roger W. Bowen, "Cold War, McCarthyism, and Murder by Slander: E. H. Norman's Death in Perspective," in Roger W. Bowen (ed.), *E. H. Norman: His Life and Scholarship* (Toronto: University of Toronto Press, 1984), p. 49.

[40]Hugh Keenleyside, *Memoirs* (Toronto: McClelland and Stewart, 1981), I, p. 220.

[41]Arnold Heeney, *The Things That Are Caesar's* (Toronto: University of Toronto Press, 1972), p. 145.

[42]*New York Times*, April 11, 1957, p. 16.

[43]Pearson, Memorandum for the Prime Minister, April 15, 1957, File E-16-3N, Pt. 4, Vol. 179, St. Laurent Papers, MG 26, L, PAC.

[44]*The Toronto Daily Star*, April 16, 1957, p. 1.

[45]United States Congress, *Congressional Record*, Vol. 103, Pt. 4 (March 25-April 12, 1957), pp. 5607-5613.

[46]McManus to Morris, October 23, 1957, Norman File, Records of the Senate Subcommittee on Internal Security (1951-1975), RG 46, NA.

[47]Eastland to Dulles, May 22, 1958, Norman File, *ibid.*

[48][illegible initials], Memorandum for the Prime Minister, July 25, 1957, Norman File, RCMP (CSIS) Papers.

[49]John G. Diefenbaker, *One Canada: Memoirs of the Right Honourable John G. Diefenbaker* (Toronto: Macmillan, 1977), pp. 267-269.

[50]An unsigned memorandum entitled "A Conversation with the Prime Minister," February 11, 1965, Add. MS. 77.53 (1.1.5), Bruce Hutchison Papers, University of Calgary. Bruce Hutchison acknowledges the authenticity of the memorandum but is unable to recall its writer. The Archivist of the University of Calgary Library to the writer, January 24, 1986. See also J. L. Granatstein, *Canada 1957-1967* (Toronto: McClelland and Stewart, 1986), p. 290.

[51]Granatstein, p. 290.

[52]Bentley, pp. 309-310.

[53]See for example, Bowen, "Cold War, McCarthyism, and Murder by Slander," pp. 46-68 and Roger W. Bowen, "Irony or Tragedy?", in Roger W. Bowen (ed.), *E. H. Norman: His Life and Scholarship* (Toronto: University of Toronto Press, 1984), pp. 195-198; Charles Taylor, *Six Journeys: A Canadian Pattern* (Toronto: Anansi, 1977), pp. 107-151; Henry S. Ferns, *Reading from Left to Right* (Toronto: University of Toronto Press, 1983), pp. 196-225. James Littleton, *Target Nation. Canada and the Western Intelligence Network* (Toronto: Lester & Orpen Dennys, 1986), *passim*.

[54]See Lamphere and Schachtman, pp. 136-137, 201.

[55]Sise to Pearson, September 17, 1962; Pearson to Sise, September 25,

1962; Pearson to Sise, May 29, 1963; Sise to Pearson, August 16, 1963; Pearson to Sise, September 5, 1963; Sise to Pearson, November 21 and 22, 1963; Pearson to Sise, November 27, 1963; Pearson to Sise, February 28, 1964; Sise to Pearson, March 6, April 6, 1964 and January 27, 1965, Vol. 7, Folder 14, Sise Papers, MG 30, D187, PAC.

[56]Dean Acheson, *Present at the Creation* (New York: Norton, 1969), pp. 696, 700-705. See also Paul Martin, *A Very Public Life* (Toronto: Deneau, 1985), II, p. 152.

[57]David Carlton, *Anthony Eden* (London: Allen Lane, 1981), p. 321.

[58]Martin, p. 397.

[59]Peter Stursberg, *Lester Pearson and the American Dilemma* (Toronto: Doubleday, 1980), pp. 220-223; Lawrence Martin, *The Presidents and the Prime Ministers: Washington and Ottawa Face to Face* (Toronto: Doubleday, 1982), pp. 1-3.

[60]See for example, Stursberg, p. 167.

[61]Robert Bothwell, *Pearson: His Life and World* (Toronto: McGraw-Hill Ryerson, Ltd., 1978), p. 216.

APPENDIX A

[1]Under the committee system of the United States Congress, committee hearings before the House of Representatives or the Senate can be either in executive or public sessions. Many witnesses before the committees are first examined in executive sessions which are secret, and anyone discussing their contents outside the privileged confines of the hearing room is liable for charges of contempt of Congress. This testimony is then repeated in public sessions. Testimony in public sessions is published and, occasionally, testimony in executive sessions is likewise published. The executive session testimony of Elizabeth T. Bentley on August 14, 1951 was never repeated in public session, and has never been published until now.

[2]Elizabeth T. Bentley was born in New Milford, Connecticut and graduated from Vassar College in 1930. She took a master's degree in language at Columbia University and continued her studies at the University of Florence. Revolted by Mussolini's fascist government, she joined a Communist Party cell at Columbia University in 1935. For further details about Bentley see Chapter 7, pp. 106-107. Also see the *New York Times*, December 4, 1963, p. 47; Elizabeth Bentley, *Out of Bondage* (New York: Devin-Adair, 1951), *passim*.

[3]Neither senators McCarthy nor Welker had any standing with the Judiciary Committee. They were probably invited as a matter of senatorial courtesy and no doubt to have some Republican senators present.

[4]Congressional committee procedure is quasi-judicial. The witness is sworn in. To bear false witness is a felony and invites prosecution under the Perjury Act. This rarely occurs, but when it does, charging, indictment, prosecution, conviction, and sentencing follow.

[5]Bentley, pp. 104, 158.

⁶Following the disclosures by the defecting Russian Embassy code clerk Igor Gouzenko, of Russian spying in Canada, Fred Rose, a member of the Canadian House of Commons, was charged, prosecuted, convicted, and incarcerated for six years under Canadian law.

⁷Like Fred Rose, Sam Carr who was the Organizing Secretary of the Canadian Communist Party, was implicated in Gouzenko's disclosures. He was charged, prosecuted, convicted, and incarcerated for six years under Canadian law.

⁸Here Bentley is in error; the correct spelling is S—i—s—e. Throughout this testimony, however, for purposes of consistency, Bentley's spelling will prevail. It is possible that she may have met Sise in New York in 1942, but the earliest that he could have arrived in Washington was in the spring of 1943. He probably left Washington in the spring of the following year, 1944. See Sise to [Pearson], March 21, 1943 and Sise to [Pearson], April 28, 1944, Vol. 43, Pearson Papers, MG 26, N1, PAC.

⁹In her memoirs, Bentley wrote that Sise had been sent by Tim Buck and Sam Carr. See Bentley, p. 158.

¹⁰As to Sise's unsuccessful rendezvous in Paris with his Russian contact, see his elliptical account of this failed meeting in a letter from [Sise] to O'Donnell, October 12, 1937, Vol. 6, Folder 7, (Correspondence 1936-1937, Spain), Sise Papers, MG 30, D187, PAC. Bentley, however, was incorrect in crediting the failed rendezvous to the Stavisky Affair. This affair had occurred several years before Sise arrived in Paris on October 1, 1937. (See Alexander Werth, *France in Ferment*, (London: Jarrolds, 1934). The incident that probably led to the failure of the rendezvous was the kidnapping, about a week before, on September 22, in Paris, by Russian intelligence of the White Czarist General Yevgeny K. Miller. French police activity at the time probably made any meeting inadvisable. See Paul W. Blackstock, *The Secret Road to World War II. Soviet Versus Western Intelligence, 1921-1939* (Chicago: Quadrangle, 1969), pp. 241-247.

¹¹Sise was assigned to Washington in December 1942 as liaison officer between the Canadian National Film Board and its American counterpart. See, for example Robertson to Grierson, Vol. 13, Folder 12, Sise Papers, MG 30, D187, PAC.

¹²Lester B. Pearson served as Minister-Counsellor of the Canadian Legation in Washington from early 1942 until early 1945, at which point he was appointed ambassador upon the departure of Leighton McCarthy.

¹³The first letter that one can find is one written from Montreal by Sise to Pearson on September 8, 1939, and sent to him at the High Commission in London. It starts with the salutation, "Dear Mike." Pearson's reply begins with "Dear Hazen." Obviously they knew each other well and probably had met when Sise was living in London, just prior to the war. Though Sise had "vacuumed" his papers before depositing them in the Public Archives of Canada in Ottawa, in his private correspondence for the 1930s he certainly made no attempt to disguise his communist orientation. One finds it hard to believe that Pearson was not aware of Sise's ideological proclivities. [Sise] to [Pearson], September 8, 1939, Pearson to Sise, October 3, 1939, Vol. 13, Folder 2, Sise Papers, MG 30, D187, PAC.

[14]According to Pearson, as Minister-Counsellor of the Canadian Legation in Washington, he was "left largely . . . the administration of the Mission as well as State Department contacts, meetings, and reporting." Minister McCarthy "looked after White House liaison and kept in personal touch with Mr. Roosevelt and [Prime Minister Mackenzie] King." Lester B. Pearson, *Mike: The Memoirs of The Right Honourable Lester B. Pearson* (Toronto: University of Toronto Press, 1972), I, p. 207.

[15]There is no doubt that Sise had psychiatric problems by late 1947 which probably first manifested themselves in Washington during the war. See, Dr. J. J. O'Connell to P. F. Sise, December 9, 1947, and P. F. S[ise] to Dr. J. J. O'Connell, December 24, 1947, Vol. 3, Folder 11, Sise Papers, MG 30, D187, PAC.

[16]On the question of the Institute of Pacific Relations as a communist-front organization see Chapter 3, pp. 20-22.

[17]See Chapter 3, pp. 16-17.

[18]In his testimony before the Canadian Royal Commission to investigate Gouzenko's disclosures of Russian spying in Canada, Grierson denied that he had any affiliations with the Communist Party. (See *The Gouzenko Transcripts: The Evidence Presented to the Kellock-Taschereau Royal Commission of 1946*, ed. by Robert Bothwell and J. L. Granatstein (Ottawa: Deneau, 1982), pp. 341-343 and also Gary Evans, *John Grierson and the National Film Board* (Toronto: University of Toronto Press, 1984), pp. 249-254. Certainly, after the Gouzenko disclosures Mackenzie King was "distrustful of Grierson and was happy to see Grierson go." (See *ibid.*, pp. 247-248). As to the FBI and probably the State Department, they took a dim view of Grierson following Gouzenko's disclosures, as well as of subsequent information received. They suspected him of communist associations. Accordingly, he was denied a visa to the United States. See *ibid.*, pp. 266-268 and [Richardson] to [Diefenbaker], February 15, 1947, pp. 051048-051051, Box 63, Series 1940-1956, Diefenbaker Papers, University of Saskatchewan, Saskatoon.

[19]Frederick Poland who worked for the Wartime Information Board, was one of those indicted but not convicted in the aftermath of Gouzenko's disclosures.

APPENDIX B

[1]Initially the word RCMP had been typed in inadvertently and this mistake was corrected in ink by an unknown hand to read Com[munist] Pa[rty].

[2]The person who Bentley identified might have been Squadron Leader Frederick Poland who was prosecuted, following Gouzenko's disclosures of Russian espionage in Canada, and acquitted.

[3]The acronym that Bentley used was incorrect. GPU stands for *Gosudarstvennoye Politicheskoye Upravleniye* which translates as the State Political Directorate which was organized in February 1922. It was the immediate successor to the "The All-Russian Extraodinary Commission," abbreviated to Cheka which directed Moscow's terror from 1917 onward. At the time

of the Spanish Civil War the GPU had been reorganized as the OGPU (*Obye-dinennoye Gosudarstvennoye Politicheskoye Upravleniye*) which translates as the United State Political Directorate. During the Second World War Russian espionage was conducted by its successor, the NKVD (*Narodnyy Komissariat Vnutrennikh Del*) which stands for the People's Commissariat of Internal Affairs.

[4]See p. 241 fn. 10 in the previous document.

[5]A perusal of Sise's correspondence and papers leaves no doubt as to the accuracy of Bentley's recollection. See Sise Papers, MG 30, D187, PAC.

[6]The word "also" appears to have been deleted in ink by an unknown hand.

[7]The word "any" has been inserted in ink by an unknown hand as a substitute for "within a."

[8]Here the name is underlined in pen and starred undoubtedly by someone at FBI Headquarters, Washington.

[9]The name was circled in pen undoubtedly by someone at FBI Headquarters, Washington.

[10]Bentley appears to be correct on this point. By the spring of 1947, Sise had concluded that he should no longer avoid divorcing his wife. See Sise to his father, April 10, 1947, Vol. 3, Folder 11, Sise Papers, MG 30, D187, PAC.

[11]See p. 11 fn. 15 in the previous document.

[12]For Joseph Katz's other espionage activities, see William Rusher, *Special Counsel* (New Rochelle, New York: Arlington House, 1968), pp. 76–77 and Robert J. Lamphere and Tom Shachtman, *The FBI—KGB War. A Special Agent's Story* (New York: Random House, 1986), pp. 74, 75, 90, 165, 168, 279-282, 296-297.

[13]The expression "left-winger" is meaningless, but it is interesting to note that in a description of the personnel of External Affairs, Pearson was placed "mildly left of centre." See Hugh L. Keenleyside, *Memoirs* (Toronto: McClelland and Stewart, 1982), I, p. 232.

[14]Initially the word was "planning" and was corrected in ink to "planting" by an unknown hand.

[15]As to Grierson's recruitment of personnel, see Gary Evans, *John Grierson and the National Film Board* (Toronto: University of Toronto Press, 1984), pp. 246-254, 258.

[16]Bentley is not precise. WAC was the acronym for the Women's Army Corps of the United States. The Canadian counterpart was CWAC, the Canadian Women's Army Corps.

[17]Categories (i), (j), and (k) were added in ink by an unknown hand. Category (h) was "documentation," crossed out when it was realized that the category had already been specified in (g).

APPENDIX C

[1]In an unsigned, untitled, and undated handwritten note of this conversation, Morris pointed out to O'Connor that the Canadians knew of the

information imparted by the committee about Norman "in view of apparent exchanges of information between the FBI and RCMP." Norman File, Records of the Senate Subcommittee on Internal Security (1951-1975), RG 46, NA.

[2]Parts of this secret memorandum about Norman can be found in Hearings, *Scope of Soviet Activity in the United States*, Part 56 (March 12 and 21, 1957), p. 3660.

[3]In Morris' unsigned, untitled, and undated handwritten note, O'Connor held that the release of Bentley's "testimony would blow whatever water was left in the boiler and would cause a tempest in a certain named friendly country." Norman File, Records of the Senate Subcommittee on Internal Security (1951-1975), RG 46, NA.

[4]See Chapter 7, p. 107.

[5]Both in the press and in the House of Commons Pearson denigrated Morris and the subcommittee. See, for example, Canada, Parliament, House of Commons, *Debates, Official Report*, 22nd Parliament, 5th Session, Vol. III (March 15, 1957) (Ottawa: Queen's Printer, 1957), pp. 2349-2350.

[6]See Chapter 3, pp. 16-17.

[7]Ludwig Rajchman was an official of the Polish communist government and its representative on the Executive Board of the UN's International Emergency Children's Fund. Rajchman's name had cropped up in the subcommittee's hearings and when the subcommittee attempted to subpoena him he refused the subpeona on the ground of diplomatic immunity. See *The Times* (London), February 21, 1957, p. 6.

[8]Among others, Stanley Ryan who served in the UN Secretariat during that period, is a case in point. Born in Leningrad, his surname was Gerschun. He changed it to Ryan and acquired Canadian nationality in 1944. Ryan was attached as press officer to the 1947 Commission of Investigation Concerning the Greek Frontier Incidents, established by the Security Council. His pro-communist antics on the commission led the Americans and British to lodge strenuous protests with Secretary General Trygve Lie about Ryan's partiality. See, Ethridge to Baxter, September 26, 1947 attached to C[yril] B. Black, Memorandum (Appraisal of the United Nations Secretariat attached to the Balkan Commission), July 21, 1947, Box 68, US Mission UN 1945-1949, RG 84, NA; [LaFleche] to the Sec. of State for External Affairs, February 26, 1947 and George to Reilly, March 20, 1947, FO/371/67065, PRO; Canadian Consulate General (New York) to the Sec. of State for External Affairs, No. 1271, October 9, 1947, Adsel Telegrams, Pt. 1, Vol. 1056, RG 25, F6, PAC; Memorandum from the Greek Embassy in Washington to the Department of State, May 5, 1947, File 501.BA/5-547, Gibson (Salonika) to the Sec. of State No. 12, March 6, 1947, File 501.BC Greece/ 3-647 and Austin (New York) to the Sec. of State, No. 327, April 8, 1947, File 501.BA/4-847, RG 59, NA; Permanent United Kingdom Representative (UN) to the Foreign Office No. 1118, April 8, 1947, FO/371/67065, PRO.

Index

MacLeod, Alexander A., 13, 14, 34, 57, 61, 78, 89, 215 fn. 14; cold-
   shouldered by Norman, 33, 58, 121
McMaster University, 46, 53, 65
MacNeil, Robert, 53, 66
McRuer, J.C., 170
Majlis, 10, 77
Maly, Theodore, 128
Mandel, Benjamin, 186, 189
Martin, Paul, 69, 70, 75, 95, 112-113
Marx, Karl, 16, 64
"Mask of Destiny," 149
Matsubei Matsuo, 41
Matthews, Donald, 159-161
Matthews, H. Freeman, 56
Memorandum: Trudeau, a Potential Canadian Castro, 238 fn. 19
Methodism, Canadian, 8
Methodist academy (Kobe), 2, 54, 66
MI5 (Military Intelligence 5), 25, 73, 80, 85-88, 91, 92, 94, 95, 98, 115,
   119, 120, 140, 146, 149, 157, 158, 182; interested in Norman, 73-74,
   76
MI6 (Military Intelligence 6), 25, 119
military intelligence, American, 25, 46, 68, 71, 90, 234 fn. 46
military intelligence, Russian. *See* GRU
Miller, Yevgeny K., 241 fn. 10
missionary children, 179
Morris, Robert, 105, 107, 108, 110, 116, 144, 146, 159, 160, 164, 169,
   172, 176, 243 fn. 1; intelligence officer, 109; interrogates Bentley, 186-
   192; meeting with State Department officers, 203-206; promise to
   Henderson, 109
Moscow Spy Trials, 14, 64
Mosley, Sir Oswald, 6
Motinov, Lieutenant Colonel, 54-55, 133
Munsinger, Gerda, 177
Munsinger Affair, 178
Mussolini, Benito, 3, 25

Narodnyy Komissariat Vnutrennikh Del. See NKVD
Nassar, Gamel Abdul, 100
National Archives, Washington, D.C., 99
National Council for Canadian-Soviet Friendship, 51, 65, 67, 84, 88, 130
National Federation of Labour Youth, 79
National Film Board of Canada, 106, 166, 187, 191, 197, 200, 238 fn. 25,
   241 fn. 11
National Press Club, 137
NATO (North Atlantic Treaty Organization), 120-121
naval intelligence, American, 13, 23
Neuberger, Richard L., 175